T0330149

Networks and Institutions in Natural Resource Management

Networks and Institutions in Natural Resource Management

Edited by

Yvonne Rydin

London School of Economics, UK

Eva Falleth

Norwegian Institute for Urban and Regional Research, Norway

Edward Elgar

Cheltenham, UK • Northampton, MA, USA

Published by
Edward Elgar Publishing Limited
Glensanda House
Montpellier Parade
Cheltenham
Glos GL50 1UA
UK

Edward Elgar Publishing, Inc.
136 West Street
Suite 202
Northampton
Massachusetts 01060
USA

A catalogue record for this book
is available from the British Library

Library of Congress Cataloguing in Publication Data

Networks and institutions in natural resource management / edited by
    Yvonne Rydin and Eva Falleth.
        p. cm.
    Includes bibliographical references.
    1. Natural resources–Management. 2. Natural resources–Management–
Case studies. 3. Sustainable development–Case studies. I. Rydin, Yvonne, 1957–
II. Falleth, Eva, 1962–

    HC85.N48 2006
    333.7–dc22   2005049718

ISBN-13: 978 1 84542 294 3
ISBN-10: 1 84542 294 5

Printed and bound in Great Britain by MPG Books Ltd, Bodmin, Cornwall

Contents

Figures

Abbreviations

AEDA	Asociàciòn en Defensa del Acuífero 23
AONB	Area of Outstanding Natural Beauty (English case studies)
ASAJA	Asociàciòn Agraría de Jóuenes Agricultores
CAMS	Catchment Abstraction Management Strategy
CAP	Common Action Problem
CAP	Common Agricultural Policy (EU)
CHASM	Catchment Hydrology and Sustainable Management
CIDA	Canadian International Development Agency (Zimbabwean case study)
CPR	common pool resources
DEFRA	Department of Environment, Food and Rural Affairs
DN	Directorate for Nature Management
EA	Environment Agency (English case studies)
ENRI	Eastern Norway Research Institute
ERP	Em River Project (Swedish case study)
EU	European Union
FC	Forestry Commission (Zimbabwean case study and English case studies)
FPU	Forest Protection Unit (Zimbabwean case study)
GIS	Geographic Information Science
HMIP	Her Majesty's Inspectorate for Pollution
LDF	Local Development Framework
LSE	London School of Economics
MOE	Ministry of Environment
MOVAR	Norwegian inter-municipal water system company (Norwegian case study)
NFA	New Forest Association
NFCDA	New Forest Commoners Defence Association (English case study)
NGO	non-governmental organization
NIBR	Norwegian Institute for Urban and Regional Research
NIVA	Norwegian Institute for Water Research (Norwegian case study)
NPA	National Park Authority (English case studies)
PBA	Planning and Building Act (Norwegian case study)

RDC	Rural District Council
RMC	Resource Management Committee (Zimbabwean case study)
RRC	Rönne River Committee (Swedish case study)
RSPB	Royal Society for the Protection of Birds (English case study)
RWA	Regional Water Authorities (English case study)
SAC	Special Area of Conservation (English case studies)
SSSI	Site of Special Scientific Interest (English case studies)
SVR	Setesdal Vesthei-Ryfylkeheiane (Norwegian case study)
SWT	Staffordshire Wildlife Trust (English case study)
VIDCO	Village Development Committee (Zimbabwean case study)
WARDCO	Ward Development Committee (Zimbabwean case study)
WG	working group
WRB	Wild Reindeer Board (Norwegian case study)
WRC	Wild Reindeer Committee (Norwegian case study)
WFD	Water Framework Directive (EU)
WWF	World Wide Fund for Nature

Preface

There has been considerable institutional innovation in pursuit of sustainable natural resource management. Organizations at many different levels, tiers and scales have been combined in more or less complex networks to tackle the thorny problem of how to promote collective action for such resource management. Our book presents a detailed analysis based on original fieldwork in an attempt to understand how such institutional arrangements work. The origins of the work lie in a conversation between Inge-Lise Saglie of the Norwegian Institute for Urban and Regional Research (NIBR) and Yvonne Rydin of the London School of Economics (LSE) during a visit by the former to London in 2001. Inge-Lise saw the potential of expanding some of Yvonne's work on social capital to understand the more general problem of collective action for resource management. A research grant application to the Norwegian Research Council ensued, based around three in-depth cases studies in Norway. Having successfully secured the Norwegian part of the project, a parallel application went into the UK Economic and Social Research Council for a project based on three UK cases. Work on the joint project began in Norway in 2002, with the fieldwork concluding in England in 2004.

The three Norwegian and three English cases form the major part of the following book. Two cases in each country look at the combined goals of landscape protection and nature conservation with an emphasis on the former in Setesdal Vesthei-Ryfylkeheiane and Cannock Chase, and the latter in Rondane and New Forest. It proved difficult to parallel the Norwegian case concerning the wild reindeer herds; the New Forest ponies were the closest we could manage. Two further cases considered aspects of water management in Morsa and the Lake District. All case studies were undertaken within a collaborative research framework, which established a common theoretical approach using the concepts of social capital and institutional capacity and a broadly applicable common methodology. The details of this methodology are given in the Appendix; it allowed for some variations to fit with specific local circumstances and to take advantage of related projects based in the case studies. The six cases thus formed a coherent whole.

We believe that general lessons about institution-building for resource management can be learnt from this Anglo-Norwegian comparison. But to widen the scope of the analysis, we invited three other researchers who had been working on resource management within closely related theoretical frameworks to contribute to this book. Drawing on their doctoral studies, these researchers contributed further water management and further land-scape/nature conservation studies. This has also expanded the geographical coverage to cover Sweden and Spain within Europe and, a quite different context, Zimbabwe in Africa. Our conclusions are therefore able to synthesize and test out the results from our original Anglo-Norwegian project with the challenge of these additional cases. We hope that this both strengthens and broadens the appeal of our analysis.

There are a number of thanks we would like to express. First, there is our debt to the funders of our joint research project, the Norwegian Research Council and the UK Economic and Social Research Council. In addition, the LSE Nordic Travel Fund supported the original visit to the LSE by Inge-Lise Saglie. Then we would like to thank all the many people who gave up their time to be interviewed and to respond to our requests for information. The research would not have been possible without them. Special thanks are due to the three researchers – Victor Galaz (University of Göteborg, Sweden), Elena Lopez-Gunn (LSE) and Everisto Mapedza (LSE) – who agreed to contribute chapters based on their own work and who generously reconsidered and rewrote their empirical fieldwork in the light of the themes of our research project. More generally, we would like to thank our respective institutions – the London School of Economics, the Norwegian Institute for Urban and Regional Research and the Eastern Norway Research Institute (ENRI) – for the supportive contexts that they provide. A rather special context for working on the project was provided by Jönnhalt Seter in Rondane, Norway and the Mortal Man Inn, Troutbeck, Cumbria! A special thanks to the LSE Design Unit for drawing the maps. Finally, thank you to Catherine Elgar for her support in securing publication of the book.

Hans Olav Bråtå (ENRI)
Eva Falleth (NIBR)
Tove Måtar (LSE)
Yvonne Rydin (LSE)
Inge-Lise Saglie (NIBR)
Knut Bjørn Stokke (NIBR)

April 2005

1. Fragmented institutions: the problem facing natural resource management

Inger-Lise Saglie

The management of natural resources has been and will continue to be of crucial importance for human life based on the simple fact that we are dependent on these resources for our survival and well-being. Our successes and failures in managing them are therefore of vital importance for us in a long-term resource management perspective. The long-term management of natural resources is a central element in sustainable development. The most quoted understanding of the concept of 'sustainable development' is 'development that meets the needs of the present without compromising the ability of future generations to meet their own needs' (WCED 1987: 40). The moral obligations of intra- and inter-generational justice would mean that natural resources should be managed so that future generations should also be able to satisfy their needs. While many would agree with these moral obligations, the actual management practices are often the subject of contention. To know whether a certain management practice is sustainable or not within a natural scientific discourse may be difficult, but the design of management systems and procedures is also a contested issue.

The starting point for the theoretical and empirical research presented in this book is the increasingly fragmented institutional setting for natural resource management and planning. The management of natural resources is most often a question of collective management involving many actors even in countries with well-developed regulatory regimes. The research questions that we discuss in this book are: How do bodies and parties involved in natural resource management succeed in developing networks and strategies in order to overcome this fragmentation; and Does this lead to an optimum situation for the planning and management of natural resources? This fragmented institutional setting includes both a fragmented public sector, as well as the necessity of cooperation with market actors and participation from organizations and individuals in civil society. In sum, this means a high number of participants each with their own agenda, preferences, norms and working routines being involved in resource management. In this chapter, we will describe the collective action problems inherent in natural resource management, the extent of institutional fragmentation creating collective action problems, and possible approaches to overcome collective action problems, focusing on networking and the new conditions of governance.

NATURAL RESOURCES: THE NEED FOR COLLECTIVE ACTION

The collective action problem is one of the main problems identified in social science literature on the management of natural resources because of the public good characteristics of resources (Olson 1965; Ostrom 1990). The collective action problem is a problem related to situations where the pursuit of individual rationality does not lead to collective rationality. This social dilemma has been described and named in many variations: the public good problem (Olson 1965), the free-rider problem (Edney 1979; Grossman and Hart 1980), the tragedy of the commons (Hardin 1968) and the management of common pool resources (Ostrom 1990; Ostrom et al. 1994). In this book we will concentrate on the concepts of 'common pool resource' and 'public good' as most appropriate for our case studies.

A common pool resource is 'a natural and man-made resource system that is sufficiently large as to make it costly (but not impossible) to exclude potential beneficiaries from obtaining benefits from its use' (Ostrom 1990: 30). These resources show two important characteristics. The first is that they are limited, which means that consumption of a resource unit implies that there are less units available to others (subtractability). When the limits of the resource are approached, the reproduction capability of the resource may be destroyed in the long run (Ostrom 1990). The second characteristic is the difficulty of excluding potential beneficiaries from access to the resource system which, in turn, creates a risk of free riders who may use the resource without contributing to its continued existence. Preventing access for users is costly and thus exclusion cost is a core problem for the management of the common pool resources. Individual rationality may lead each actor to use the common resource as much as possible for their own gain. If all actors think alike, the resource will be overused. Everybody has a collective interest in the long-term existence of the natural resource for future use, and consequently everybody has an interest in cooperation to achieve this. However short-term individual rationality may lead to overuse and depletion. The problem is to act collectively to restrict access and to secure participation in maintaining or creating the resource. A herd of wild reindeer can be an example of a common pool resource, see Chapter 6 on Rondane. The resource is divisible and limited in the sense that over-exploitation of the resource may lead to its depletion.

In economic theory, a public good is defined as a good that may be enjoyed by all members of a group irrespective of whether they have contributed to its supply (Olson 1965; Dasgupta and Heal 1979; Samuelson and Nordhaus 1989). The temptation for each actor is not to participate in the supply of the good, while remaining able to enjoy its benefits. The problem is if all actors were to think in the same way, the public good would not be produced and everybody would be losers. All actors share the same interest in the public good being supplied, which implies that everybody has an interest in cooperation. The dominant strategy may however be not to participate. According to Olson (1965), large groups cannot produce public goods unless coercion or selective incentives are involved. In a large group each individual contribution may be small, thus a missing contribution does not significantly reduce the possibility of the public good being supplied. This is the case for taxes. The single contribution from each taxpayer may be small compared to the total amount. This allows for the situation where an individual avoiding taxation is still able to enjoy the benefits of for example public roads, hospitals, concert halls and welfare institutions. The underlying logic in this argumentation is the rational behaviour of 'the economic man' as a strategically egoistic actor trying to maximize his own utility. Examples of public good may be open-access areas for outdoor recreation or landscape aesthetics. In both cases however, their characteristics as a public good may be questioned as not everybody takes part in outdoor recreation, and aesthetic appreciation may vary. However if there is sufficient social and political support for such amenities to be framed as a public good, this could lead to actions such as securing property rights, taking legal measures to secure public access to a piece of land or continued financial support to secure certain management practices in a landscape.

A shared characteristic between the concepts of public good and common pool resource is the difficulty of excluding potential beneficiaries, and therefore both allow for free riding. In both situations, the need for some form of collective action arises. In the public good tradition, much focus has been on the necessity for collective action in order to ensure the supply of goods. In common pool resource theory more emphasis has been on the necessity of collective action in order to avoid the overuse of the resource, possibly making it extinct. This is because there are differences between the concepts with regard to subtractability. While the emphasis in the public good concept is on its character of indivisibility in its enjoyment such as the light from a lamp post, a major theme in common pool resources is on the subtractability of the benefits, for example overfishing. The subtractability of a common pool resource is a feature shared with private goods (Ostrom 1999).

Institutional regimes define the access to a resource and hence the possibility for free riding. Such institutional arrangements vary from country to country, but property regimes are always (or usually) important in defining access to the resource. Berkes (1989) argues that common property resources may be held within open-access property, communal property, state property and private property regimes. These categories are not mutually exclusive. State ownership may secure open access as is the case with the right to roam in US National Parks, or common property rights as in the case of *statsalmenninger* in Norway where the right to graze benefits the local community. In some cases access to state properties is highly restricted, as for example in the case of military areas. Private property may also sustain open access rights as in the case of *allemannsretten* in Norway or the 'right to roam' in England.

Examples of open-access regimes are parks and recreational areas. The number of users in such a regime may be very high, and consequently the potential contribution from each user is relatively small, leading to a more pronounced free-rider problem. In an open-access common pool resource, there is consequently a threat of its depletion (wear and tear by use). In a public good situation, the possibility of securing the means for its supply may be more difficult as the potential user group is very large (for example financial contributions in order to secure the public rights of access to land, or the maintenance of certain farming practices). Another example of a property regime is provided by communally managed properties, such as the commons in England or the *allmenninger* in Norway. In a communally managed property right, the number of people with access to the resource is limited, although the number can still be high. The difference with the open-access regime is that the actors are clearly identified. Often, there is some kind of organization of the 'commoners' or the group that is entitled to a particular 'right' on common or so-called public land. The potential number of free riders is reduced but, as for example in the case of the New Forest, the commoners are only one of several groups whose use influences the quality of the natural resource. The institutional arrangements may define communal management over a broad or a more narrowly defined spectrum of issues. In the case of Rondane, the communal management of the wild reindeer herd includes management of hunting, but also management of the habitat for the reindeer, which thus becomes a 'thicker' cooperation covering several issues. The common right of the commoners in the New Forest case may be a 'thin' communal property rights cooperation only covering common grazing.

In practice there may be problems of drawing distinct lines between the public good and the common pool resource characteristics of a natural resource. These unclear borderlines follow from the multifunctional characteristics of natural resources and the way natural resources yield different environmental benefits to different user groups. A natural resource can show different collective action problems depending on the function and the corresponding user group.

In the case of water, water quality may be a public good making it possible for the public at large to go swimming. In this capacity it is indivisible. It cannot at one and the same time be clean for one person and unclean for another person. However water may also be a common pool resource as is the case with water abstraction (see Chapter 9 on the Lake District) or with the exploitation of water as a sink for emissions (the Chapter 8 on the Morsa river basin). Overuse of water as a 'common sink resource' will lead to unwanted changes in the state of the natural resource in the form of pollution.

In the case of the Morsa river basin (Chapter 8) the public good characteristics of clean water for fishing and swimming are threatened. But Morsa is also a common pool resource as a 'sink' for emissions and the collective action problem is to prevent free-riding on this common pool. The 'user group' for Morsa as a sink are mainly home owners and farmers. In the case of the Lake District the collective action problem is concerned with water abstraction. In this capacity water is a common pool resource for specified user groups and the task is to manage the use of and the access to the resource.

Public goods theories have been developed for goods that can be produced, for example a lighthouse that shows its light for everybody whether or not they have contributed to its supply. The management task is to convince, persuade or coerce the actors to contribute to its supply. In the situation where resources can be overused and possibly depleted, as emphasized in common pool resource theories, the management task will be to handle the problem of access to the resource. Natural resources may have traits of being a common pool to be exploited, but may also have traits that require active supply. An example of this latter case is where continued and specific agricultural practices are needed to maintain a culturally valued landscape.

In the case of cultural landscapes, such as in the New Forest case dealt with in this book (Chapter 3), the management task is to both regulate and steer access to the resource as well as ensuring its maintenance. The number of visitors makes it necessary to direct where they may walk and to maintain the paths in order to reduce wear and tear. In this respect the natural resource shows common pool resource characteristics of subtractability and overuse. The user groups are tourists as well as local residents. Another task is to secure continuous grazing by the ponies in order to keep the landscape open and not overgrown, showing public good characteristics. The user group in this respect is the commoners. As most landscapes are, to a greater or lesser extent, cultivated and changed by management practices, both the problem of securing a contribution to the production of the good as well as of managing access to avoid the problem of overuse may exist side by side.

The user group for a specific resource may differ enormously on a scale from the global to the local. In the sustainability discourse we are all users in the sense that the long-term management of natural resources will be an inheritance for following generations. In this function, any natural resource is constructed as a public good. In the UN Convention on Biological Diversity, the long-term survival of ecosystems, species and the gene pool is considered as a public good for all in order to secure the future for coming generations. In such a framing, the survival of a species is clearly indivisible in its nature. It cannot at the same time be extinct or non-extinct for different groups of people or individuals. However it may be a highly disputed matter whether a species is extinct, should be maintained or not, or whether one particular management practice will lead to extinction. The inherent indivisibility of the public good remains, however. It is a good for all, not for just a few, if the species is maintained.

But there are also more localized user groups benefiting from a specific natural resource, for example as a source of income as in the case of fishing or reindeer herding. In this function, the natural resource shows more traits of being a common pool resource. It is such local use of resources that is investigated in this book. A natural resource can also have a function in terms of local amenity, for instance as an area for quiet enjoyment and outdoor recreation. In this function it is a public good in a localized setting as in the case of Cannock Chase (Chapter 5). These amenities become increasingly important in post-industrial societies where non-working hours and realization of the 'good life' seem to take up more time and resources.

In practice the same natural or man-made resource may be multifunctional, showing varying property rights corresponding with its different functions and thus creating tensions among its users. A privately owned wood is an example of such a multifunctional resource with varying degrees of access for different user groups. The right to make an income from forestry is a right belonging to the owner with strongly regulated access, but the public at large may have a right to pick berries or mushrooms and to roam freely in the same wood. In the latter case, it is an open-access property regime. The life-sustaining properties of the wood may be providing a habitat for a possibly endangered species and can therefore be framed as a common good where the 'user' is mankind at large. In this case the right to make an income from the timber may be in conflict with the public interest in protecting endangered species as framed in the UN Convention on Biological Diversity.

In this spectrum from the global to the local, we are in this book concerned with the local use of a certain natural resource, and the local user groups' actions to maintain or supply this environmental good by overcoming local collective action problems. Table 1.1 summarizes the collective action problems that we examine in our various case studies.

Table 1.1   Summary of collective action problems examined

Case Study	Nature of the Collective Action Problem
New Forest, England	Collective management of recreation, forestry and grazing by Forestry Commission and commoners needed to maintain landscape and ecosystems
Setesdal Vesthei-Ryfylkeheiane, Norway	Collective management of recreational uses (cabin development, off-road traffic, tourism, hunting and fishing) needed to maintain landscape and reindeer herds
Cannock Chase, England	Collective management of recreation (including mountain-biking) and of changes in land uses to 'horsiculture' and residential development on the edge of the Chase needed to maintain landscape and its quiet enjoyment
Rondane Region, Norway	Intensification of recreational use in form of cabin development, tourist facilities and roads threatening wild reindeer herds needs collective response
Mafungautsi, Zimbabwe	Collective management of the forest is needed to maintain the sustainable use of its resources and its biodiversity and meet the needs of local communities
Morsa River Basin, Norway	Level of water quality depends on collective control of discharges from agriculture and dwellings
Lake District, England	Potential collective action needed in context of impending climate change and possible water shortages; current collective action needed to protect salmon populations
Castilla-La Mancha, Spain	Collective action needed to avoid overexploitation of groundwater resources in three aquifers
Em and Rönne Rivers, Sweden	Water population and eutrophication a problem that requires collective action among a range of water users

OVERCOME COLLECTIVE ACTION PROBLEMS

The proposed solutions to the collective action problems differ within the academic debate. According to Olson (1965), only regulatory means including coercion and incentives can solve this dilemma. Privatization has been put forward as a solution in order to make individual rationality consistent with collective rationality (Hardin 1968). Because private property regulates access it has been advanced as a solution to the free-rider problems of common pool resources. We take issue with relying solely on these approaches.

The critique of the narrow utilitarian view on human behaviour is that man is not driven solely by a desire to maximize economic utility, but that norms and values are important behavioural factors (Etzioni 1988; Elster 1989; Hjelseth 1993). Norm-driven behaviour may lead to cooperation in maintaining the resource base, as the actors may see this as appropriate behaviour in certain institutional settings. This leads us to explore the institutions which with their norms and rules frame the actors and their decisions. This institutional approach is explored in more detail in Chapter 2.

To act collectively means that all actors using the resource base must come together and agree upon the rules. Common pool research has sought to find examples where co-management has occurred and been successful, as an alternative to market and regulatory solutions. Co-management can cover a wide range of arrangements, but includes at least some kind of power-sharing between governmental bodies and user groups at varying levels (Zachrisson 2004). This research tradition has identified some characteristics that make the success of co-management more probable (Singleton 2000; Agrawal 2001; Dolšak and Ostrom 2003; Zachrisson 2004). Common management of a natural resource is more likely to succeed if the resource is small in size and has stable and well-delineated boundaries. A small size may mean that the user group is small, and a well-delineated boundary will clearly identify the beneficiaries. Common management is also more likely to occur if its use results in few negative externalities. This also reduces the number of actors involved, and also a possible tension between those that benefit from the resource and those that potentially suffer from the actions. The resource should also be as mono-functional as possible. This will also mean coordination of fewer actors, and it also means that possible tensions between different user groups are reduced. Furthermore it is advantageous if the user group is small, homogeneous, has shared norms and possibly a history of cooperation. Shared norms may reduce potential conflicts, thus making it easier to agree on strategies. A history of cooperation may also mean that institutions for cooperation are already there, thus reducing the cost of cooperation.

However many natural resources are multifunctional, some cover large territories and they are unstable and varying. Local communities in today's post-industrial societies are integrated in networks reaching far beyond the local level, they are not necessarily homogeneous and they may have few shared norms. Uneven spatial distribution of costs and benefits and consequently possible uneven distribution of costs and benefits between user groups may follow from the multifunctional character of a natural resource (Naustdalslid 1994). In the River Rönne case discussed in Chapter 11, the cost involves measures to reduce the pollution in upstream municipalities while the downstream municipalities will enjoy the benefits. In an economic rationality perspective, this is a situation that may reduce the possibility of achieving collective action without strong incentives or coercion. On the other hand, soft sanctions and a sense of moral obligation may increase the possibility for collective action.

THE PROBLEM OF INSTITUTIONAL FRAGMENTATION

Developed countries have established institutional settings based on administrative borders, and management of natural resources must often find its solutions within these settings. Collective action problems may occur because of a fragmented institutional setting that necessitates cooperation between a considerable number of actors with highly varying norms, interests and powers to act. Such fragmented institutional settings may also exhibit free-riding situations among organizations, not only among individuals. This leads us to explore the extent of institutional fragmentation.

Fragmentation of institutions is a common problem facing developed societies. The problems related to institutional and organizational fragmentation may cause collective action problems across territorial and sectoral boundaries and between tiers of government. A possible consequence of institutional fragmentation may be that no one 'owns' the problem, and therefore no one takes the responsibility for solving it. This is the classical problem related to the commons. In developed countries with well-developed regulation regimes however this is rarely so. It is rather the case that the agencies involved are organized so that their administrative geographical boundary is not fitted to the geographical boundary necessary to solve the problem, or that the agencies have the responsibility but not the necessary means or resources to solve the problem. The means are distributed among other agencies and private partners.

The main problem in most cases is therefore that the cost involved in coordinating such a high number of actors may be high. Time- and resource-consuming processes to facilitate joint action may mean that such processes are less likely to occur. Such costs involve the establishment of norms and routines for cooperation as well as negotiations for the appropriate framing of the problem, the possible measures to deal with the problem, and the distribution of tasks and possible costs among the actors. Then there is also the question of implementation of measures when actors return to their daily routines. We can see in the cases presented here that special arrangements are needed to keep the implementation under surveillance, as for example in the Rondane case (Chapter 6) in this book.

In both Britain and Norway (the context for the majority of our cases), uncoordinated planning between sectors and a plethora of plans for a single territory have been singled out as a major problem when planning for and managing natural resources. This was one of the strongest messages of the report *Environmental Planning* from the Royal Commission on Environmental Pollution (2002). The same message came from Planlovutvalget (Commission for New Planning Legislation) in the Norwegian context. This commission specifically pointed at the fragmented systems of laws involved, turning planning into a complex, uncoordinated and often wasteful exercise in time and resources (NOU 2001: 7; NOU 2003: 14). It is a common trait in both countries that a high number of different strategies exist for one particular area. A number of sectors with their separate systems of agencies and laws frequently make their own separate strategies and plans covering the same geographical territory. Decisions taken within different sectoral planning systems may even be contradictory and involve time-consuming processes to clarify the formal status of the decisions taken.

While the town and country or spatial planning system has been looked upon as the main coordinating system by the commissions in both countries, large sectors remain outside this system. In Norway, farming and forestry are sectors that are largely outside the land-use planning system, although the activities in these sectors are of vital importance for the management of land and natural resources.

There are historical, practical and pragmatic reasons for the division of governmental tasks. The range of issues handled by public authorities in our present complex society must of necessity be organizationally divided. Such sectoral agencies are often specialized, based on a certain accepted knowledge base and often staffed by members of certain professions guarding special interests. Usually there are also historical reasons for the agencies. Agriculture is a sector with long established institutions, while institutionalization of environmental issues is new in comparison. In Norway the Ministry for Agriculture (under various names) was established in 1899. In the field of environmental protection, new agencies have been set up including a pollution control authority, and a directorate for nature management in Norway. There are multiple governmental agencies with different territorial boundaries and operating on different governmental levels, often exercising power over several tiers. However this distribution varies between the sectors, thus making a very fragmented organizational figure for management.

The best scale and territorial boundary for the management of natural resources may differ considerably, and is a disputed issue. But in many cases, the delimitation of a natural resource does not follow administrative boundaries. This mismatch between the delimitation of the object of management and the operating administrative boundaries easily increases the number of actors by fivefold or tenfold as can be seen in the case studies in this book. The cost of interaction increases considerably in consequence.

An example of the discussion of the right scale for the management of natural resources is the discussion on the ecosystem approach advocated by international conservation organizations. Ecosystems are 'complexes of plant, animal and micro-organism communities and their non-living environment interacting as a functional unit. They are dynamic systems in which organisms survive subject to a complex web of interactions' (McNeely 1999: 11). However ecosystems may vary in scale from tiny ponds to the entire globe. 'Implicit in the eco-system approach is the idea that "ecosystem" refers to a rather large scale, sufficient to affect human conditions' (McNeely 1999: 11). This large-scale ecosystem approach is also known as the 'bioregional approach'. The concept is not very precise and does not give clear indications of the delimitation of such bioregions. What is clear however is that there is a widespread agreement that management has to be comprehensive with regard to the relationship between human actions and the natural resource, and that relatively large-scale approaches must be applied. Very often, this also means either that management has to be exercised across existing territorial and functional (sector) boundaries through coordination and networking, or that a new organization and institutional arrangement better suited to the managing task must be developed. One example of the latter approach is the EU Water Framework Directive, where the river basin is the territory for management, for which special organizational arrangements must be made according to the directive. Several of our cases address such river basin management.

GOVERNANCE, NETWORKING AND FRAGMENTATION

In the late twentieth century there has been an accepted shift towards governance. This shift can be viewed as a problem with regard to increasing fragmentation, but at the same time governance is also a form of co-management and thus can be suggested as a means to overcome fragmentation (Singleton 2000; Lundqvist 2004a). The term 'governance' is often used in contradistinction to 'government'. In the latter concept, the focus is on formal, hierarchical public authority. The governance approach looks beyond these formal structures, focusing on the actors participating both inside and outside the formal allocation of power. Governance is used both as a descriptive and as a normative model, but as Montin (2000) points out, the borderline between these two latter perspectives on governance is not always clear.

Governance is not a concept with only one meaning. However it broadly refers to new and innovative theoretical perspectives for understanding changing processes of governing (Rhodes 1997) and associated new institutional frameworks (Rhodes 2000). These perspectives include a change in the meaning of government, a new process of governing, a changed condition of ordered rule or a new method by which society is governed. Governance is about a situation where policies are defined and implemented within different kinds of networks, rather than within public hierarchies or markets alone. No single actor, public or private, has the knowledge, the instruments, the resource capacity or the authority to tackle environmental problems unilaterally. In other words, no sovereign actor is able to direct or regulate alone. The public role is, in this perspective, not to direct and control in a traditional sense, like traditional government, but rather to coordinate and create partnerships to achieve a common purpose (Montin 2000). Dependency and reciprocity are important elements in network relations, not competition as in the market or hierarchy as in government. Governance is thus regarded as a third form of management (Rhodes 1998).

Cars et al. (2002) point out that the shift from government to governance is a consequence of economic, technological and social change across Europe. Castells (1996) calls these changes the emergence of the 'network society'. This presents new challenges for the planning system. In Britain, many of these changes have been promoted by national policy 'through strategies of privatization and deregulation, while encouraging "partnership" between municipalities and other stakeholders. By the late 1990s, with a new, more social democratic government, there has been more emphasis on initiatives to promote integration at the local level' (Cars et al. 2002: 8). Cars et al. see the emergence of governance as horizontal integration, or more focus on place and territory as loci of integration instead of traditional functional and sectoral management.

From and Sitter (2002) point out that governance has also developed as a result of the decentralizing and liberation of the public sector. These public sector trends have contributed to a generally fragmented form of management, and new forms of governance have emerged as a result. Whether governance has replaced or just supplemented traditional government is viewed differently by different authors. Rhodes (1996) takes the first view in his article 'The new governance: governing without government'. Vabo (2002) argues that governance as a replacement for government is a more familiar description within an English rather than a Norwegian context, where public actors still have a key role to play. This is certainly the case in Norwegian nature resource management, even in the situation where public actors are dependent on private actors to achieve their purposes. In such situations, governance literature highlights new roles for public actors, including new attitudes (Helgesen 2002) and logics (Stoker 1998). Rhodes (1996) focuses on the following strategies to handle management by networks: incorporation, consultation, bargaining, avoidance, incentives, persuasion and professionalization.

There is also a normative dimension of governance concerned with the question of 'good governance'. In this tradition, the norms and values of actors within public agencies are important. The interests and goals of private participants must be accepted as legitimate by the public actors (Singleton 2000). They must also accept the policy goals and values of other public sector organizations. The role of public agencies must not be to maximize sectoral policy goals, but rather they must be willing to negotiate compromises (Stoker 1998). Instruments for the negotiation of compromises are also important. This is a question of both autonomy and resources. The actors, especially government actors, must have some degree of flexibility of action or bureaucratic discretion (Singleton 2000), or what Stoker (1998) describes as an open-endedness. This is important in order to have the ability to make credible commitments. A policy based on coercive instruments, or command-and-control, will not facilitate cooperation. Rather, mutual trust between different actors and groups is important.

The normative approach has been criticized for several reasons (Elander and Blanc 2001). Firstly, new fora for decision-making are often less open and transparent than is expected of traditional government decision-making. Real decision-making often takes place behind closed doors. Secondly, as an extension of the first point, new forms of partnership tend to build fortresses around themselves, that is, some groups and interests are excluded from participation. Thirdly, partnerships and other 'new' governance fora for decision-making do not include any mechanisms for democratic accountability. Lundqvist (2004a) argues that there have been unclear schemes of coordination and comprehensive but non-transparent involvement of stakeholder interests. He sees this as problems of ecologically rational and democratically acceptable multilevel governance. Two different but not mutually exclusive ways to increase democratic legitimacy can be described (Hovik and Vabo 2005). The first is to link the decisions made in governance fora to decisions made by elected councils. The second is to extend the number of participants in the network.

These new forms of governance have led to a new and growing general interest in evaluating collaboration – and especially partnerships. Sullivan and Skelcher (2002) distinguish between (1) outcome-focused evaluation; (2) applying process-outcome evaluation; (3) evaluation of communities in collaboration; and (4) community-led evaluations. Our focus will be a process-outcome evaluation, using the concepts of social capital and institutional capacity. We explore the conceptual frameworks further in Chapter 2.

2. Institutions and networks: the search for conceptual research tools

Yvonne Rydin

Chapter 1 has characterized natural resources as exhibiting public good traits and requiring management of access to prevent free-riding. As discussed there, the actual property regime under which natural resources are 'owned' may vary, from open-access regimes to communally managed common property to private ownership under a market system to state ownership. But the underlying common pool characteristics of resources such as water systems, landscapes, the atmosphere, biodiversity and forestry mean that resources can be depleted or degraded through the collective overuse of the resource by many individual actors. Collective management can resolve this by setting rules for individual use, but the key problem facing natural resource management is how to enable such collective action. To achieve this would require the many individual resource users to come together and agree. The ability to access the resource and to free ride on the management actions of others inhibits such collective action. This is then further inhibited by the fragmented nature of the institutions that have been established and evolved for natural resource management. Our case studies have investigated how collective action can be enabled to prevent individuals free-riding and, ultimately, to manage the resource involved in a sustainable manner in a variety of institutional contexts.

In order to investigate this, a conceptual framework is needed that identifies the key factors and relationships shaping the balance between free-riding and collective action for sustainable management. This chapter sets out such a framework. Following the lead of others, such as Elinor Ostrom (1990, 1992), who have investigated common pool resource management, we adopt an institutionalist approach. The implications of this are explored in the next section. In particular the important role of networks within institutions is emphasized. However institutionalism is itself a broad church and there is a need for a more precise specification of the ways that collective action can be promoted. To this end, the chapter examines two key concepts: social capital and institutional capacity. These are slightly different yet overlapping ways of conceptualizing the nature and operation of networks within institutions. There are strengths and weaknesses in both cases, but the comparative account of these two 'middle-range' theories allows key issues and research questions to be identified.

These issues and questions inform the following case studies. The research for the three English and three Norwegian cases was undertaken within a tight collaborative research framework that followed these issues and questions closely. To broaden the analysis of the book as a whole, three authors working within the institutionalist paradigm on natural resource management were also asked to contribute case studies. In each case, the research was informed by a concern with networks and some aspects of social capital and/or institutional capacity. Wherever possible, the lines of connection between the discussion in this chapter and the case study analysis have been highlighted. The conclusion returns to the main concerns of this chapter in the light of the results of all nine case studies.

THE INSTITUTIONALIST FRAMEWORK

There has been a recent rapid rise in interest in the institutional arrangements underpinning various aspects of our economic, political and social lives. The core of the institutionalist perspective is the insight that organizational arrangements on their own do not provide an adequate explanation of dynamics and outcomes. A focus on organizational arrangements can detail (often in diagrammatic form) the links between different departments, divisions and other units within an organization or the formal links between different organizations involved in some form of joint working. Thus in policy contexts, organizational analysis will identify the internal divisions of a government department or municipality. It will also set out the formal connections implied by procedures for developing and implementing policy, which may extend across more than one organizational unit, involving various government departments, agencies and municipalities. Similarly within civil society, organizational analysis can help map out the links between non-governmental organizations as well as their internal arrangements. Even the economy can be understood from this perspective, in terms of both the internal organization of the firm and other economic actors and the ways they form sets of connections to facilitate the circulation of goods, materials, intermediate products, finance, technology and so on.

But institutionalism argues that attention to such organizational arrangements only gets one so far. It does not reveal how the linkages within and between organizational units are activated. The central claim of institutionalism is that insights will be revealed by looking at the more cultural dimensions of how organizations work. March and Olsen, in their path-breaking book *Rediscovering Institutions* (1989), clearly set out these more cultural aspects, defining institutions as:

> the routines, procedures, conventions, roles, strategies, organizational forms, and technologies around which political activity is constructed. We also mean beliefs, paradigms, codes, cultures and knowledge, that surround, support, elaborate, and contradict those roles and routines (ibid.: 22)

The combination of the formal and informal, the explicit and implicit is a key feature of institutionalism. It suggests that any organizational analysis of the links between actors – whether within the same unit or across different units – needs to be supplemented by attention to these informal, cultural dimensions. Institutionalism is particularly useful for studying situations of governance, where policy implementation and formulation involves a wide range of actors (see Chapter 1). The formal and informal networks between these actors help explain how governance processes work. The cultural dimensions of the links between actors in these networks advances the analysis even further.

This emphasis on the informal as well as the formal is important because it underpins the processes by which actors within organizational networks learn how to operate within those networks. They need to understand their allotted role and develop appropriate behaviour for that role. This involves being able to undertake the required everyday routine practices but also expressing the norms that are associated with that role. Organizational arrangements can only operate because actors develop such roles and acquire such norms. Therefore considerable effort, including self-reflexive effort, goes into getting actors to behave and take decisions in line with these roles and values; this is termed the 'logic of appropriateness' (March and Olsen 1989; see also Rydin, 2003, Chapter 3). This involves rewarding appropriate behaviour and penalizing behaviour that falls outside these bounds in a variety of ways. There is therefore a strong connection to prevailing norms within an organization. The outcomes of organizational behaviour will depend, at least to some extent, on how the various actors perform their allotted roles. If the organization is to be effective – however it defines this – then actors' behaviour that leads to effective outcomes needs to be encouraged. However institutional norms may not necessarily be oriented towards success or effectiveness. Institutionalist analysis also highlights how ineffective or suboptimal patterns of behaviour among actors can become embedded within organizations.

Institutionalism is therefore useful for understanding why things go wrong and continue to go wrong, as much as for understanding how organizational arrangements succeed. It is an actor-centred account that manages to see organizations as comprising actors with their own sense of agency, but also as sets of arrangements that place some constraints and pressures on those actors. It sees the informal as being as important as the formal. And it looks to the detail of everyday engagement between actors and how they take the mass of individual decisions during their daily activities to understand collective outcomes at the organizational level. Different emphases have been placed on the actors' motives. Some emphasize that political institutions are norm-shaping and meaningful, and have an integrating effect on actors in relation to a given social and political community. March and Olsen (1989) are representative of this tradition. Others emphasize a new economic institutionalism in the public choice tradition: see for example Knight (1992). Our approach follows that of March and Olsen.

The core of an institutionalist analysis therefore comprises two elements. First there is the need to map organizational arrangements and understand how these create linkages between actors. This is network analysis, a task that can be undertaken with more or less sophistication. Some network analyses content themselves with identifying actors, the links between them and the frequency of contact. Some go further and consider the nature of the relationships between the actors within the network, looking at the resources that are used by actors in relation to each other. Some may seek to quantify this through the use of software that measures features of the network such as range, density, centrality and the existence of important nodes (Dowding 1995). At some level though, a network analysis will be a foundational element of an institutionalist perspective on a problem. In all our case studies, the key actors are identified and the way that they form into a network is discussed.

The starting point is usually a formal network analysis, that is, the stated and public connections between actors. Bomberg (1998: 167) defines a network in policy contexts as:

> an identifiable and policy-concerned set of public and private actors who depend on one another for resources such as information, expertise, access and legitimacy. Most networks form around functions (implementation, regulation) and/or specific policy sectors (agriculture, environment)

These may be outlined in a formal document, particularly if the network has its own organizational character as a unit, a partnership or some such identifiable body. However the institutionalist emphasis on organizational culture and on routines established and reproduced through actors' repeated behaviour, also draws attention to the potential existence of more informal networks that are not set down in writing or explicitly stated. Therefore the network may be identified through the responses of actors in interviews as to the other actors that they are in contact with. This may produce a different pattern to the formal network. Such linkages may be based on social contacts between actors outside work. It may involve the influence of contacts between actors in one context that extends to contacts between them in another context. For example connections between farmers' representatives and local municipal officials over subsidies and other financial matters may impact on their relationships within a formal network trying to plan land uses in the area.

In contemporary conditions of governance, these networks will be widely drawn to extend across the barriers between the public sector (or the state), the economy and civil society. Network analysts need to be alert to the involvement of actors from all three sectors. But these sectors cannot be treated as unitary. They are also fragmented across tiers, scales and functional sectors, as discussed in Chapter 1. Therefore networks will typically connect actors at multiple points within the state, economy and civil society. These actors will also be members of multiple networks and thus analysts need to be aware of overlaps between networks and mutual influences between networks. The different position of an actor in different networks is also important; a local politician, say, may hold a nodal position in a local authority network but just be one representative among many in another network, say organized on a regional scale. Neither should networks be considered as unbounded. Each network will exclude as well as include certain actors, and the character of the boundaries that are drawn will be important for defining that network and how it operates. In these ways, a distinction can be drawn between issues networks, policy networks and (the more exclusive) policy communities (Dowding 1995; Rhodes 1997).

The institutionalist emphasis on cultural dimensions of organizations (seen as networks) further emphasizes the significance of actors being members of multiple networks. For actors may be subject to different 'logics of appropriateness' within the different networks and they may be pulled in different directions by the different roles and norms that they have to accommodate. They may also play an important role, acting as a node that connects to other actors in a variety of policy locations. Such nodal actors may be termed policy champions or brokers or entrepreneurs (see Chapter 5 in this volume). One interesting feature of a network that tries to combine actors from very different backgrounds, perhaps explicitly to overcome a collective action problem, is how these different pressures from the actors' 'home' networks and this new network affect each other. It is precisely because such multiple pressures may jeopardize efforts at joint working that the analysis of the cultural dimensions of organizations and networks is so important.

So the second element of an institutionalist analysis will be an attention to the norms, values, routines and everyday working practices of those within networks to reveal the normative pressures towards a particular pattern of behaviour on the part of actors, how actors construct their roles, and the extent to which these are embedded or amenable to change. With any attempt to bring together those who have not previously worked together, as with initiatives for collective action on resource management, then the potential for developing new patterns of decision-making and the extent of institutional inertia will be particularly important. Such cultural dimensions will be revealed through interviews, document analysis and non-participant observation of the working of the network.

The strengths of institutionalism therefore lie in its value for understanding networks in conditions of governance, its emphasis on the formal and the informal, and its highlighting of the cultural dimensions of relationships between actors that become embedded in everyday life. This book examines how the formal and informal networks linking actors shape the prospect for collective action to support sustainable natural resource use. But it must be recognized that there are also weaknesses in the institutionalist approach, which relate to its broad applicability. This very breadth of applicability can also be a weakness as it lacks specificity in identifying crucial factors or relationships. As such, institutionalism is more of a framework for analysis that requires supplementing with other 'middle-range' theories appropriate to the specific context being discussed (Hall and Taylor 1996). Any choice of supplementary middle-range theory will imply an emphasis on certain factors at the expense of others; such specification is the point of such theory-building. For the problem at issue here – how to engender collective action for sustainable natural resource management – two particular middle-range theories seem appropriate. They both focus, in different ways, on how relationships between actors can be built and strengthened and they have both been developed and applied in local environmental planning contexts. For this reason the concepts of social capital and institutional capacity will be discussed to build a more nuanced institutionalist account.

THE SEARCH FOR CONCEPTS (I) SOCIAL CAPITAL

The social capital literature is of particular interest to those concerned with natural resource management since Elinor Ostrom's work has shown how, in certain contexts, the development of social capital can help build institutions to overcome collective action problems where common pool resources are involved (Ostrom 1990, 1992, 1999). Social capital is understood here as constituted by dense networks of relationships between actors based on trust, mutuality (meaning a recognition of mutual interdependence and hence interests in common) and reciprocity (meaning a relationship whereby the behaviour of one actor can occur in the justified belief of another actor behaving in a certain way). Within networks, reputations for behaving in a certain way consistently are important for embedding norms of trust, mutuality and (particularly) reciprocity. Actors are able to take decisions in the belief – supported by evidence of past behaviour – that others will behave in a consistent and mutually beneficial way. They can trust each other to take decisions individually that will be to the advantage of all within the network. This applies to all actors, so that each actor's behaviour will be matched by reciprocal behaviour on the part of others. The whole scenario is based on all actors having an understanding of their mutual interdependence. Social capital can therefore be detected by prevailing norms within the network of trust in each other, recognition of mutuality and the expectation of reciprocity.

This works to enable collective action and prevent free-riding. The argument developed by Ostrom is that actors within a collective action problem face a particular incentive structure, in which the incentives to collaborate are outweighed by the disincentives. This is primarily because of the opportunity to free ride on the efforts of others. Putting effort into a collective action initiative will incur certain current costs and is unlikely to reap equivalent benefits for the individual actor. What social capital can do is create links between actors based on sets of moral obligations that alter the balance between these incentives and disincentives. The shame and loss of reputation that is associated with failure to engage in collective action becomes a strong incentive to collaborate. Or, put more positively, collaboration can also occur due to behaviour being encouraged and reinforced through praise and an enhanced reputation. The networks of social capital become a key way of establishing that collaboration is mutually beneficial and of disseminating information about and attributing blame to those who do not collaborate.

Such mechanisms work particularly well in small, homogeneous groups who are already expected to behave in similar ways and who can be readily monitored for inappropriate behaviour. Thus Ostrom favours building up small groups with strong social capital as a way of encouraging actors to come together to self-manage common pool resources. Such self-management is expressed through the creation of rules for resource management by the actors within the network. She further argues that such mutually agreed rules for resource use will contribute to the sustainable use of the resource, since this is in the long-term common self-interest of the group as a whole. Another aspect that is emphasized in Ostrom's work is the need for such rules to include generally recognized ways of handling conflicts over resource allocation. The existence of social capital then ensures that these rules are followed and that conflicts are resolved in a non-destructive way.

Based on Ostrom's work it would seem that the concept of social capital would be useful for analysing fragmented natural resource institutions. However Ostrom's own work was heavily based on studying the specific resource of water and largely located in developing-country contexts, particularly agrarian rural contexts. It may not be as appropriate for developed-country situations or for other types of natural resource management. In addition there are lessons to be learnt for the Ostromian perspective from the broader literature on social capital that has been instigated by Robert Putnam's use of the concept to understand local democracy and local economic development, first in the Italian and then the USA contexts (1993, 2000). This literature has sought to examine the ways that social capital in a locality can contribute to greater civic engagement among the local community or communities, enable better policy delivery and underpin more robust economic performance.

One important contribution that Putnam and others have made is to clarify that what Ostrom was discussing was a very specific kind of social capital, characterized as bonding social capital. This operates within an identifiable and delimited network and seeks to create strong ties between the actors in that network. Bonding social capital is usually associated with the local level and, further, with specific localities. The term 'community' is often used rather uncritically to describe the networks held together by bonding capital; indeed analysts concerned with urban regeneration often look to bonding social capital as a tool for strengthening local communities in the pursuit of such regeneration (*Urban Studies* 2001).

There are three problems with the strong normative emphasis on bonding social capital. Firstly, such bonding capital can have a 'dark side' (Beall 1997; Wilson 1997; Woolcock 1998: 158; Gargiulo and Benassi 2000). This concerns the extent of social monitoring that it involves, which can often be resisted by members of a local community. Strong local ties can be experienced as repressive by some members of a community or network. In addition there is nothing in the bonding social capital concept that ensures that it will be used to further a liberal agenda. It may be used to promote sustainable natural resource management and thereby support the livelihood of local communities, as Ostrom suggests. Putnam has suggested that it can support innovation and local economic development to the benefit of areas with strong bonding capital. But it can also be used to tie a community together for entirely negative reasons, as with the strong bonding capital represented by communities ruled by the Mafia and similar gangs. The Capulets and Montagues in *Romeo and Juliet* both exhibited strong bonding capital with tragic results. It is therefore important to see the arguments for building social capital in the context of broader arguments for enhancing democracy and meeting the challenge of a transparent and inclusive polity.

Secondly, the emphasis on bonding capital as a characteristic of specific localities may inhibit the treatment of issues where there is a strong non-local dimension. The tendency to equate the concern with bonding capital with the search for better planning of a local area or place is apparent in much of this literature. Bærenholdt and Aarsæther (2002) convincingly argue that there are implicit and unacknowledged assumptions about territoriality and place involved in the use of the concept and Woolcock (1998) is similarly critical of an overemphasis on the local in social capital work. Selman also points to the assumption 'that the social capital locked into communities is locally grounded' (2001: 27). This restricts attention to local actors when discussing social capital. Yet with many natural resource management problems, the involvement of non-local actors will be a key concern. Focusing just on an overly localized bonding variant of social capital may not be appropriate for such resource management.

In most of Ostrom's case studies, the communities were defined around local water resources (say, a river) and bonding social capital was seen as a way of enabling them to work together in a sustainable way. Representatives of different local communities were then brought together to handle the management of the underlying common pool resource (say, a river basin) in a mutually satisfactory manner. Typically a pyramid structure was proposed whereby local communities sent representatives to a gathering of a relatively small number of such communities; these gatherings sent representatives to a higher-tier gathering; and so on until the appropriate regional or other geographical scale was reached. This is an attempt to use the tool of social capital that had been demonstrated to have value at the level of the local community, at the broader trans-community scale. However this ignores the problems of considerable transactions costs involved in such pyramid structures. It also assumes that the role that bonding capital plays at the most local level is also appropriate at higher tiers. In effect it seeks to replicate the horizontal linkages typical of bonding capital at successive higher tiers.

The third problem with the overemphasis on bonding capital is the lack of attention to other forms that social capital may take. In particular analysts have pointed to the benefits of 'weak' links, as opposed to the strong links represented by bonding capital (Granovetter 1973). The term 'bridging capital' has been coined to describe the basis of such weak ties. Whereas bonding social capital seeks to build links between like members of a network, bridging social capital is about the work that needs to be done to build those links between unlike members and between different networks. The search for bridging social capital recognizes that effective bonding capital can sometimes inhibit initiatives by cementing a group into a close common identity that sets them apart from other actors, when links between all the actors could achieve positive change. Rydin et al. (2003) details how bonding social capital within a local community organization was acting to prevent urban regeneration efforts that required links across a mixture of very different actors, often operating at different tiers of government and/or over different geographical scales.

The distinction between bonding and bridging capital is now accepted as a key element of social capital theory. The two different types of social capital are seen as performing very different kinds of function (Brown and Ashman 1996). Bonding capital works to bring a limited group of actors, often very similar in at least one characteristic, together into a close set of relationships imbued with common values and a strong sense of reciprocity and mutual responsibility. This is often easier to achieve where the boundary around the group is clearly set, dividing insiders from outsiders. Bridging capital, on the other hand, is defined by its ability to bring unlike actors and sets of actors together. As such, it just describes links that are typical of many networks. The usefulness of describing this as a kind of social capital lies in the possibility that such links are also imbued with common values and a sense of reciprocity. Bridging social capital, like bonding social capital, is an institutional concept and therefore goes beyond the typical descriptors of network analysis.

This is a strength of bridging social capital as an analytic concept, but it does have some significant limitations. It can potentially be applied to a wide range of circumstances, just as network analysis itself can be. This means that it lacks specificity. Are all linkages equally useful? If bonding social capital relates to a bounded group of actors, are there no limits to the extent of bridging capital? How weak do links have to get before they are not contributing to collective action?

One particular issue that needs to be resolved in using social capital concepts in analysing policy situations is that such situations tend to involve both strong links between like actors and weaker links between unlike actors in different organizations. This could be analysed just in terms of networks, but then some of the cultural strength of institutional analysis would be lost. Bonding capital on its own overemphasizes the links between members of a community (however defined) and underemphasizes the contribution of weaker links. But bridging capital adds relatively little other than identifying that not all links between actors are of the strong bonding type.

One suggestion has been to identify a third type of social capital, bracing capital (Rydin and Holman 2004). This recognizes that specific policy situations require contacts between a limited set of actors; there has to be an edge to the set of actors involved and unlimited bridging is not helpful. However within this limited set there is a need for elements of bonding among specific groups of actors, cementing those specific relationships in more depth. The metaphor of 'bracing' is meant to suggest the need for scaffolding to achieve a specific policy task, which has definite outer boundaries and covers a limited amount of policy space, has links across the whole policy space (bridging) but particular points where more intensive links are needed to support the required policy work. This compares with the strong glue of the 'bonding' metaphor and the indiscriminate linking of 'bridging'.

So bracing social capital would operate within a delimited set of actors, allowing for strong bonds to be built between at least some of these actors, but the set would range across different local communities and groups, across sectors, across tiers and geographical spaces. In particular it would allow for a mix of horizontal and vertical linkages whereas most of the social capital literature focuses exclusively on horizontal linkages (Pretty and Ward 2001). As such the concept of bracing capital is much more appropriate to contemporary situations of governance where partnerships comprising local, regional and even national actors seek to work together, and where such actors may come from local communities, the state at various levels, quasi-state organizations and private sector businesses. The challenge within such partnerships is to build the right mix of weak and strong ties to hold the partnership together and collectively achieve the desired goals.

The need to go beyond the current usage of the social capital concept in contemporary conditions of governance has been pointed to by political scientists. However they have chosen to frame this problem in terms of the overemphasis of the social capital concept on civil society and the lack of attention to the role of the state in shaping the nature of that civic action (Lowndes and Wilson 2001; Maloney et al. 2000). In response Maloney et al. use the concept of 'political opportunity structure' to point to how the state shapes the demand for civic involvement that strong social capital can supply. Similarly Lowndes and Wilson point to four aspects of institutional design that, they argue, explain how state agency is involved in civic engagement. These are: the state's relationships with the voluntary sector; opportunities for public participation; the responsiveness of state decision-making; and the arrangements for democratic leadership and social inclusion. The problem with these developments of social capital literature is that it remains within a sharp dichotomy between state and civil society, seeing social capital as an attribute of civil society and the state as potentially shaping it. Yet governance refers to a much closer and more involved interconnection between the state and civil society (and the business sector). Seeing bonding social capital as influenced by decisions and actions of the state is a very partial account of how communities can be involved in governance structures such as partnerships.

A broader reinterpretation of the social capital concept to apply to link-ages within but also beyond civil society is more appropriate. This would marry the network analysis of complex governance structures that go beyond the locality and the community with the distinctive social capital emphasis on relationships of trust, mutuality and reciprocity. One of the research themes of this book is to explore how far such a reinterpretation of the social capital literature is useful in understanding attempts to over-come fragmented institutions for natural resource management and instead enable collective action for sustainable resource management. Before exploring this through our case studies though, it is appropriate to consider an alternative institutionalist approach to see if it has something distinctive to offer to our analysis.

THE SEARCH FOR CONCEPTS (II) INSTITUTIONAL CAPACITY

The social capital concept appears therefore to have considerable potential for analysing situations of fragmented institutions for natural resource management, provided adjustments are made for the kind of linkages found within contemporary governance. However its main strength – the distinctive focus on relationships of trust, mutuality and reciprocity – may also turn out to be a weakness. Are there other key factors that should be incorporated into a research framework? With this question in mind the institutional capacity concept is also worthy of discussion. While the social capital literature can be considered as highly focused and based on a tight causal mechanism (particularly in Ostrom's work), the institutional capac-ity literature is much more broadly drawn; variants are used to analyse both economic and policy processes.

Typically an institutional capacity model is multidimensional. For example Healey et al. (1999, 2002) build on work by Innes et al. (1994) who identified three different kinds of capital that could be activated in rela-tionships between actors: intellectual, social and political. Actors could hold such capital vis-à-vis other actors and use these to achieve their ends and influence the decision-making of others. The use of such capital would activate the networks that the actors were involved in. The focus on such capital is therefore useful for exploring the dynamics of a situation and how change might be achieved, and it draws attention to the range of resources that may be activated through networks as opposed to the rather narrower focus of the social capital literature. Healey et al. (1999) renamed these three types of capital as knowledge resources, relational resources and mobilization capacity; together they comprise institutional capacity. In another variant, Davoudi and Evans (2004) see institutional capacity as comprising four types of capital, echoing Innes et al. again. These are intellectual capital, social capital, material capital and political capital.

Proponents have found institutional capacity to be useful in a variety of contexts. Healey et al. (1999) used it to explore urban planning and, in particular, urban regeneration projects, to see how successful urban change is achieved. In a related area of work, Amin and Thrift (1994, 1995) use the institutional capacity concept alongside that of 'institutional thickness' to identify the qualities of territorial milieux that promote innovation and related economic development, while Davoudi and Evans (2004) tackle waste management from this perspective. In the expectation that it might be similarly useful in terms of natural resource management, it is worthwhile examining the different elements.

Material capital is only explicitly mentioned in Davoudi and Evans's approach, perhaps because it is such an essential element of any network analysis that it can be taken for granted. Such analysis looks at both the linkages between actors and the flow of resources through those linkages. In most network analysis these resources are largely taken to mean finance, political authority and the ability to exercise regulatory powers. This is the automatic background for an institutionalist analysis that then looks beyond such linkages and material resources.

Davoudi and Evans include social capital as a second dimension. This has of course been discussed at length above. In Healey et al.'s framework this is termed 'relational resources', the term 'social capital' having been dismissed as a confused 'portmanteau term' (1999: 121). This raises the question of whether the term 'relational resources' provides additional analytic capacity beyond the social capital concept. Healey et al. use relational resources to refer to the way that actors are embedded in networks and tied together by bonds that have moral significance, connoting rights, obligations and levels of trust between actors. This seems very close to any definition of social capital. They suggest that social capital can be specified along a number of different axes:

- range, that is, the key actors and how they relate to other members of the network with an emphasis on the factors that hold the actors together in the network;
- morphology, referring to the 'architecture' of the network including density (or thickness) and identifiable patterns such as flat, equal networks as compared to tiered, hierarchical ones; spatial reach is also relevant here;
- network integration, which looks at how the multiple networks in a locality are integrated with each other; and

- power relations, which are invoked to discuss how relationships are held together and to acknowledge the active work involved in managing relationships within networks; there is also a nod here to the more structural forces that constrain and shape the operation of networks and to the potential for actors to influence these structural forces.

Of these axes, morphology is a standard network descriptor, as are elements of range. The emphasis on factors that hold the network together is resonant of bonding capital, while the reference to network integration could be considered an aspect of bridging capital. There is clearly considerable overlap between the social capital and institutional capacity concepts here. Either approach could be used to distinguish, say, a small network with many actors held together by trust and strong bonds but isolated from other networks, from a broader network that is part of a network of networks, with a large number of weak links and specific nodal points to which a limited set of actors have access.

The final axis referring to power relations is rather different in character and connects with the identification of mobilization capacity as a key element of institutional capacity. Mobilization capacity is defined as the ability to activate knowledge (discussed further below) and relational resources in a proactive manner. It is therefore presented as the dynamic element in the model and characterized in terms of opportunity structure, arenas, repertoires and change agents. Opportunity structure refers to the perceptions among actors that change is possible and desirable, as well as perceptions of constraints. It is linked to the selection of issues for mobilization and the extent to which there is agreement on this issue agenda. Arenas identify the loci where mobilization may take place, and repertoires refer to the techniques of mobilization that actors may use. Finally, the need for innovators is pinpointed in the term 'change agents', a term close to that of 'policy entrepreneur' used in political sciences. In Davoudi and Evans's framework the discussion of power and mobilization capacity is rolled together under the heading of political capital. This refers to the mix of capacities that give actors the power to achieve an objective, the 'capacity to act' in Stone's terms (1989).

The difficulty with these attempts to explicitly consider power within a network framework is that they suggest that power is a distinct element separable from the other aspects of the networks' operation. Rather power, whether understood as the ability to achieve an objective or to make other actors behave in a certain way, is an integral aspect of how networks work. It is implicit in all relations between actors and all mobilizations of resources through networks. There is a sense in which social capital, with its policing and monitoring dimensions, is also involved in creating, maintaining and expressing power relations. Power is also involved in the way that knowledge (discussed below) is constructed and used within the networks. It is not possible to limit the discussion of power to just one aspect of institutional capacity. Rather it is made manifest through the operation of the entire network.

This then raises the question of how the dynamics of such network operations are conceived. As discussed above, the identification of categories of mobilization capacity or political capital suggests that these dynamics are a distinctive aspect of institutional capacity. But the corollary of separating out the dynamics in this way is that the other aspects must in some sense be static. Despite statements to be found in both Davoudi and Evans and Healey et al., that institutional capacity is a relational concept and that its constituent parts (like social capital) are also relational and not stocks or assets attributed to actors, the separation out of mobilization as a distinct element can only reduce the other elements to such stocks and assets. A similar problem can be found in Lowndes and Wilson's work on social capital and institutional design (2001). Here they talk of the 'creation' and 'mobilising' of social capital, implying that it must be a stock (2001: 631).

An alternative view is to see the dynamics of a network as involving the activation of the relationships inherent within that network, including the various linkages and resources that flow along the linkages. Power is expressed through these dynamics. It becomes the sum total of the network relationships understood in terms of capacity to achieve outcomes and influence the behaviour of others. The activation of resources within the network will be a key element of such power being expressed. Power and power relations cannot therefore be separated out in the way suggested by some analysts. Relationships between actors and resources may be latent, that is, not actually activated. But their activation is implicit in the relationships and potential resource flows. Actual activation will be contingent on actors' decisions and behaviour in a particular situation. But mobilization is always a possibility, not a separate capacity. This suggests that the categories of mobilization capacity, relational resources and political capital add little that is distinctive to an institutional network approach that incorporates the insights of social capital literature, beyond reminding one of the range of resources that may be activated through networks.

The same cannot be said of knowledge resources, which are also given a prominent role in the institutional capacity approach. Again, knowledge is here understood as a relational concept with an emphasis on interactive learning through the relationships in the network, rather than on knowledge as an asset that individual actors bring to the process. Furthermore, knowledge is seen as socially constructed within these interrelationships.

This opens up the term 'knowledge' to mean that all those claims that are *recognized* with the network are knowledge. Local as well as aspatial knowledges may be accredited; experiential as well as experimental; tacit as well as formal. The question is how knowledge claims are expressed and recognized with the network.

Four different research questions are posed by Healey et al. in relation to knowledge resources. Firstly, there is the question of who is considered to hold accredited knowledge claims, leading to the possibility of drawing up a 'knowledge map'. This is assumed to be closely tied to the specific locality, which in Healey et al.'s work is the focus of analysis. Secondly, the underlying knowledge frames, which give meaning to the flow of information within the network, should be unpacked. Thirdly, there is the important issue of how knowledge is transferred around and between networks and, within one network, from one arena of discussion to another. Finally, the openness of the network to learning and absorbing new knowledge should be assessed, particularly in relation to local traditions and the potential for new knowledge to mesh with established ways of looking at the locality and local policy. Davoudi and Evans discuss knowledge under the category of intellectual capital and identify the same four key aspects.

These are all aspects that are not automatically highlighted within either a network analysis or a social capital framework. Here there is a distinctive contribution that the institutional capacity approach can bring to understanding institutions, and this is a key strength that we will wish to take forward in discussing our cases. The role of knowledge resources in framing issues, in providing a basis for either bonding or bridging between actors and for shaping the identity of actors within networks, are all issues that we will wish to explore.

Another aspect of the institutional capacity framework that Healey et al. develop is the emphasis on the role that external forces on the one hand, and local place-based tradition on the other, play in enabling institutional capacity. External pressures would include, in our context of natural resource management, the characteristics of the common resource pool and its current state of productivity or degradation. It would also include pressures on the network from higher tiers of government, often national government but also including transnational bodies such as the European Union, as well as economic conditions, such as the market for the natural resource product in question. Healey et al. use this distinction between local capacity and external forces to put more emphasis on the prospects for place-based governance, which builds on local traditions to develop a strong sense of local ownership of the area, local identity and distinctiveness of local networks. All these are held to enhance the operation of institutional capacity. This is not a necessary conclusion of this insight but does suggest the value of identifying external forces and changes as part of research into local institutions.

These emphases on knowledge resources and on external factors are elements we would wish to bring into our analysis, along with a broadening of the resources that can be operationalized in a network. However other aspects of the institutional capacity framework seem less helpful. Furthermore it is important to recognize the strongly normative element to some institutional capacity work that may confuse its more analytic application. For example Healey et al. use the concept to argue for the positive role of local action in reaction to external forces. They also develop an a priori theoretical description of the most successful type of initiatives on the assumption that success is related to the development of institutional capacity. That is, they argue that on the basis of these categories it is possible to identify the networks that will be successful in achieving their specific objectives. These are networks that reach a wide range of stakeholders who are held together by rich bonds, but also have clearly identified nodal points that enable multiple opportunities for access from outside. In addition there need to be good links between networks and also good access to holders of power (through regulation and resource allocation) beyond the networks, ideally characterized by open, sincere and trusting relationships. This sounds idealistic and raises a number of questions. Are there any conflicts between these multiple requirements? What are the barriers that prevent such ideal network attributes being established? How realistic are these recommendations? What are the costs of such an approach, including the costs of network maintenance? Do these costs increase over time?

This normative approach can distract from the analytic use of the institutional capacity concept to see whether central government action may not be a more appropriate way to achieve a particular end. A similar issue is identified by Lowndes and Wilson (2001) in relation to the social capital literature, where they criticize Putnam for eliding democratic goals with policy performance goals. They argue that Putnam makes a case for social capital enhancing policy performance, and then conflates the two ends; since the democratic goals are a *sine qua non*, this results in a strongly normative argument for developing social capital.

These examples emphasize the importance of keeping an open mind on the benefits of developing any particular type of network and associated institutional arrangements. It is a research question to investigate the type of institution that exists in a particular situation, to see how it is working and to make a judgement on the goals it is achieving. Only on the basis of such research can policy recommendations for institutional design be put forward. This is the task of this book and the final section summarizes the research questions arising from this discussion of institutions, networks, social capital and institutional capacity.

EXAMINING CONCEPTS THROUGH CASE STUDIES

In the following chapters, we use these concepts of institutions, networks, social capital (bonding, bridging and bracing) and institutional capacity (particularly the role of knowledge resources) to investigate how collective action over natural resource management is fostered (or not) in situations of fragmentation. While the case studies vary and each highlight rather different aspects of the research task, there are some common themes running through them.

There is an emphasis on identifying how actors are linked together through network arrangements, both formally and informally. We consider how these linkages extend across sectors, across tiers of government and across space and localities. Since the institutional framework also alerts us to the importance of how norms and values are established for networks, we look for evidence of how such norms and values are shaped and shared through the network. Following on the discussion above, we consider how a variety of resources are mobilized through the networks. These might include financial resources along with regulatory powers and authority. Third party backing may often be an important constituent of such authority. To these, the social capital approach would add the important elements of trust, reputation and the ability to require reciprocal action, as well as the exercise of sanctions and penalties (both 'soft' and 'hard'). And from the institutional capacity perspective, the particular role of knowledge resources can be identified in all their complexity. The institutional capacity framework also identifies the importance of external factors and how these may influence the operation of local networks.

We also consider our cases in terms of the level and extent of collective action that results. We look at this in slightly different ways in our different contexts but in several of our cases we are considering a process of strategy development. Where this is concerned, three levels of agreement between parties can be identified: the extent of agreement on the everyday practice of the network; agreement on the process of developing strategy; and agreement on the actual visions in the strategy itself. Beyond this there is the extent of agreement and cooperation in implementing this vision through various processes and procedures. Then there is an assessment in terms of policy outcomes, meaning not only the plan or strategy but also the implementation of that plan or strategy, the generation of common norms between parties and the impacts on the ground. This last aspect can be measured in terms of environmental impacts and changes in actors' perceptions, as well as judged against actors' ambitions for collective action. We are particularly interested to find evidence of change operating as a virtuous (or vicious) circle, whereby relationships between actors reinforce trends, hopefully towards greater cooperation and collective action. Finally, we consider how these processes of cooperation are linked to the legitimacy of the policy process and of the democratic (or otherwise) political systems in which our cases are embedded.

3. The New Forest, England: cooperative planning for a commons

Yvonne Rydin and Tove Måtar

All landscapes are unique and all landscapes have their histories but the New Forest stands out in Britain's crowded spaces for a number of reasons. This area in the south of England is a landscape of beauty close to major metropolitan areas. It is a habitat of considerable importance and fragility. The social history of the area can be traced back almost a millennium. And the area is based on a pattern of property ownership, known as common-ing, which makes it one of Britain's few commons. We begin our account of the area by describing this history and outlining the nature of the New Forest as a commons.

The New Forest was a royal hunting ground, principally for deer, dating back to the time of William the Conqueror in the later eleventh century. The naming of the area as a 'forest' dates back to this time, when it referred to its properties as a hunting ground and food larder, rather than as an area full of trees. In 1079 William the Conqueror 'afforested' the area, meaning he brought it under Forest Law, designed to protect the 'beasts of the chase'. Such beasts were red deer, fallow deer, roe and wild pig. The name 'New Forest' can therefore be somewhat misleading as the area is neither new nor entirely a forest, that is, woodland. Even during William's time much of the Forest was heathland (Hampshire County Council 2004).

In the seventeenth century and well into the eighteenth century the Navy's need for timber for shipbuilding dominated the use of the Forest. A growing conflict between forestry and the existing grazing rights of com-moners (discussed further below) in the Forest emerged. In 1851 the regis-tration of all Rights of Common on unenclosed land within the boundary of the Forest began, to be finalized in 1852 when the 'Register of Decisions on Claims to Forest Rights' was published. Then in 1877 a New Forest Act was passed which meant that the Crown gave up its powers and no more land could be enclosed beyond that which had already been enclosed by the reign of William III. The act was also called the 'Commoners' Charter' as it provided for a balance between the Crown's need for timber and the commoners' need to use the Open Forest for grazing. This went someway towards resolving the conflict between commoning and forestry.

In 1923 the responsibility of managing the Forest was handed over to the Forestry Commission from the Office of the Woods. The Forestry Commission is a public agency set up in 1919 specifically for the purpose of ensuring that Britain was self-sufficient in timber. In fact it achieved this goal in 1984. As forestry production has decreased in importance, so the Forestry Commission has increasingly concerned itself with the recreational use and the nature conservation value of its forest areas. Its more commercial activities have been hived off to a sub-agency, Forestry Enterprise. Altogether the Forestry Commission manages 10 000 km² of land, with the New Forest amounting to 375 km² (Forestry Commission 2004).

The main uses of the New Forest are now a combination of timber production (although this has declined in recent years due to the low prices of timber), recreation and nature conservation. The demand for recreation and contact with nature are considerable since the New Forest is surrounded by the large urban areas of Southampton (population 221 100), Bournemouth (163 700) and Portsmouth (183 973) (see Figure 3.1). The area of the Forest itself is home to some 60 000 people but over 15 million people live within a 1.5-hour drive from the Forest. In addition people come from further afield to visit the Forest. A visitor survey from 1996–97 estimated that there were 18 million day visitors to the Forest; today's estimate is around 22 or even as high as 25 million a year, a rapid increase and a substantial total number. As a result both domestic and even some international tourism are important contributors to the local economy. In fact, tourism provides the single largest economic input to the Forest. In 2001 the value was estimated to £156 million providing for around 30 per cent of all jobs (New Forest Committee 2004).

The nature conservation value of the Forest is as important as its recreational value. As discussed above, and contrary to the impression that might be conveyed by its name, the New Forest is not dominated by trees. There are areas of woodland and these are diverse, combining a variety of coniferous and deciduous species. The areas for timber production, which are fenced to keep the Forest animals out, consist of mostly conifers and some broadleaves such as beech and oak. However with changed market conditions, the area of new treeplanting for timber has declined. The Open Forest, which is where the commoners' animals graze, consists of many different types of habitats, such as dry heath, humid heath, wet heath, valley mire, associated heath communities and ancient and ornamental forests. The New Forest is the largest remaining area of lowland heath in Britain. All of this results in a very varied and broad flora and fauna including

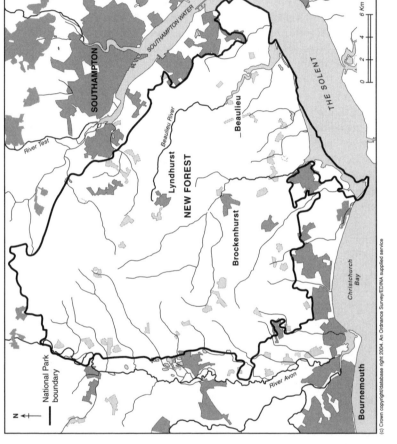

Figure 3.1   New Forest

birds, invertebrates (for example beetles, butterflies and moths), reptiles, bats, mammals (such as deer, squirrel, badgers) and fungi, many of which are endangered species.

Central to the maintenance of the ecology of the Forest is the presence of the ponies. The New Forest ponies are semi-wild and have been present in the Forest since medieval times. They roam freely in the Forest and on the heathland and have also been important for the local economy. Small in stature – the height can vary from under 122 cm to a maximum of 148 cm – they do not disturb the fragile habitats. Rather their pattern of grazing is the main reason why the heathland has not been encroached on by scrubland; they have been called 'the architects of the Forest'. The maintenance of the population of ponies and the particular system by which the ponies are managed is essential to the continuing value of the New Forest as a landscape to be enjoyed for recreational and nature conservation reasons. And this brings us to the role of the New Forest as a commons, because the management of the ponies is synonymous with commoning as a practice.

Commoning describes the activities of the New Forest commoners. These commoners own specific plots of land in the area to which common rights to use the Forest are attached. These entitle commoners to take specified materials and products from land belonging to others within the Forest. In practice, this means that commoners have the right to graze their ponies on other land within the Forest. The New Forest is therefore not a commons in the sense that access is open to all; it is not *res nullius*. Rather it is a commons in the sense that a specified group of people – the commoners – have a specific set of rights (largely grazing) that they can exercise. In 1858 six rights of common were registered for the New Forest (Forestry Commission 2004):

1. The Right of Pasture: the right to put out ponies, cattle and donkeys on the Forest.
2. The Right of Sheep: the right to turn out sheep on the Forest. Very few properties own this right and none is exercising it.
3. The Right of Mast: the right to turn out pigs in the autumn season to feed on green acorns and beech mast that are poisonous to cattle and ponies.
4. The Right of Fuelwood: the right to collect wood for fuel. This right is nowadays confined to a few commoners; most rights have been sold to the Forestry Commission as the supply has caused them inconvenience.
5. The Right of Marl: the right to take limey clay for the improvement of agricultural land, this is no longer practised in the Forest.
6. The Right of Turbary: this right allows the commoner to cut turf, or peat, for fuel; this right is also not practised any more.

The underlying property rights of ownership of the land rest with the Crown and other local freeholders, including of course the commoners' own freehold rights in specific plots of land. This is a specific case of *res communales* (Berkes 1989). The net result of these common property rights held by commoners is that 5000–6000 animals are turned out each year. In 2001 the figures were 3885 ponies, 2890 cattle, 172 pigs and 83 donkeys. According to the Forestry Commission there were 455 practising commoners in the Forest in 2000 (Forestry Commission 2004). The set of rights and responsibilities bound up in commoning have evolved to manage the potential collective action problem posed by multiple owners of common grazing rights in the Forest. However the issue today is not potential overgrazing by the Forest ponies and other foraging animals, but rather the combined effect on a valued landscape and fragile ecosystem of the multiple uses of the Forest by commoners, local residents and tourists from further afield. This is the modern collective action problem facing those concerned with the long-term sustainability of the Forest.

Specific problems include the physical effects of erosion from people walking in the Forest, the disturbance to the wildlife and the knock-on demands for changed land use. There are demands for more car parking and for camping sites arising from the numbers visiting the area. To try and manage the visitors, several roads have been closed, thus reducing the impact on the adjoining forestland. Whether this has been sufficient is hotly debated. There is a division of views between those seeking to reduce the overall level of demands on the area and those who would be satisfied by more active management of that demand. For this latter group, the economic contribution of Forest visitors is important to the locality and they seek a form of management that will ensure greater expenditure in the local area by these visitors, through overnight hotel stays or the use of local pubs and restaurants. The Forestry Commission, with its reduced income from timber, is also interested in generating returns from more tourism.

In this context, the loss of active commoning would be a real problem. It is seen as essential to the conservation of the area; in effect, New Forest commoners undertake some of the key management activities of the area through their grazing practices. However commoning is not economically viable today. None of the commoners can make a living through New Forest livestock. The cattle and pigs are sold at market and there are special pony sales held at Beaulieu in the Forest, but prices for the ponies are not high. The Department of Environment, Food and Rural Affairs has signed an agreement with the commoners under the Countryside Stewardship scheme that provides subsidies for those grazing their ponies on the land. This amounts to £4 million over ten years, roughly £2000 per commoner per annum. But not all commoners have shown much interest in the scheme, not least because it seeks to regulate the grazing of animals. Most commoners now have other forms of employment and commoning is seen as a source of supplementary income, albeit one with significant cultural roots.

In addition to livelihood concerns, commoners have been faced with the problems of high and rising local accommodation costs. The south of England is a high-price housing market, buoyed up by the economic growth of the main urban areas, the numbers commuting to high-income London and the substantial demand from those moving into the area for their retirement, often from even higher-priced housing markets. This puts most local housing to buy beyond the reach of commoners, with their precarious livelihoods. The local council, the New Forest District Council, has put in place a number of affordable housing projects specifically for commoners but this is unlikely to solve their housing difficulties. These economic pressures on commoners may have considerable environmental impacts on the Forest if they result in a decline in commoning.

The problem in the New Forest is therefore a need to balance the demands for recreation and the economic benefits from tourism on the one hand, with the impacts on the landscape and ecology on the other, having due regard to the importance of the economically beleaguered commoners in maintaining the unique character of the area. To achieve this requires a number of different actors, with different interests in the area, to understand their mutual interdependence.

BUILDING A NETWORK

The various actors within the New Forest have evolved specific institutional arrangements to try and recognize this interdependence and collectively manage the Forest. Before describing these arrangements, we will outline the different actors involved. It should be noted that as of our research in 2004 the New Forest had not yet been formally designated as a National Park; this occurred in March 2005. We discuss the implications of this designation process at the end of the chapter although, as will become apparent in our discussions, the increasingly likely prospect of National Park designation affected some of the networking processes in the New Forest.

The first actors to consider are the local authorities for the area, directed by elected local politicians. The majority of the New Forest lies inside the New Forest District Council; the total population for this local authority is around 169 518 (NFDC 2001). However a small part of the Forest falls within the jurisdiction of Salisbury District Council. In addition, the Test Valley Borough Council borders the New Forest. Above this district council tier of local government are the county councils. New Forest

District Council and Test Valley Borough Council fall within Hampshire County Council while Salisbury District Council lies within Wiltshire County Council's remit. The local authorities are individually and jointly responsible for local planning of the area, including land use and transport planning, as well as having an input into nature conservation and economic development. There is a lower tier of local authorities comprising numerous parish and town councils. In the New Forest area there are 41 such councils. However they have little in the way of formal responsibilities, resources or powers. They are primarily consultative bodies although they can undertake projects of specifically local interest.

In addition to local authorities there are a number of regional offices of governmental agencies that are involved in the New Forest. Such agencies each have their own functional planning remit, their own management structures and quasi-corporate mission. They are responsible to central government through the Department of Environment, Food and Rural Affairs (DEFRA), but are essentially arm's-length bodies and have been so since the 1980s when the last Conservative government began a programme of distancing such agencies from central government and its departments. There are four such agencies relevant to the New Forest case.

The Forestry Commission has already been mentioned as directly involved in managing much of the land within the New Forest for the Crown, the ultimate landowner. Then there is English Nature, the body charged with promoting nature conservation and England's contribution to biodiversity. It is a significant source and repository of ecological knowledge. English Nature directly manages a number of national nature reserves and in 1969 a Minute of Intent was signed between the Forestry Commission and English Nature whereby the commission recognized the Forest as having the status of a National Nature Reserve and agreed that consultation needed to take place on every issue of importance. English Nature is the body that liaises with all landowners and organizations, often non-governmental organizations, such as the local Wildlife Trusts or Royal Society for the Protection of Birds, who can be responsible for areas of nature conservation importance.

The Countryside Agency is the national body with, as its name suggests, current responsibility for the countryside. As such it promotes the use and enjoyment of the countryside, representing recreational interests, and it handles many of the numerous special schemes for the management of the countryside in pursuit of a balance between production, recreation and environmental goals. However although it had its origins in rural development, the agency does not have overall economic development responsibilities in rural areas, this having been removed to the regional development agencies when they were set up in 1998 (operative in April 1999). The

Countryside Agency is also the government agency responsible for National Park designations and therefore has been a key player in the designation of the New Forest.

The roles of English Nature and the Countryside Agency are currently in flux following a review by the Department for Environment, Food and Rural Affairs. The two government agencies are from 1 April 2005 due to establish a distinctive new body which has been named the Commission for Rural Communities. The new body is supposed to become the rural advocate, expert adviser and independent watchdog (Countryside Agency 2005).

The fourth agency is the Environment Agency, charged with pollution control, water management and waste management, the latter in conjunction with local authorities. Its remit within the New Forest has been limited but it has taken an active role in the LIFE 3 biodiversity project mentioned below because of the implications for water management.

There are two main organizations representing the commoners. The New Forest Commoners' Defence Association has about 700 members of which about 400 are practising commoners. The NFCDA was founded in 1909 in response to increasing conflicts between the activities of the urban population, which was spreading to the Forest's fringes, and the grazing of commoners' animals. The NFCDA has through the years had an active role in raising the profile of and securing the commoners' right to graze animals in the Open Forest (NFCDA 2004).

Then there is the Court of Verderers, which is a statutory body set up under the New Forest Act 1877. The name 'Verderer' comes from the Norman 'vert', meaning green, and refers to their roles as guardians of the Open Forest. The court has two main roles: to manage the animals in the area through the regulation of commoning; and to contribute to spatial planning and development control decisions. Also, under the Countryside Act of 1968 the Forestry Commission has the powers to provide for tourist, recreational or sporting facilities, but these powers are only exercisable with the consent of the Verderers of the New Forest. The court comprises ten Verderers, five appointed by organizations with an interest in the Forest and five elected directly by commoners. The Verderers meet every month in an open court where anybody is free to make a presentment (a verbal statement made to the court). The court thereafter considers the presentment and gives a judgment during the next meeting (Verderers 1997).

In addition, within civil society, there are numerous groups active in the New Forest. These range from dog walkers to cyclists, ramblers, kite flyers, off-road cyclists and conservationists. As we will see, these are also represented in the New Forest organizations.

There has been a long history of bringing together the various actors within the Forest into networks, largely in response to the recognition that there were conflicts between the different interests in the area. For example the New Forest Association (NFA) was established in 1867 and attracts members from organizations such as the Verderers, Hampshire Wildlife Trust, the Commoners' Defence Association, New Forest parish councillors as well as individual landowners. The association states that it is dedicated to sustaining and protecting the traditional character of the New Forest. The NFA is also a strong supporter of commoning and promotes public understanding of the tradition and its modern relevance to the Forest (NFA 2004). This association now finds itself located within the contemporary networks for planning the New Forest area. There are two formal networks, one more extensive and consultative, the other more focused on specific collective action.

The extensive network is termed the New Forest Consultative Panel, a name that fully reflects its role within the management of the area. It is a forum for about 70 different organizations with fairly flexible rules of membership. It predates the more formal and narrowly drawn New Forest Committee, discussed below, having been established in 1971 in response to some vocal conflicts over the management of the Forest. The panel is made up of representatives from all parish, town, district and county councils in the New Forest. Furthermore it includes representatives from amenity, conservation and voluntary groups (for example New Forest Friends of the Earth, Hampshire and Isle of Wight Wildlife Trust, Hampshire Council for Youth Services, Hampshire Field Club and Archaeological Society), sporting and recreational organizations (for example New Forest Equestrian Association, Camping and Caravanning Club, New Forest Beagles), and land management and statutory bodies with responsibilities in the New Forest (for example Forestry Commission, English Nature, National Trust, Verderers of the New Forest, DEFRA). The panel meets on a bimonthly basis to discuss issues affecting the New Forest area. It is used as a sounding board for ideas from the committee and the statutory bodies in the New Forest. This open discussion can perform a useful function in raising issues for further attention but the very openness and informality of the panel discussions that enable unrestricted consultation render the panel less useful for promoting effective collective action.

It is the New Forest Committee that is the main forum for establishing the nature of collective action and the key network for undertaking initiatives that will promote such action. The committee was established in 1990 following a proposal by a Review Group, itself set up in 1986 by the Forestry Commission to consider the conservation of the traditional character of the Forest for future generations. The impetus for creating the committee lay with the local office of the Forestry Commission and its concern over the continuing conflicts about tree-cutting and forest management.

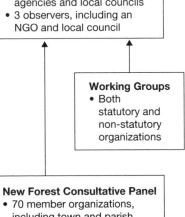

Projects and Partnerships

LEADER +
- Overseen by a local action group, including members from statutory and non-satutory organizations plus local authorities

LIFE and LIFE 3
- Statutory and non-statutory organizations plus local authorities (LIFE coordinated by NFC, LIFE 3 coordinated by Hampshire County Council)

PROGRESS
- Joint project with similar areas in the Netherlands and France (led by Countryside Agency)

Formal Networks

New Forest Committee
- 9 member organizations, including government agencies and local councils
- 3 observers, including an NGO and local council

Working Groups
- Both statutory and non-statutory organizations

New Forest Consultative Panel
- 70 member organizations, including town and parish councils, NGOs, government agencies, local interest groups

Figure 3.2   Networks and partnerships in the New Forest

Meeting every two months, the committee comprises nine member organizations, all of which have a statutory role in the management of the New Forest. The four government agencies reviewed above are all represented and so too are the key local authorities (Test Valley Borough Council has only observer status). The Verderers of the New Forest are full members but the New Forest Commoners' Defence Association again has only observer status. This suits the Commoners' Defence Association as it means they do not pay fees and feel that they retain a degree of independence, which is important to their membership. Other observers are the National Farmers' Union, the Country Land and Business Association and the New Forest Association of Local Councils (representing town and parish councils).

These formal extensive and intensive networks appear to cover all the main relationships between actors in the New Forest (see Figure 3.2). Research revealed very little in the way of other informal contacts. Interview questions on the most important actors consistently resulted in mentions for the members of the New Forest Committee. The only minor exceptions to this were references to the 'general public' living in the Forest and the National Trust, a major non-governmental organization (NGO) and local landowner. However the committee clearly represents the main networking activity involved in the management of the Forest area. Our research suggests that the formal network of the committee has been extremely influential in establishing a cooperative framework for collective action to resolve problems within the Forest. We now explore how this cooperation has been established, beginning with the joint work undertaken by the committee on preparing a strategy for the New Forest.

DEVELOPING A STRATEGY

The New Forest Committee was founded in 1990 by the Forestry Commission with central government support. Its first Annual Report stated that it was formed to 'co-ordinate the activities of the six national and local government bodies which have greatest involvement in the life and future of the Forest' (Forestry Commission 2004). The first New Forest Strategy was published in 1996, mainly directed toward statutory bodies, that is, government agencies and local authorities. The review of the strategy deliberately sought to engage a broader range of stakeholders. It was timed with a view to a possible forthcoming designation as a National Park (discussed further below) and hence the possibility that the strategy could form the basis for the National Park Plan. The review process started in 2001 when a work plan was drawn up and a Strategy Review Group consisting of around 100 stakeholders was formed. The group met six times in 2001–2002. Then in the summer of 2002 a formal public consultation on the strategy was held which resulted in 120 responses. These were then incorporated into the revised strategy. The consultation process sought to include all groups in the New Forest in the development of the strategy. The groups that were the hardest to reach were young people and businesses. Consultation was held through workshops, formal consultation, and meetings with statutory bodies, input from local schools and informal discussions with members of the public.

Interviews suggest that there was a good level of participation at most workshops, although this was not consistent throughout the strategy development process. About half a dozen commoners attended all the public meetings on the strategy. The early stages of interaction were characterized by conflicts between local residents and those representing visitors to the Forest. In addition there was considerable opposition to any development in the Forest. As the discussion progressed, issues of nature conservation and local heritage figured more prominently along with the need to promote local economic development. Working through these issues meant that by the end of the process there was a considerable degree of common agreement on the need for a comprehensive and balanced approach to all these issues.

The New Forest Strategy was published in 2003 and sets out the problems and possible ways forward under the headings of:

- conserving the Forest (with reference to the landscape, cultural heritage, biodiversity and general environmental quality),
- living and working in the Forest (covering commoning, farming, forestry and woodland management, tourism, sustainable development, affordable housing, business and employment opportunities, and village and town centres),
- enjoying the Forest, and
- implementing the strategy.

This last heading, of implementation, is now the most important for taking the common strategy forward. The strategy itself carries no statutory or resource-led force. Implementation is dependent on the ideas within the strategy being incorporated into the decision-making and plans of the constituent organizations within the committee and on specific projects aimed at implementing specific aspects being funded.

The first step towards implementing the strategy has been for the New Forest Committee to produce an Action Plan. There was a public consultation on this in 2004 in the form of a 'Priorities for Action Questionnaire' sent to some 350 local organizations, asking them to consider 131 proposals grouped under 15 topics. The result of the scoring exercise was a clear emphasis on four topics favoured by 75 per cent of all respondents. These were: landscape protection; understanding and enjoying the Forest's special qualities; managing recreation; and transport. The top ten priorities for action were:

1. protecting the landscape from inappropriate or intrusive development including cumulative small-scale development and intensified recreation;
2. protecting and increasing the stock of affordable housing;
3. building on the partnership approach to sustainable tourism;
4. producing a recreation strategy for the whole Forest;
5. revitalizing village centres;
6. agreeing and implementing an education strategy for the Forest;
7. implementing Forest Design Plans for the Crown Lands enclosures;
8. planning policies for high-quality building and open space design;
9. updating regularly the assessment of housing needs;

10.   working with regional and adjoining authorities to take the special
      character of the Forest into account.

The eleventh priority was to support sustainable commoning.

The Action Plan is to be published in 2005. Thereafter one will need to look to a variety of other local documentation to see how the New Forest Strategy is influencing local decision-making. These documents include the local spatial planning document, the Forestry Commission's own management strategy and the National Park Plan in due course. In addition there is the possibility of specific implementation initiatives being undertaken in the form of projects. There is already a history of such projects in the New Forest, projects that are both based on and in turn consolidate partnerships between local organizations. In each case funding was obtained from the European Union (EU) and the creation of a local partnership was a precondition for obtaining EU finance.

The first is the Forest Friendly Farming Project, funded under the LEADER+ stream of European funding. This dates from 2001 and aims to develop practical ways of supporting farming, commoning and woodland management in the New Forest. It is managed by the New Forest District Council and coordinated through the New Forest Committee. The actual initiatives under the Forest Friendly Farming Project are delivered through a partnership of local and central government organizations, with the support of local volunteers and a small staff team, itself funded by the New Forest District Council and Hampshire Wildlife Trust. Examples of the initiatives developed through Forest Friendly Farming include developing a Forest Friendly Farming Accreditation Scheme.

Secondly, there is a collection of projects funded under European LIFE funding, the EU's specific environmental financial instrument. The focus of these projects is management for biodiversity. The first project was set up in 1997 with a partnership coordinated by the New Forest Committee and included the Forestry Commission, English Nature, the National Trust, Ninth Centenary Trust, Hampshire Wildlife Trust, Wiltshire Wildlife Trust, Hampshire County Council, the Verderers of the New Forest and the Royal Society for the Protection of Birds (RSPB). Since then the partnership went on to receive continuation funding under further rounds of LIFE funding (LIFE 2 and LIFE 3). However by the time of the LIFE 3 the partnership had slimmed down to just English Nature, Environment Agency, Forestry Commission, Hampshire County Council, the National Trust and RSPB. The main aims of these projects, taken together, have been to produce a management plan for the area, to increase the amount of land owned and managed primarily for nature conservation and to restore over 4000 hectares of the New Forest to favourable conservation status. The emphasis under LIFE 3 has altered slightly to focus on wetland restoration. This £2.9 million project aims to restore 10 km of damaged watercourse and 600 hectares of surrounding wetlands by the end of 2006. The Environment Agency is a key player in this project because of the emphasis on watercourses. Restoring mires has however caused some concern among the commoners, who in the past drained mires and lowland valley bogs in order to create more grazing for their animals. Mires have since then been listed as extremely rare habitats, Ramsar wetlands and Sites of Special Scientific Interest (SSSIs) (Forestry Commission 2004).

The third project is termed PROGRESS (The Promotion and Guidance for Recreation on Ecologically Sensitive Sites) and is being undertaken in collaboration with the Alterra Research Institute in the Netherlands and the Royal Forest of Fontainebleau in France. This aims to compare recreational tourism in the New Forest and Fontainebleau, with a view to reducing the negative impacts of recreation and developing improved management of the forest areas and better communication with visitors. The lead organization within the UK for this £2.7 million project is the Countryside Agency but there is a forum of some 22 other bodies guiding the project.

All these more specific projects reinforce the linkages established within the New Forest Committee and suggest paths for implementing some of its key policies in addition to shaping the individual plans and strategies of key local organizations.

BUILDING COOPERATION

The development of the New Forest Strategy has been an important focus for the activities of the New Forest Committee. However the strategy itself is not the only significant test of the successful operation of the committee. Arguably the building up of a culture of cooperation among the members and also observers has been more significant. We have termed this cooperation rather than collaboration (Healey 1997) because, in our view, the form of co-working falls short of the ideal of collaboration described by Healey and other theorists seeking to embed Habermas's communicative rationality within the planning process (Habermas 1984, 1987). This would involve full and undistorted communication between parties, based on a mutual desire to understand each other's positions and move towards a consensus (Rydin 2003, Chapter 2). Such collaboration involves much more than just negotiation and instrumental compromise, yet these are often the key elements of engagements between actors in any policy process.

There has been considerable movement towards agreement between the actors within the New Forest Committee. However it would seem to us to be an exaggeration to describe this as collaboration in any meaningful sense. There is agreement but not consensus, negotiation on the basis of individual interests rather than mutual identification, and compromise rather than a common vision. Cooperation is nevertheless a considerable achievement and can be based on a common understanding of actors' mutual interdependence and hence of the policy problem at issue. In this section we explore the different ways that this cooperation has been built up over time.

An important first point to make is that there was a definite need to build cooperation between actors. There had been considerable tensions between actors, for example between groups that are first and foremost concerned with conservation and groups that are more concerned with keeping the Forest as an area where people can live and work and enjoy nature. The New Forest Committee was established in recognition of these tensions and with the expressed intention of trying to improve the situation. There was a particular need for more common management of the area and the need to form a vision that everybody could agree to. The committee sought to do this through establishing concrete projects based in partnerships between sets of actors, that got actors into the habit of working together, as outlined above.

The extent of cooperation between local organizations has been enhanced by the continuity of the same personnel within the various organizations making up the networks in and around the committee. This means that the work that goes into establishing relationships between actors is not wasted and that a collective memory of cooperation is retained within the network. This has also supported the creation and growth of trust between parties to the network, an essential element of social capital that seems to be in evidence within the committee.

Widespread consultation on the New Forest Strategy has also been a key element in building cooperation. The New Forest Committee actively sought to involve all groups in the community during the preparation of the strategy. As was shown above, there were repeated rounds of consultation. The New Forest Consultative Forum was a considerable asset here. However the preparation of the New Forest Strategy also happened to coincide with that of the New Forest District Council's Local Plan, which was being revised. There was no formal cooperation on the consultation efforts for the various plans and strategies and this led to some concerns with potential 'consultation fatigue'. The simultaneous consultations were seen as a negative rather than a positive feature, since they might make people confused.

Nevertheless the production of these two planning documents at the same time holds out some potential for policy integration. Certainly it will be an important test of the strategy's influence and the extent of collective agreement among parties whether the local spatial planning document supports and reinforces the strategy. This local planning document is currently the Local Plan but, in due course, will be the Local Development Framework (LDF) under recent national reforms of the local planning system. Such a plan is intended to provide the framework for decisions over new development in a locality. It reflects a mixture of influences: central government policy guidance, professional judgement, but above all local political priorities. However any such spatial plan is not a zoning ordinance and its implementation in turn depends on proposal-by-proposal decision-making through development control (the granting or otherwise of planning permission for development by the local authority). Therefore implementation of the strategy in terms of managing new development will ultimately depend on this process of development control. The common framing of planning problems and solutions – developed through networking in the committee – will be more important than the formal conformity of the Local Plan (or LDF) and the New Forest Strategy since this common framing will influence how the local authorities undertake development control.

The relationship between the Forestry Commission's management plan and the New Forest Strategy is equally important. The Forestry Commission's management plan was also being revised at the time of the development of the strategy. This document guides the commission in detailing its activities in managing the Forest over the short and medium term; it is not primarily an indication of local political priorities. The Forestry Commission did not engage in any widespread public consultation on its management plan; its main consultation effort occurred around 1999–2000 when it entered into an extensive process of talking to people about its vision of the Forest. But there was considerable effort to coordinate the strategy and its management plan. The particular importance of the Forestry Commission management plan lies in its role as the largest *de facto* landowner in the Forest and the significance of its management decisions for the future of the area. It was widely anticipated that the Commission's plan was bound to be a primary consideration when drawing up a National Park management plan (see below). The New Forest Committee were also hoping that its strategy might serve as a basis for the National Park's plan. This therefore provided additional pressure to bring the Forestry Commission's plan and the New Forestry Strategy into line.

These conduits for the implementation of the strategy are important. The specific mechanisms for achieving implementation remain unclear in many cases. There is a general reliance on the various local policy and planning documents integrating with each other. Where a policy falls clearly within the remit of a statutory authority (an agency or a local authority) then the expectation is that this body will 'pick up' the policy and take responsibility for it, as a corollary of its involvement in the strategy development process. Elements of the strategy should therefore find their way into other plans, strategies and documents. Yet as the discussion of the New Forest Strategy, the Local Plan and the Forestry Commission's management plan indicates, institutional fragmentation at the level of document production persists.

The strategy also clearly states that one of the purposes of this revision of the strategy is to 'extend the implementation process beyond the main statutory organisations, and bring together a broad range of interested organisations and communities to work together on the actions of relevance to them' (NFC 2003). The intention seems to be that the New Forest Committee will form a variety of partnerships with selected groups of actors in order to achieve outcomes. How this will be achieved remains an open question although it does have a track record of establishing some useful project partnerships, as explored above. However it has to be recognized that moving from the strategy to the project level requires the cooperation developed within the committee to be extended further into scenarios where resource allocations are involved and the prospect of win–lose outcomes becomes more apparent. Here conflicts which were resolved at the more general level within the committee can become more apparent and less tractable 'on the ground'. Some actors have voiced doubts about the efficacy of the committee arrangements at this implementation level. It may be that some priorities in the strategy will be easier to implement than others. Most of the priorities however will require good communication and cooperation between all local actors.

Although the committee is regarded as the main organization for networking within the area, in our interviews the committee only ranked seventh in the list of more important actors in the Forest. The Forestry Commission as the main *de facto* landowner was ranked first, followed by the agencies (English Nature and the Countryside Agency) and the local authorities, together with the Verderers who achieved joint second ranking. This reflects the view of some local actors that the committee itself should have more power. This might though undermine the committee's action as a network where responsibilities and powers are dispersed rather than concentrated. However without effective implementation, some actors thought that the committee might lose some legitimacy and momentum in its activities anyway. This tension between concentration of power in the pursuit of efficacy and networking in the pursuit of genuine collective action is also apparent in the discussions surrounding the designation of the New Forest as a National Park.

DESIGNATION AS A NATIONAL PARK

The institutional arrangements that we have analysed have operated against the backdrop of the designation of the area as one worthy of special protection. In 1991 the New Forest Committee drew up a proposal for defining the Forest as a Heritage Site. The New Forest Heritage area is approximately 58 000 hectares, around 90 per cent of the proposed National Park boundary. However there had long been proposals for designating the area as a National Park, dating back to 1947. In the event, the New Forest was not included in the first wave of National Park designations under the 1949 National Parks and Access to the Countryside Act. But in 1994 central government announced that the same enhanced planning policies would apply in the New Forest Heritage Area as operated in the designated National Parks. Then in 1999 it was suggested that there should be a specially designed administration for the Forest that would take into account the unique character of and problems facing the Forest. This followed practice in the Norfolk Broads in East Anglia and the discussions about the management of the South Downs in southern England.

When it became apparent that central government was inclined to extend the number of officially designated National Parks, having so designated the Norfolk Broads in 1989, the idea of the New Forest being added to the list was raised. At the same time similar discussions were being held concerning the South Downs and there were firm plans to create Scotland's first two National Parks at Loch Lomond and The Trossachs and Cairngorms under the National Parks (Scotland) Act 2000 (the original 1949 legislation had not applied to Scotland). In 1999 the Countryside Agency started the designation process for the New Forest and in 2000 a draft National Park boundary was presented for consultation, a process which took two years. In 2002 the Countryside Agency published a Designation Order for a New Forest National Park under the 1949 National Parks and Access to Countryside Act. Between 2002 and 2003 a public inquiry to examine the boundary and administrative arrangement was held, and finally in June 2004 the designation of the New Forest National Park was confirmed by the Minister for Rural Affairs.

The prospect of National Park designation had been anticipated by those active in New Forest planning for some time. Many had viewed it as a threat, or at least a form of uncertainty for the area. The desire to develop the New Forest Strategy was partly a reflection of the perceived need to establish a locally grounded base for management of the area before any National Park was established. For some the strategy should form the basis of the National Park Authority's plan, a kind of prototype plan. However the likelihood of this happening is unclear. In London, the London

Planning Advisory Committee produced a draft plan for the Greater London Authority, its 'endowment' to the new authority when it began work in 2000. However the Mayor of London largely ignored this draft and preferred to devise his own distinctive strategy (West et al. 2003). The same process may happen in the New Forest. In addition, there has been some concern about the boundaries of the park. These exclude some parts of the New Forest area that have been part of the Heritage Area for many years and have therefore been protected by the equivalent planning status of a National Park, protection which they will now lose.

In 2002, when submitting the Designation Order to central government, the Countryside Agency proposed that 'special arrangements' regarding the management and setting up of a National Park Authority in the New Forest would be considered appropriate, reflecting 'the needs of this unique part of the country' (Countryside Agency 2002). This meant that the actors in the New Forest were hoping that the management structure after designation would be more or less the same as before, with the New Forest Committee retaining its importance. However it was decided that the New Forest National Park Authority should follow the pattern in the rest of the National Parks in the UK. DEFRA proposed that the New Forest National Park Authority would consist of 22 members, 6 of whom would be directly appointed by the Secretary of State, 12 would be nominated by the local authorities and 4 by the parish councils for subsequent appointment by the Secretary of State.

The New Forest National Park Authority began its existence from April 2005 but will not take on all its responsibilities until April 2006. It is clear that the New Forest Consultative Panel will continue to be an important asset to the management of the New Forest National Park and it is hoped by many local actors that the Committee will form the core of the National Park Board. However there are likely to be other members as well. This raises the more general question of how the formal apparatus of a National Park will affect the cooperation that has been fostered through the New Forest Committee. There should be an element of continuity in planning for the Forest and in the relationships between actors within the Forest. However the authority will have different responsibilities and functions to the non-statutory committee. It will therefore have to operate in a very different way. The concern of many is that the patterns of cooperation built up over time may be disrupted by the more formal mechanisms of the park authority. Some of the local actors, even land owners and statutory bodies, have stated that they would not wish to be a part of the National Park administrative body because their needs could be better looked after from the outside (see also Smith 2005).

THE SOURCES OF AND LIMITS TO COOPERATION

In this final section, we bring together the key findings of this case study and reflect on the value of the concepts introduced in Chapter 2, focusing particularly on the different kinds of social capital, the use of resources, the importance of knowledge resources in building institutional capacity and the impact of external factors.

Our case has shown that effective networking was established through the New Forest Committee and that this dispelled some of the distrust that had existed prior to its operation and instead institutionalized cooperation. The committee has brought together the key actors within the local area, so that a formal network has been able to carry the burden of building relationships between actors. The committee has built cooperation through a mix of extensive and widespread consultation and specific projects building partnerships within specific sets of actors. The process of developing a strategy helped consolidate the network, although some concerns still remain over the implementation of all of the strategy's proposals. The pursuit of effective implementation may put a strain on the looser cooperation of networking to date, a strain that may become even more apparent with the advent of the National Park.

Returning to our concepts of Chapter 2, it would seem that the concept of social capital has considerable applicability in this case. We have seen how actors within the network developed relationships of trust, a key characteristic of social capital. This has further been fostered by the longevity of the membership of the key network. There was also recognition of reciprocity between some actors, particularly between the Forestry Commission and the commoners. This provides a good basis for moving towards collective action according to the social capital framework. Sanctions were not used to enforce collective action, not even soft sanctions of blame. But the actors were keen to demonstrate a positive working relationship with each other; positive encouragement to maintain this worked more effectively than blame for not joining in.

The main type of social capital that was operating within the New Forest Committee was bridging capital but operating within a specific and limited set of actors. The core network of the committee had links out into the broader set of stakeholders concerned with the Forest, but the research emphasized the centrality of this relatively limited set in taking the lead on policy for the Forest. There was also evidence of bonding capital, but this was mainly within the commoning community; there was no evidence of bonding acting as a precursor to bridging as in the Setesdal Vesthei-Ryfylkeheiane case study in this volume. This community of local land-holding families and individuals exhibited strong bonds keeping the group together, maintaining the identity of commoners as a distinct group and pushing for the interests of commoners. It is also closely connected to the cultural nature of the commoners as a social group. The existence of such bonding capital was essential to enable the commoners to be represented by one or two individuals within a bridging network such as the New Forest Committee, and for the cultural dimensions of commoning to be fully taken into account within the committee's deliberations. It was important that the representatives of commoners could be relied on to represent the larger group. Furthermore it was important that that larger group accepted decisions and commitments reached by representatives. Bonding capital ensured this two-way link between the commoning community and their representatives within the committee. It is interesting to note though that the strength of bonds within the commoning community led to it having slightly weaker bridging ties, through desiring a degree of distance from the other members of the committee. This combination of some strong bonding capital and bridging capital linking together a limited set of actors suggests that the revised concept of bracing capital has some relevance here. The efficacy of the New Forest Committee network depended on this combination.

Resources remain a key factor in shaping the management of the area. Networking has been instrumental in releasing resources to the extent that partnership between actors was essential for securing EU funding for a number of specific projects. However this is a limited demonstration of the ability of networks to create resource opportunities. Part of the push towards National Park designation arose from the view that this would bring funding opportunities with it. The continued livelihood problems facing the commoners and the implications this has for the environmental sustainability of the area mean that resource inputs are still required for successful management of the area. The lack of available resources is one of the key reasons that doubt has been expressed over the implementation of the New Forest Strategy.

One resource that the local actors did hold was knowledge of the local area. Such local knowledge was an important asset that was activated through the network of the committee. This constitutes an understanding of the local ecology, the practicalities and potential of grazing practices, and the experience of managing both livestock and visitors to the Forest. The committee played an important role in exchanging this knowledge since it resided among a number of different actors; no one actor had a monopoly of such knowledge. Commoners, Verderers, government agencies and local authorities all had a contribution to make in generating a common pool of such knowledge. Some of this was more technical, based on surveys whether of biodiversity or visitor movements; other was more experiential and based on the commoners' long family histories of putting animals out to graze in the Forest. An appropriate management strategy for the sustainable use of the Forest relied on this combination of knowledge being brought together and the committee provided an effective network for doing so.

However there were other arenas where knowledge resources seemed less important. In the Local Plan arena and in the debates over the designation of the National Park, political considerations often dominated over decision-making legitimated through recourse to sources of knowledge. Although a technical study was commissioned from consultants Environmental Resource Management to assist in the determination of the park boundaries, this was balanced with a public consultation exercise involving individuals, local authorities and other organizations. Similarly there was relatively little overt emphasis on building up knowledge resources through learning from past experiences, as with the periodic evaluations of practice that are common in the Norwegian cases in this volume.

Finally, we have found a potential gap in this case between the outputs of collective action in the form of joint strategy development and outcomes in terms of changed decision-making in the Forest. This is a significant outstanding issue in terms of the implementation of the New Forest Strategy. The work of the New Forest Committee, and its associated consultative forum and project partnerships, has provided the potential for such implementation. In terms of the institutional capacity framework, it suggests that cooperation of the kind found in the New Forest may create a form of mobilization capital. However this does not guarantee outcomes. This is partly because of the remaining requirement to mobilize other material resources, but also due to the importance of external factors. The problems of falling timber prices, falling pony prices and rising house prices remain problematic for the area and potentially undermine the sustainable management of the area. European Union funds have been relied onto pump-prime local projects, but much emphasis is now being laid on the National Park designation bringing in funds.

However the new organizational arrangements for the National Park may also threaten the carefully built up cooperation institutionalized in the New Forest Committee. Since our research for the purpose of this book ended in 2004, the New Forest Committee has been disbanded and since April 2005 the National Park Authority has taken up its central role within the New Forest. The National Park Authority is expected to continue working in partnership with other organizations in the New Forest. Planning policy responsibilities will remain as they are now until April 2006 when the National Park Authority becomes the sole local planning authority for the area. Regarding other policies, for example those concerning tourism, house prices, traffic and commoning, Ministers have recommended using the existing strategy for the New Forest as a basis for the National Park Authority's work. It waits to be seen if the specific combination of bonding and bridging capital involved in the network's bracing capital, which has proved so effective in terms of strategy development, creating a sense of mutuality and common framing of problems and solutions, will survive the change in organizations.

4. Setesdal Vesthei-Ryfylkeheiane, Norway: local co-management in a protected area

Eva Falleth

Setesdal Vesthei-Ryfylkeheiane (SVR), the southernmost mountain region in Norway, ranges from 800 to 1200 metres in elevation and features a typically alpine landscape. The area in this study covers approximately 2600 km² of mountains and is protected under Norway's Nature Conservation Act of 1972. Mountain regions such as the SVR represent important wilderness areas, and include some of Norway's most vulnerable natural habitats and most fragile ecosystems. This wilderness area and its wildlife face crucial challenges, such as the reduction and fragmentation of land, and increased off-road traffic. Accordingly, public management devotes special attention to nature conservation and the protection of habitats for endangered species of flora and fauna.

SVR is classified as a Nordic alpine habitat (NOU 1986). The mountains are home to the southernmost herd of wild reindeer in Europe and the wild reindeer is an endangered species. Norway ratified the Bern Convention on the Conservation of European Wildlife and Natural Habitats from 1982 which assigns Norway an international responsibility to protect the wild reindeer and its habitat (Andersen and Hustad 2005). Nature conservation is a national responsibility in Norway, as in most other countries (Brandon et al. 1998). In 1986 the Ministry of the Environment recommended the creation of a National Park in the SVR. The proposal met considerable local resistance amid arguments that nature protection was unnecessary, and that local participation was crucial for sustainable development.

SVR was declared a protected area where special regulations apply in 2000. Local resistance had gained support, but not enough to put a stop to the Storting's (the Norwegian parliament) desire for nature conservation. For the first time, a pilot management project was set up in a protected mountain region in Norway. In 2001 each of the municipalities involved was granted statutory powers to administrate the SVR in cooperation with a stakeholders' advisory group. The challenge facing them was to develop an agreement and collective action among all the stakeholders to take joint responsibility and avoid harmful impacts on the wilderness area. The situation was complicated by the fact that what constitutes a 'harmful impact' was up for debate.

SVR is an area of major environmental importance, but it is also host to several kinds of human activities (see Figure 4.1). Approximately 15 000 people live in the eight rural municipalities adjacent to the mountains, and about half a million live in the greater metropolitan area. While the rural communities have traditionally used the mountains for grazing, fishing and hunting, the greater metropolitan area regards the SVR primarily as an area for outdoor recreation such as hiking and skiing. Today, summer homes and private and public mountain cabins are scattered across the mountains. There is a great demand for more cabins and more off-road traffic. Since the 1960s the area has also been developed for the production of hydroelectric power. All of this threatens the vulnerable alpine environment, including its wildlife and its ecosystems.

Studies in Norway indicate that land management is highly fragmented and that public management in such areas is more like a 'battlefield of regimes' than cooperation between actors (Skjeggedal et al. 2001). There seems to be no common approach to development, and land use planning is subject to many objections and exemptions (Holsen 1996; Tennøy 2000). There are many, and varied, actors in the SVR, with disparate levels of formal power, and different approaches and objectives. The original problem in the SVR was that in the absence of a set of rules, individual actors (predominantly the local municipalities) were acting as free riders on the preservation of the wilderness. Numerous cabins had negative small-scale impacts on the wilderness, but this situation was exacerbated exponentially by the large-scale impacts of bigger dams and new roads (FM 1984). The increase in traffic, especially in off-road vehicle traffic, has had a very adverse impact on wildlife. No comprehensive agreement existed for how to manage the SVR.

The actors include public authorities, voluntary organizations, landowners and commercial enterprises. The public institutional setting consists of eight local municipalities with elected local councils, three elected county councils above them, three county governors (representatives of the national state at the county level), and an elected Wild Reindeer Committee. Altogether there are about 100 local and regional branches of NGOs, local public boards and community-based organizations (Hovik and Falleth 2003). Almost all the community-based organizations organize farmers and private landowners in order to promote their interests in rural development, farming, hunting and fishing.

There are 418 land properties with a heterogeneous land ownership structure. The State Forest Authority administrates what was formerly a

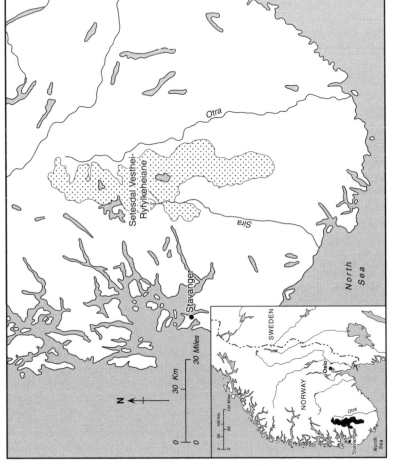

Figure 4.1   Setesdal Vesthei-Ryfylkeheiane

private nature reserve (810 km²) and a local mountain board administrates an area of Crown land (132 km²). The rest of the properties are in private hands and mostly (60 per cent) owned by local farmers. There are four large semi-public hydroelectric companies that operate several large dams and minor roads under the terms of national licences. There is also a dense network of marked footpaths and approximately 30 public cabins owned and administered by the Norwegian Mountain Touring Association. The Air Force also uses the SVR regularly for military training.

THE ACTORS AND THE NETWORK

The formal actors in SVR are, first of all, the eight local municipalities with statutory powers in the protected area. The county governors (who normally have statutory powers when it comes to nature conservation) and the elected county council (which has statutory powers for land use planning) play consultative roles. The numbers of stakeholders increase dramatically if we add non-governmental organizations and all the governmental agencies engaged in significant activities within the area. Empirical studies indicate two main groups: on the one hand, the environmental NGOs, the Ministry of the Environment, the Directorate for Nature Management and the county governors who campaign for nature conservation, and on the other, the farmers' and landowners' organizations and the local municipalities who are opposed to nature conservation (Glosvik 1996a, 1996b; Daugstad et al. 2000; Falleth 2004).

There is also tension between local and national management. In general, those who advocate nature conservation are critical of local management (Glosvik 1996a, 1996b; Daugstad et al. 2000; Falleth 2004), arguing that the municipalities do not have the capacity to prioritize nature over development. Their expertise is in local land use planning in the municipalities, which often rates development and private landowners' wishes more highly than nature conservation (Holsen 1996; Tennøy 2000; Falleth et al. 2003). Others want local municipalities and the landowners' organization to hold on to land management authority. This cleanly divides the actors into those who support nature conservation and those who oppose it. This study however identifies actors that have the capacity to break such 'shackles of the commons' (Schattschneider 1975), straddling the institutional barriers between nature conservation and local management. Examples include environmentalists who advocate both nature conservation and local management, and the local farmers' organization that proposed a multi-purpose plan for all the municipalities.

Several networks have attempted to manage the SVR through joint action, the most important being the local network that drafted a multi-purpose plan in 1994, the environmental champion network that advocated local management in nature conservation, and the bridging network that devised the pilot management project.

A LOCAL NETWORK

When the environmental authorities proposed a National Park in SVR (NOU 1986), local and regional authorities responded negatively, referring to an ongoing regional planning process that followed up the Mountain Plan from 1974. The Ministry of Environment decided to extend this process in order to protect the area. In 1989 the county governors announced the intro-duction of nature conservation as a goal. Local stakeholders were critical, believing nature conservation to have a unilateral focus on environmental values. They also questioned the striking differences between the National Park Plan which proposed a national park covering 550 km^2, and the regional Mountain Plan which proposed landscape protection covering 4200 km^2. Local actors also deplored the loss of the formal right to partici-pate when the regional and participatory process was turned into a formal designation process.

A few knowledgeable and resourceful people with strong connections to local municipalities, the political system and farmers' organizations, decided to oppose the proposal for nature conservation. They thought that collective, proactive action would be more effective and constructive than individual, reactive comments against nature conservation. Consequently, they decided to put together a multi-purpose plan combining strategies developed by the farmers' organization, land use planning where statutory authority was conferred on the local municipalities pursuant to the then new Planning and Building Act (1985), and strategies from a national initiative to improve environmental management in local municipalities (Hovik and Johnsen 1994).

Their ideas were submitted to the county councils through the political system, and the further planning process followed formal procedures in land use planning, paying attention to local knowledge, the documentation of human activities and the potential for sustainable development in the SVR. The process was characterized by broad, representative participation by four working groups and a steering committee. However local actors were in the majority. Actors from the environmental authorities and organiza-tions took a critical stance and believed the process was designed to benefit local interest networks, contending that broad participation merely gave the process a greater degree of legitimacy. This local 'bottom-up' process was the opposite of conventional 'top-down' nature conservation, where power is devolved to the county governor. The multi-purpose plan was adopted by the three county councils in 1994, but was ignored by the Ministry of Environment. Instead a nature conservation proposal was completed in 1996. With substantial capacity to mobilize, the local networks again used the political system to raise a private member's bill in the Storting in 1996 in opposition. The Storting unanimously recommended protecting the SVR as a landscape of outstanding beauty, but also censured the environmental authorities for their ignorance of local participation, and recommended a pilot project in the SVR based on local nature conservation management. The county governors were mandated to work out a local administrative model in cooperation with the local network.

NETWORK OF ENVIRONMENTAL POLICY CHAMPIONS

The ongoing reorganization of environmental policy and administration ran parallel to the multi-purpose planning process. This had already started in the 1980s, with the new Planning and Building Act of 1985 which empowered local municipalities, but it was given a much broader focus in the 1990s through nationwide reform and improvement of the capacity for local environmental management (Hovik and Johnsen 1994), and a gradual delegation of administrative power in nature conservation and agricultural management. However these changes did not apply to the management of mountain and national parks, as they were regarded as too valuable and too complex to be administered at the local level. Nevertheless some officers within the environmental authorities also wanted to delegate power to the local municipalities in such protected areas as well. They became policy champions within an almost invisible network. They had a two-pronged, most delicate objective: to promote local management within environmental authorities and to the local municipalities.

THE PILOT MANAGEMENT PROJECT

A model for the pilot project was set up in 1998. The power to administer the nature conservation regulations and claims was delegated to the eight local municipalities. There is no formal regulative framework to require cooperation, but it is highly recommended by the environmental authorities through the management model, which instructs the local municipalities to

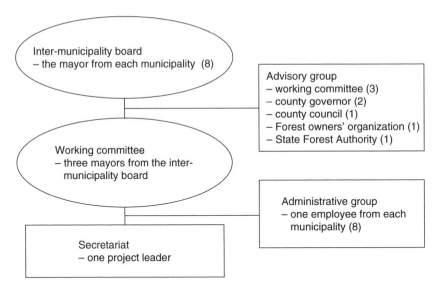

Figure 4.2   Local management model in Setesdal Vesthei-Ryfylkeheiane

work out a joint management plan. In 2001 the local municipalities formalized an inter-authority enterprise consisting of a steering committee comprising the eight elected mayors from the local municipalities, an executive committee of three mayors, a project leader, an administrative group comprising officers of the eight municipalities and an advisory group consisting of eight representatives from the most important stakeholder group. This organization was extended in 2002 by conducting an annual open meeting and including three observers in the advisory group. Figure 4.2 presents the local management model. The municipalities' administrative costs are fully covered by the Directorate for Nature Management.

The enterprise's initial mandate was to draft a joint management plan. Work on this started in 2001. The administrative group zoned the SVR and drew up policy guidelines. Proposals for zoning and guidelines were discussed regularly in the steering committee, the administrative group and the advisory group. The mayors promoted this process, and the final proposal for a management plan reflects local policy as well as national nature conservation policy. The proposal was controversial: an attempt by eight different municipalities to develop a joint policy about off-road traffic and spatial development, but also an attempt to build a bridge between the municipalities and the more restrictive environmental authorities. The plan was sent for a public hearing, and then finally adopted by the local municipalities and the environmental authorities in 2004. The resultant enterprise is now in the process of developing into an innovative advisory institution for the eight municipalities. They have initiated a broad process to plan for sustainable development on the fringes of the SVR, a new and controversial policy area in which Norway has little experience but which has recently become the subject of strong political focus. The local management model is also developing common routines and activities for the stakeholders and their dealings with each other. These attempts seem gradually to be developing operative norms for joint actions based on consensus.

The effort to identify a common policy also involved a process of defining new roles for stakeholders, who all either gained or lost power in the pilot project. The local municipalities tried to dominate, demonstrating their positions of newfound power by restricting the participation of those stakeholders opposed to local management who had lost power and influence, that is, the environmental organizations, the Reindeer Committee and the county governors. They in turn tried to gain access through appeals to the Ministry of the Environment. These tensions prevailed until common norms based on transparency and trust were developed. Since then, oppositional stakeholders have gained access to the advisory group, and information flows more freely. The project leader is trying to resolve conflicts professionally, addressing the right actors at the right level. The critics have responded to these changes by expressing increasing trust in the local municipalities' management and, in particular, in the project leader. The reversal from defensive towards more transparent processes seems therefore to have turned distrust among stakeholders into a significant level of trust.

The level of trust is however delicate. Stakeholders are still replicating conflicts. One example is the debate about public trails and cabins in the most vulnerable areas. The Ministry of the Environment decided on the location of these trails and cabins back in the 1970s, despite local protests. Local municipalities proposed relocation to less vulnerable areas, that is, to areas with considerable infrastructure. The Mountain Touring Association was willing to relocate some cabins and trails, but not into areas defined by infrastructure, and not as long as private boats were allowed on nearby dammed reservoirs. They regarded this as a revival of old conflicts designed to demonstrate local power, and the issue has been a setback to the growth of mutual trust among these stakeholders. That being said, this conflict runs much deeper than public trails and cabins. It is more about local communities' long-standing hostility towards the Mountain Touring Association, regarded by some private landowners as an organization that has too readily been granting permits in the SVR.

Today the tensest conflicts are between the Wild Reindeer Committee and the local municipalities. The latter want to incorporate wild reindeer management into the pilot project, while the Wild Reindeer Committee prefers cooperation. The conflict is complex, and includes disagreement about knowledge and strategies to protect their habitats. It has led to distrust of local municipalities' land use strategies and the Reindeer Committee's herd management. The conflict has become institutionalized through different management systems, and has escalated because of conflicting professional knowledge about the wild reindeer's tolerance for human activity. This conflict remains unsolved, and has set back the process of devising and implementing a joint strategy in the management plan.

NETWORKS OF OPPOSITION

There are still stakeholders who play no part in any collective action in the SVR. Their approaches are quite different from those of the actors within the pilot management project network because their objectives and strategies seem impossible to combine with the joint strategy in the pilot project. One of these networks of opposition comprises local snowmobile users who advocate a more liberal, or an unregulated, off-road traffic policy. This is not a formal network, but a loose local bonding network based on a common interest in strong opposition to current national and local policy on off-road traffic. Members of the network act as individuals, although some are members of local snowmobile clubs, while others are elected municipal politicians.

Another oppositional network is that of landowners advocating fewer governmental regulations and limitations on the right of public access. Their policy goes beyond both land-use planning and nature conservation management, arguing for the value and the sovereignty of private land ownership. Their opinions are visible at open meetings, through public hearings and in the media.

IMPLEMENTATION AND OUTCOME

Networking has yielded many results but there is a major distinction between outputs in terms of plans and strategies and outcomes in terms of individual decisions that affect collective action. The networks in the SVR have succeeded in making plans and devising strategies. The local politicians and the farmers' organization drafted a multi-purpose plan in 1994, and raised a private member's bill in the Storting in 1996. The county governors and the local municipalities created a plan for the pilot project in 1998. And eight local municipalities, in cooperation with the Advisory Board, devised the management plan in 2004.

The most crucial issue is the extent to which the management plan of 2004 will be implemented by the stakeholders. Although they have agreed on it as a collective strategy, this study has discovered that this level of agreement varies between stakeholders, creating a somewhat delicate setting for implementing the plan. For example, the wild reindeer stakeholders and some of the environmental authorities and organizations tend to regard the plan as overly liberal because it paves the way for more human activities and reduces the protection afforded to nature; at the same time, some of the local municipalities regard the management plan as overly restrictive.

The implementation of this plan by each of the stakeholder groups is an indicator of the extent to which joint action will actually take place in the SVR. The formal power of stakeholders to follow up the management plan differs, and their level of implementation must take account of these differences. The eight local municipalities have the statutory authority to administer physical development and off-road traffic by granting exemptions to the nature conservation regulations; furthermore they also have responsibility for information, management and monitoring. Their implementation will therefore depend on following the guidelines for this in the management plan. Other actors' implementation of the management plan will depend primarily on the extent to which it affects their own activities in the SVR. Further description of the networks' performance will therefore be divided between the local municipalities on the one hand, and the other stakeholders in the advisory group on the other.

LOCAL MUNICIPALITIES

The local municipalities carry responsibility for the public management of the SVR within their own municipal boundaries alongside the inter-authority enterprise that monitors landscape changes based on satellite photos and cultivates an information strategy and a sustainable development strategy on the outer fringes of the SVR. Most implementation of the joint agreement will however take place in each municipality with the statutory authority administering the nature conservation regulations. This mainly consists of administering applications for exemptions, for example it is in general forbidden to build in the SVR and to traffic the protected area with off-road vehicles, but it is possible to obtain exemptions from this regulation if the activity is necessary to agriculture, hunting or recreation and does not threaten nature conservation. The management plan includes guidelines for granting such exemptions.

The municipalities granted 457 exemptions (32 for construction and 425 for off-road vehicles) between July 2001 and July 2004. The rate of acceptance of applications, 95 per cent, is similar to the rate of acceptance of exemptions from land use plans (Falleth 2004). Most exemptions for traffic are given for snowmobiles (68 per cent), while almost all exemptions for construction are given for minor enlargements of existing cabins and summer homes. While there is general disagreement among stakeholders about this high level of exemption, very few exemptions are in fact illegal, or contravene the guidelines in the management plan. The most controversial in respect of legality have been two exemptions for private cabins in particularly vulnerable areas, and two permits for organized family tours with snowmobiles.

There is political tolerance for this controversial local management. There is also political tolerance for the different levels of collective action in the municipalities. Different policies existed in the municipalities before the SVR was declared a protected area, and current practices still vary in terms of the number of permits issued, the conditions for granting permits and the limitations placed on each permit. In general, the political climate seems to be shifting slightly in the direction of a more restrictive policy, as outlined in the management plan. According to the more conservative stakeholders, the more liberal municipalities interpret the guidelines in the management plan in favour of local development rather than weighing them against the loss of natural resources. The local authorities have however adjusted their policies as a result of the guidelines in the management plan, and this formal change can be regarded as the first sign of joint action, notwithstanding the different groups' different assessments of human activities and nature conservation.

THE ADVISORY GROUP

The management plan caters primarily for the local municipalities' formal management of the SVR, but it also includes strategies for the resolution of other problems, for example the reduction of traffic in the most vulnerable areas. It aims to restrict the traffic to the power plants, relocate part of the network of public cabins and trails belonging to the Mountain Touring Association, and to cut down on airborne military exercises. Individual stakeholders' activities are however generally regulated by their own institutional arrangements, although efforts are being made to accommodate both the management plan and their respective mandates for activities in the area. The Norwegian Mountain Touring Association is willing to relocate one cabin and related trails to less vulnerable areas, but not into areas featuring significant infrastructure. Their members want to hike in unspoiled natural surroundings. The State Forest Authority and the Wild Reindeer

Committee have reduced their sales of hunting licences, but report that this reduction is not permanent. The Norwegian Air Force has limited its military activity in the area – for the time being. These groups state that further policy changes must be matched by policy changes on the part of the municipalities. Other stakeholders participate to an even lesser degree in the collective action. The hydroelectric companies argue that their first priorities are their concessions and the upgrading of the security of their dams, rather than implementation of the management plan.

CONDITIONS FOR COLLECTIVE ACTION

There are several theoretical approaches to explain the conditions leading to collective action. As discussed in Chapter 2, this study focused on the two approaches 'social capital' and 'institutional capacity' to highlight the interrelationships between the actors in a network in order to explain collective action. The study confirms that the existence of a formal network and the quality of the interrelationships between members of the network are important. Bridging social capital dominates in the SVR, but this is a very challenging way to mobilize collective action, not least because relationships among actors are influenced by divergent and even conflicting institutional settings.

Reciprocity seems to be the crucial characteristic for effective social capital in this case, but open and inclusive procedures, broad participation and shared knowledge and problem-framing also seem to be important for holding the network together. The bridging network has produced innovative solutions. Such findings are not new. The effect of weak ties and such a network's power to innovate new solutions was identified by Granovetter in the 1970s (Granovetter 1973). Collective action in the SVR seems to be contingent on the creation of a bridging network, the development of social capital consisting of common routines and reciprocity, and the development of shared knowledge. But its capacity for mobilization is very vulnerable owing to low levels of trust.

A BRIDGING NETWORK

The research identified three distinct networks governing the SVR. The first consisted of local municipalities and farmers' organizations that put together a multi-purpose plan. The second consisted of environmentalists who advocated local management in the SVR. The third bridging network brought together the key actors in the two other networks. The third group's focus was on devising a pilot project based on local management, but the members did not share the values of the nature conservationists. One important prerequisite for collective action in SVR is that the bridging network has resulted in more representative participation by stakeholders. The development of such broad representation has been a complicated and conflict-ridden process. The network was transformed from being a focus group revolving around a few actors with shared ideals, to an open and inclusive network with heterogeneous stakeholders. This has enhanced its legitimacy.

The current pilot project consists of a core group from this bridging network, extended by more stakeholders represented on the formal boards of the pilot project. However the farmers' organizations, which had been an important driving force, lost enthusiasm when the SVR became protected. Their objective was primarily to prevent the SVR from being declared a protected area. Their proactive position at the core of the network dwindled to a reactive position in the advisory group. Conversely, the stakeholders from the Wild Reindeer Committee and the Mountain Touring Association, which were not initially on the advisory group, improved their positions through an increasingly inclusive way of working. Another interesting characteristic of the three networks is that a few key people from the municipalities and the environmental authorities have been key actors since the 1980s, independently of formal structures. The fusion of the two earlier networks into the bridging network has led to closer cooperation among these key individuals.

The structure of the current network can therefore be divided into a core network involving key individuals, the network formalized through the pilot project, and the network of affiliated actors. The actors in the core network hold different positions in the formal organization of the pilot project, and they also have affiliated networks that include public authorities, the political system and several voluntary organizations. The capacity of the pilot project increases when the key actors use their affiliated networks to gain support for the creation and implementation of policy. The network also facilitates the flow of knowledge. The management plan for the SVR differs from plans that focus primarily on nature conservation. Since it includes nature conservation, participation, varied human activities and information, it might be called an innovative strategy for nature conservation.

SOCIAL CAPITAL

Social capital is usually defined by trust, reciprocity and reputation as important characteristics of the interrelationships inherent in collective action. Trust is regarded as being at the very heart of this (Ostrom 1998; Putnam 1993; Coleman 1990). While trust is important for networking in the SVR, it is not the most important factor contributing to the creation of the bridging network and the associated collective action. The first two networks seem to have been more firmly based on trust than the last bridging network. Several stakeholders in the bridging network distrusted each other, but decided to participate in the pilot project because they considered comprehensive management by stakeholders in the SVR to be crucial. Trust between key actors subsequently developed to a significant degree when they realized that the other stakeholders were also trying to make the management plan work. Other studies have also reached similar conclusions about the limits of trust in bridging networks (Bærenholdt and Aarsæther 2002). Trust at high levels seems to be absent from the affiliated networks outside the pilot project (Hovik and Falleth 2003). Outside the core, in particular, it rested on the shoulders of the project leader and her open and inclusive way of administering the network.

A marked impression is that reciprocity among stakeholders is decisive for sustaining the network. The level of reciprocity also appears to affect the networks' capacity to act collectively, for example the deadlock between the municipalities and the Mountain Touring Association over the reduction of traffic. There is growing concern about potential free riders who seem to be trying to manipulate the management plan or who argue that they are unable to participate in the implementation of the plan because of their own institutional limitations. Lack of reciprocity is therefore seen as affecting the level of trust in the network. Accordingly, reciprocity is crucial for developing trust.

The last important element of social capital is the availability of sanctions to restrict free riders. Should local management be unsuccessful, one critical sanction in the SVR would be the withdrawal of statutory authority. The mayors however are not overly concerned about this potential sanction. On the contrary, they are not willing to bear the burden of local management if the cost is loss of legitimacy within their municipalities. Those previously opposed to local management now consider the pilot project promising, and they are not willing to use the removal of local power as a sanction against the municipalities in order to promote a more restrictive local policy. The loss of face is also regarded as a 'soft' sanction to avoid free riders. Although such soft sanctions are of some value for the core actors in the SVR, their value to those on the fringes of the network is limited.

Mayors are reluctant to intervene in another municipality's implementation of the management plan by applying soft sanctions. This affects the mayors' collective ability to monitor municipal practices. This lack of internal control also allows the mayors opportunities to use the pilot project as a platform for putting into practice local policy that had been bogged down in the ordinary system of governance. The pilot project has therefore enabled mayors to take solo initiatives in conflicts with the national wild reindeer management, with the Mountain Touring Association and the hydroelectric companies. Most crucial though to understanding the lack of soft sanctions among stakeholders is the mutual understanding of the delicate and legitimate balance that has been struck between taking part in the joint collective action and maintaining legitimacy within their own organizations. This is particularly true for the elected mayors who depend on the political confidence of their constituencies, but other stakeholders also seem to consider losing legitimacy within their own organizations as more critical than gaining legitimacy within the pilot project. Strong bonding capital enhances the attachment to legitimacy within such organizations.

SHARED KNOWLEDGE

The study indicates that shared knowledge seems to act as a substitute for the absence of joint norms and values. Cars et al. (2002) suggest that developing shared knowledge is critical to collective action in institutional networks such as exist in the SVR. In the SVR, this shared knowledge is the sum of several documents, produced over a lengthy period of time, about environmental and human values in the SVR. It includes preliminary studies on nature conservation in the SVR, which document environmental values and human encroachment (whereas the preliminary studies for the multi-purpose plan in 1994 document human activities). This knowledge however has not been updated recently nor is it regarded as of importance as a resource within a network. There is no shared knowledge about what has a harmful impact on wild reindeer. This disagreement has created a very tense relationship, accompanied by distrust between stakeholders.

Preferred knowledge, and the means of producing it, differs strikingly between local municipalities and environmental authorities. The environmental authorities and the Wild Reindeer Committee give priority to professional knowledge, while the local municipalities give priority to local knowledge, a distinction reminiscent of the concept of formal and tacit knowledge (Cars et al. 2002). The local municipalities and the environmental stakeholders allocate different priorities to the knowledge necessary for decision-making in the SVR. The major focus in the municipalities is sustainable development, while environmental authorities focus on nature conservation. These differences express the tremendously disparate underlying standards and cultures of the environmental authorities and the municipalities.

OTHER SIGNIFICANT EXPLANATORY VARIABLES

Theories of social capital traditionally focus on the strengths in interrelationships between actors in a network in order to explain collective actions. This internal focus is insufficient for an understanding of collective action in the SVR. It seems that the actor's capacity to interpret external factors such as policy changes, and to translate this into the local setting, is of major importance for the networks in question and their performance. The theory of institutional capacity provides a framework for an understanding of such networking as a dynamic development of cooperation in the interface between internal and external changes (Healey et al. 1999; Cars et al. 2002). It is a model suited to the description of the networking and policy development in the SVR. The merger of the local environmental networks occurred because external policy changes in transfer of statutory authority in environmental policy to local municipalities made this a fruitful alliance. However the network is also coloured by a new focus on the commercialization of hiking, fishing and hunting in the recent agricultural policy (Recommendation No. 1 (2003–2004) to the Storting). For remote areas such as the SVR, much of this new policy is about new ways of using the mountains.

The availability of earmarked national funding to the municipalities is of the utmost importance in holding them together in a network that features a low level of social and institutional capacity. The combination of collective norms and rational choices is important for the municipalities taking part in the collective action. Similar combinations of norms and rational choices have been found in other studies about joint action in respect of an environmental issue (Pennington and Rydin 2000).

CONCLUSION

The main conclusion is that voluntary networks are not an easy means of environmental management. This is particularly true because comprehensive environmental management will most often include a fragmented institutional setting and a variety of stakeholders from different and even conflicting institutions. Findings from the SVR indicate that formal settings and structures are important for identifying which bodies are participating in a network, and how participation is working. Problems occur when representatives of institutions are forced to cooperate, because there may be a clash between network norms and institutional norms.

This limits the value of theories about networks and collective actions with high levels of social capital and based heavily on trust and sanctions.

Prerequisites for collective action by networks in the SVR are: some funding in the absence of sanctions; an inclusive and reciprocal process in the absence of high levels of trust; the presence of policy champions to overcome institutional limitations; the development of shared knowledge in place of norms; and a changing context which presents opportunities for new alliances and new policy-making. All the networks in the SVR evolved when policy changes opened new opportunities. Funding and social capital in the form of weak ties appear to hold the network together. However the fragmented institutional and territorial structures place considerable responsibility on networks to adapt comprehensive management needs to transboundary natural resources. The study indicates that despite the many challenges, the development of a significant bridging network is one way to overcome such limitations.

But how far do social networks actually succeed in sustainable resource management? The most crucial challenge for networks in natural resource management is not merely to draw up strategies and plans, but also to implement them. The innovative aspects of creating a new plan or strategy is easier than implementation, and makes it possible to focus on opportunities, while the implementation of strategies and plans is about the actual change in activities. Making plans is about creating possibilities, while implementing them is more about balancing traditional conflicts between conservation and development. Failing to implement a plan or strategy may also be about upholding legitimacy within one's own institution at the expense of legitimacy within the network, and shared knowledge in this context seems to entail a relatively high tolerance for free-riding. Striking a balance between legitimacy in the network and within individual institutions is the very essence of the challenge. That does not appear to be contingent on trust. In this case, the social resources shared by actors in the pilot project are rather about local and institutional linkages, multilevel and territorial, offering a clear parallel to the 'bracing social capital' explained as a blend of bonding and bridging social capital (Rydin and Holman 2004) or as finding a smooth balance between the bonding and bridging aspects of social capital (Hulgård 2004).

5. Cannock Chase, England: a policy champion for a local landscape

Yvonne Rydin and Tove Måtar

In a highly urbanized society such as England, open space near to concentrations of population is always at a premium. Nowhere is this more true than of the West Midlands conurbation, an area of some 2 575 000 people centred around the city of Birmingham but encompassing the urban settlements of Stoke-on-Trent and Stafford. To the north of this conurbation and right next to the M6 lies the area of Cannock Chase, some 68 km² of forestry and heathland bounded by Rugeley, Stafford, Cannock, Pye Green and Hednesford. Cannock Chase is an important local resource for landscape, recreational, nature conservation and historic reasons.

Its landscape value is reflected in its designation, since 1958, as an Area of Outstanding Natural Beauty (AONB) – the smallest AONB on the English mainland but long recognized as important nevertheless. AONBs are designated by central government in order to conserve and enhance the natural beauty of an area and are the primary national landscape protection measure. Recreational use of an area is not a reason for AONB designation, but AONBs can be used for recreational purposes provided that this is consistent with conservation measures. Indeed the needs of local communities, including their recreational needs, are taken into account in the designation process. Within Cannock Chase the recreational demands on the area have also been recognized by the creation of a country park covering 30 km² of the AONB. This makes it one of the biggest country parks in Britain. Such parks are designated by local not central government and are intended to provide a recreational resource for local populations. They typically include visitor facilities, waymarked paths and some interpretation of the park's special features. Staffordshire County Council is the lead authority in the case of the Cannock Chase Country Park and runs the visitor centre at Nine Gates (see Figure 5.1).

The nature conservation value of Cannock Chase is recognized through statutory designation of parts as Sites of Special Scientific Interest (SSSIs). Such SSSIs are designated by central government, through the nature conservation agency English Nature, in recognition of their contribution to

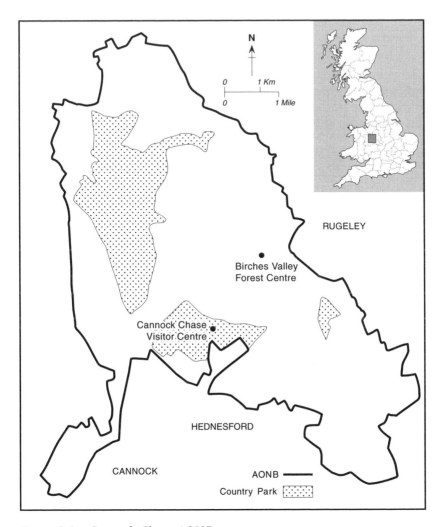

Figure 5.1   Cannock Chase AONB

national biodiversity. About 14 km^2 of the Chase heathland, woodland and valley wetland habitats is protected through this designation. In addition, many of the Chase's SSSIs were identified in 2001 as candidate Special Areas of Conservation under the European Habitats Directive, which aims to create a network of protected sites across Europe for endangered plants and wildlife habitats. This recognizes their European as well as national ecological importance. Cannock Chase is the largest surviving lowland heathland in the Midlands. The heaths are quite unique in their flora and fauna and carry a mix of species such as for example the rare hybrid bilberry, locally referred to as the 'Cannock Chase berry'. There is also a wide range of wildlife, including many rare species. Examples of such birds are the nightjar, woodlark and skylark. Four of six protected British reptiles, including the slow-worm and grass snake, are also found on the Chase. Wild deer can still be found here; fallow deer are the most common, but red deer and muntjac are also present.

The Chase is dominated by heathland but in many places bracken has taken over. The landscape needs to be actively managed to protect the heathland, so there are several projects working with bracken control, woodland thinning and scrub clearing. Historically the bracken would have been kept under control through animal grazing, but this practice is no longer economically viable and so other mechanisms need to be put in place (Cannock Chase AONB Unit 2003). Unlike the New Forest case study in this volume, there is no tradition of common grazing to maintain such landscapes.

Finally, there is also the value of the area as a historic site, capturing knowledge of the area's past in terms of its industrial development and involvement in twentieth-century wars. Cannock Chase was one of the first sites of industrial production in Britain. There is a history of iron production in the area dating back before Roman times. Production increased under Roman rule and then again after the Norman invasion in 1066. Waterpower for mills, iron ore from Rugeley Quarry and charcoal from the forests provided the key local ingredients but devastated much of Cannock Forest with rapid deforestation. However this very resource exploitation created the conditions for establishing the heathland that is now such a valued landscape and habitat. With the industrial revolution of the eighteenth and nineteenth centuries, the focus of economic activity shifted to the main urban areas, which grew rapidly. This was reinforced in the economic restructuring of the twentieth century when the West Midlands saw new phases of industrial and economic expansion. Traces of the area's industrial heritage though can still be seen in part of the Chase in the form of slag heaps, water races, sluice gates and forge foundations (Francis 1985).

As Cannock Chase's importance as a site of industrial activity declined, it came to play an increasing role in military activity. It was used during the nineteenth century as an area for military manoeuvres and during the First World War army camps were set up in the Chase. The area was ideal because the Army had knowledge of the terrain and there was little agricultural land within the Chase, so that food production would not be affected by the use of the land for training. In addition it was centrally located within England and close to a number of mainline railways, enabling the transport of troops. These camps were dismantled in 1919 after the cessation of hostilities.

However with the advent of the Second World War the Chase was used again for military training, this time by the Royal Air Force. The resulting camp was used by the RAF until the 1950s, with the huts finally sold off in 1959 and subsequently dismantled. The Chase was also used for National Service Training between 1950 and 1956. A poignant reminder of this military past remains in the form of a German war memorial site within the Chase. This was chosen in the 1960s as the final resting place for all Germans who died on British soil during the two World Wars (Whitehouse and Whitehouse 1983).

The Chase is therefore a rich area of value from many different perspectives. Some of the area's significance can be measured on the national or even European scale, as with the nature conservation designations, but much of its significance resides in its value to local residents as a site for recreation, education and visual amenity. Ironically the main pressures on the area come from these same local residents. The area is not a major draw for visitors from elsewhere in England or for overseas tourists (as is the case with the New Forest and Lake District) but it is heavily visited by the local population. A visitor survey in 2000 estimated that there were 1.5 million visitors per annum to the Chase. The problem with such heavy visitor use is that it threatens to degrade specific habitats and the landscape more generally. Heathland is not a very robust ecosystem and can be readily damaged by excessive traverse. It is proving particularly vulnerable to the local growth of 'horsiculture' as riding stables replace traditional agricultural uses in the context of declining farm incomes. Horses create more damage to the ground cover than say cattle, and are extensive users of pastureland. There are waymarked bridle paths in the Chase but riders do not always keep to these and there has been significant erosion of heathland areas as a result. There have been similar concerns regarding mountain-biking in the Chase. These create disturbance to some other recreational users as well as damaging habitats.

There are concerns that these pressures would increase with any population growth and associated residential development in the area. Figures actually show a decline in population in Staffordshire over the last few decades. Staffordshire had 1 039 000 inhabitants in 1989, 810 000 in 1998 and 808 000 in 2002; this trend is similar in all lower-tier authorities within Staffordshire. This might suggest that there is no cause for concern and that any such concerns are the result of misconceptions. However there is reason to suggest that residential development, if not population growth, may put pressure on the Chase. Housebuilding has continued to grow even if population has not. There were 309 000 dwellings in 1991 and by 2002 that number had risen to 339 000. As well as creating more demand for recreational use of the area, such residential development is also putting a more direct pressure on the Chase, since more and more of the land immediately around the Chase is being proposed for development by housebuilders and also some local authorities. Developers favour building in proximity to the landscape of the Chase, where the houses carry a premium. Currently there is no agreed 'buffer zone' that could protect the edges of the Chase from such development. Such a buffer zone would be a prime target of free-riding by local authorities. To be effective it would be important that all local authorities rejected proposals for development in a buffer zone. If one local authority chose to ignore this, then other local authorities would suffer the negative externalities of growth.

One other development pressure on the Chase arises from the continued quarrying of sites. As indicated above, there is a long history of minerals excavation in the area. The Chase still contains Europe's largest single deposit of sand and gravel and there are currently two substantial quarries operating, with an agreed plan for expanded extraction lasting until 2042. This mining activity has created some concerns about the management of the excavation, the extent of negative environmental externalities and the implementation of the restoration plans.

The Cannock Chase is therefore an area valued for multiple reasons, already used by large numbers of people and subject to pressures for intensified use. There is a need for collective management of the many individual uses of the Chase, and collective planning for changes of land use within the Chase and further development around its edge. Otherwise the very landscape that is so valued by local people will be degraded. This would also adversely affect nature conservation sites of national and European significance. The interesting feature of the Cannock Chase area though is that it has been effectively managed to avoid such degradation, to resolve conflicts between the different demands on the area and to build collective action for protecting its long-term sustainability. The rest of the chapter examines how and why such collective action was built up and institutionalized. It also discusses the question of whether these arrangements are sufficiently robust to handle any future development pressures.

A PARTNERSHIP OF LOCAL ACTORS

As with all our case studies, there is a range of actors with a stake in the Cannock Chase: central and local government, elected and non-elected, governmental and non-governmental. We start with the local authorities. A two-tier system of local government currently operates in the area, that is, a county council with a layer of district councils (sometimes called borough councils for historic reasons) below that. The Chase falls entirely within the boundaries of Staffordshire County Council. The County Council is also the second-largest landowner in the Chase (after the Forestry Commission discussed below). There is no private landownership in the Chase since all the area was originally owned by the family of Lord Lichfield, who gave the land to the local authority; the Forestry Commission subsequently bought the greater part of the estate.

The lower tier of local government comprises Cannock Chase District Council, Lichfield District Council, South Staffordshire District Council and Staffordshire Borough Council. As might be expected, the majority of the land of the Chase falls within Cannock Chase District Council. It is therefore the main planning authority for the area in terms of developing a Local Plan (soon to be a Local Development Framework under central government planning reforms) and controlling development through decision-making on planning applications. However both Lichfield and Staffordshire consider themselves stakeholders in the future of the AONB through their residents' use of the area.

In terms of central government agencies, the key actors are the Forestry Commission, the Countryside Agency and English Nature. These agencies were introduced in Chapter 3 on the New Forest. Within the Chase, the Forestry Commission is the largest landowner, owning 25 km^2, around two-thirds of the heathland and woodland areas of the Chase or around 40 per cent of the AONB as a whole. As with many of their other estates, the Forest Commission has a multifaceted role here. Some of its land is managed by Forest Enterprise as a commercial timber concern, although this has been adversely affected by the falling price of timber. But the Forestry Commission also runs a visitor centre at Birches Valley, where a cycling centre for mountain-bikers has been set up in an attempt to manage this activity in a positive manner. The visitor centre also provides information on the Commission's management of its estate for recreational and nature conservation purposes.

While the Forestry Commission may be the largest landowner, the Countryside Agency is the lead governmental agency since it has formal responsibility for AONBs within England. It proposes the designation of such areas but also continues to support them through advice, information, research and, most importantly, funding. As we will see, this has proved very important in establishing a network for the Chase AONB because the Countryside Agency funded the core unit for developing a management plan for the area. As Chapter 3 outlines, the Countryside Agency is currently undergoing restructuring but this falls outside the timescale of our research.

The remaining agency, English Nature, has a statutory role in such AONBs but its local office is reported as having been less involved than the other agencies. This is partly because it has been struggling with a reduced budget and internal reorganization, but also because of the role of a key non-governmental organization, the Staffordshire Wildlife Trust (SWT), which is particularly active in the AONB. The SWT is one of 47 local wildlife trusts around the country, bringing together local nature conserva-tionists, often with considerable local knowledge about habitats and species, for campaigning, wildlife-watching, educational and even direct manage-ment activities. This local trust comprises around 10 000 members and has been very active in the Chase. Another local NGO is the Friends of Cannock Chase. This organization has been recording a falling number of members; the figure stands at around 200. Nevertheless the Friends have been active in collecting information and undertaking voluntary work within the Chase, including heathland restoration.

There are also active NGOs representing other interests such as horse riders, dog walkers and mountain-bikers. As mentioned above, in the past there have been particular problems with mountain-biking in the Chase. Attempts to create a set of rules that all bikers would adhere to in order to minimize erosion have been unsuccessful. In a classic case of free-riding, too many bikers ignore these collective rules in pursuit of their own enjoy-ment. However there has been progress towards more effective collective action through the self-organization of the bikers into a group, enabling them to be involved in the discussions of the management of the Chase. This has also provided a conduit for the views and concerns of others about mountain-biking to find a way back to the bikers themselves.

The various actors interested in the Chase are therefore fairly well organ-ized. But historically they lacked an organizational arrangement to bring them together. There was a loosely drawn Joint Advisory Committee but the general opinion of current actors is that this was not very effective. While development pressures were not too excessive this did not cause any problems. However with the increasing demands on the area, there were occasional but repeated conflicts between the different interests. These have now largely been resolved and it is evident that the key means of achieving this has been the creation of the AONB Partnership. This partnership includes all those with a stake in the Chase, although as will be explained below, the role of the partnership within the management of the AONB is a little more complex than this suggests.

In addition to this key network, there is a broader regional partner-ship that is relevant: the Staffordshire and West Midlands Heathland Partnership, sponsored by the Staffordshire Wildlife Trust. As its name implies, this covers a much larger area than just Cannock Chase. Furthermore its focus is limited to bringing together those interested in heathland management. This is narrower than the remit of the AONB

Partnership with its coverage of forestry and minerals areas as well as heathland. However the Heathland Partnership provides the possibility of linkages between two networks and mutual learning concerning heathland management. This could provide useful knowledge inputs into the AONB Partnership. It also promotes more specific examples of collective action at the project level, implementing changes on the ground in the Chase.

INSTITUTIONALIZING JOINT WORKING

The existence of the AONB Partnership brings the various actors with an interest in the Cannock Chase together and creates the potential for collective action. However it is the particular role of the partnership within the broader management structure for the AONB that has realized this potential. This is illustrated in Figure 5.2. The partnership is here given its full name: the Cannock Chase AONB Advisory Partnership. It is a network with regular meetings and sits within a management structure that comprises a variety of different organizations. This structure has evolved over time, drawing on the elements that have seemed to work most effectively. In December 2003 it was formally agreed by the parties in the network.

As can be seen, there are a number of different elements to the management structure that essentially creates a layered (but not hierarchically tiered) set of opportunities for involvement. At the bottom of the organogram is the AONB Unit, the small unit of three staff responsible for servicing the partnership. The next layer up the main spine of the organogram comprises the Officers' Working Group with representatives at official or bureaucrat level from the five local authorities, and the three agencies. This therefore provides a small group of less than a dozen people who can work on plan development and negotiating specific problems. Then there is the formal Joint Committee of the management, its constitutional heart. This involves politicians from the local authorities; under the local government reforms of the new Labour government in 2000, local authority politicians (or councillors) have been given either executive or non-executive status denoting the tasks they take on within the local government administration. Those on the Joint Committee are executive local authority councillors. They are joined by representatives of English Nature and the Countryside Agency, but only in an advisory role. We have termed this the constitutional heart of the management because these elected politicians have the political legitimacy and official authority to take decisions on behalf of the AONB.

However the wider legitimacy of the management structure is based on a broader involvement of stakeholders. This is represented in the next layer

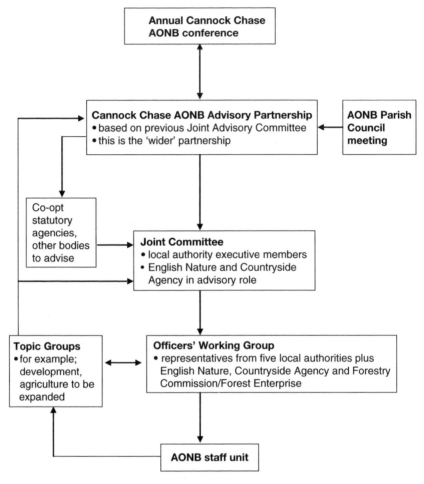

Figure 5.2   Structure for Cannock Chase AONB management and governance

up the organogram with the AONB Advisory Partnership. This was based on the earlier looser Advisory Committee but has a more formal status within the new management arrangements. While membership of this Advisory Partnership is broadly drawn, the membership is delimited to representatives of specific groups. The final layer up is a completely open Annual AONB Conference to which the wider public and any other interests are invited.

These five layers of consecutively more open involvement in the management structure are supplemented by advice from other bodies. The 13 parish councils in the Chase have an AONB meeting that sends its view to the Advisory Partnership. From time to time statutory agencies and other bodies are co-opted to advise the Joint Committee following discussion at the Advisory Partnership. Topic groups are also set up to consider specific issues affecting the Chase, such as development or agriculture. The membership of such topic groups is drawn up as the issue demands from the broader stakeholder community, with servicing from the AONB Unit. The conclusions of discussions within the topic groups are inputted into the most appropriate point in the partnership, whether the Officers' Group, the Joint Committee or the Advisory Partnership.

This arrangement has both strengths and weaknesses. Its strength is that it allows for the participation of a wide variety of actors, each in a format that suits them. Many participation efforts are ineffective because they hit the underlying problem of imbalance between the costs and benefits of participation to the individual actor. As set out in Chapter 2, the costs of participation to an individual or an organization are certain, immediate, often substantial and fall on that individual actor. The benefits, by contrast, accrue in the future, are uncertain, may not be significant for each individual actor, and often benefit whole groups, particularly where environmental assets and services are concerned. Balancing up these costs and benefits results in much lower participation than might be expected when just the interests of actors vis-à-vis the policy issue are considered.

Thus in the case of the Chase, the various stakeholders – while recognizing that the future of the area is important to them – may decide not to get involved in efforts to collectively manage the Chase because the costs of their involvement in time and effort outweigh the anticipated and likely impact of that involvement. For example mountain-bikers (or dog walkers or wildlife groups) may not come to meetings given that they are not sure their demands and needs will be met by the collective decisions. This management structure however allows each set of actors to participate in a way that minimizes the imbalance between costs and benefits. In addition, the burden of participation falls more lightly on those that do not have a work-related incentive to be involved. And finally, the AONB unit takes on much of the burden of everyday support through its servicing of the partnership and its constituent elements, thus again reducing the burden of involvement to the essential elements. The role of the topic groups performs a similar function.

The weakness lies in the complexity of the structure, which makes the workings of the management less transparent than they might be. It is also the case that while the overall burden of participation is reduced for many stakeholders, for a few centrally involved individuals the burden is actually increased through their multiple memberships of several different groups and committees. For example English Nature representatives could find themselves attending the Officers' Working Group, the Joint Committee and the Advisory Partnership, as well as certain topic groups. This may eventually undermine the commitment to this pattern of working.

Joint working has also been enhanced by having the focus of developing a specific document, a Management Plan. Under the Countryside and Rights of Way Act 2000, there is now a statutory requirement for all AONBs to have a Management Plan in place by April 2004. Indeed a key impetus for establishing the partnership was the recognition that stakeholder involvement was essential to developing such a Management Plan for the AONB. Cannock Chase was already subject to a voluntary plan produced in 1993 but the 2000 legislation required formalization of such a plan; furthermore the passage of time meant that the voluntary plan needed updating and revision. The plan took just under two years to complete, being finalized in April 2004. It covers issues such as managing the landscape, managing visitors, education and the quality of the environment, as well as discussing how to achieve the visions set up for these topics and providing for an action plan.

The partnership played a key role in developing the plan through structured and inclusive representation of all relevant interests. There was also more open consultation. At the start the local community were asked for their opinions in an 'issues report' via a questionnaire. During the work on the plan, the public were encouraged to participate through various innovative methods, and interviewees considered that the plan process had been an open and inclusive one. However it was clear that the network represented by the partnership made a specific contribution. This can be defined as the ability of the partnership to generate a consensus or at least an agreement on what future management of the Chase should look like (see also Ravenscroft et al. 2002 for similar conclusions in the case of local access forums). Interviewees emphasized that the formal structure of the partnership arrangements was not at the expense of generating a sense of inclusiveness. The sense of co-working was repeatedly stressed and interviews repeatedly referred to trust between actors, a recognition that they depended on each other for the Chase having a sustainable future. Cooperation became the norm in meetings within the partnership over the two years of its existence.

This is now being carried through to certain aspects of the implementation of the plan. For example a planning protocol is being worked on by all the local authorities, which would give the AONB Partnership a potential role in planning deliberations. The partnership could be involved in the preparation of plans as a consultee, but importantly could also be consulted on individual planning applications that might affect the Chase, particularly its landscape and nature conservation functions. This form of arrangement could be significant in overcoming free-riding by individual local authorities in allowing some development near the Chase, as discussed above. It could operationalize a form of 'buffer zone' around the Chase.

THE ROLE OF A POLICY CHAMPION

The generally satisfactory nature of the process of developing the Management Plan and the way that the partnership network was able to contribute positively can be attributed to the role that the AONB unit played. When asked to nominate the five most important actors working on Cannock Chase, most respondents mentioned the County Council, followed by the Forestry Commission, the Cannock Chase District Council and the Countryside Agency. The AONB Unit was mentioned next along with English Nature and Lichfield District Council. But this probably underestimates its significance. A small unit is here being compared with major authorities and agencies. The qualitative material from our interviews makes it clear that the unit has been highly influential in consolidating the network of the AONB Partnership.

An AONB officer was appointed in 2000 when a revision of the 1993 voluntary management plan was initiated by the Staffordshire County Council. The AONB Unit was set up in 2002 with funding mainly from the Countryside Agency but also from the five local authorities. The specific function of the unit was to coordinate the consultation process and oversee the production of the management plan for the AONB. However this is to describe the unit's work in rather procedural terms. It is clear from our interviewees that the key work that the unit did was more in the nature of building links and, further, relationships between individuals. Furthermore it was the work of the unit's leader that was particularly important. Her talent in creating better mutual understanding between actors and a culture of co-working within the partnership was highly praised by interviewees. Having worked for another AONB before coming to Cannock Chase it might have been a good choice to bring in an outsider into the process as she could begin the task from a 'fresh slate'. The various members of the partnership certainly knew each other but they had not worked together in the way required of plan preparation. Several of our other cases, such as the Morsa and SVR cases, also point to the value of bringing in an outsider in this way.

That in some circumstances a key individual can play an important role in policy processes, is recognized within the policy studies literature. Such individuals are variously termed policy brokers, entrepreneurs or champions (Dunleavy 1991: 34). What these individuals can contribute is that they seem able to negotiate the surrounding institutional context, bring together resources, motivate individuals and create consensus. This is not to suggest that the right individual can achieve all this in any context. Rather that where the circumstances are favourable, a key individual is often still necessary to activate the potential inherent in those circumstances. They become, in the terms of the institutional capacity framework, a focal point for mobilization capital.

In the case of the Cannock Chase AONB, the key contribution of the unit's leader as a policy champion was to persuade the other actors of the value of co-working and the benefits of developing a common vision for the area's future. However it may be that the role of the leader and the unit as a whole will change now that the plan has been finalized. There is a possibility of altering the partnership structure now that the emphasis is shifting from plan development to challenge of implementation. Such implementation falls to the AONB Unit although this will necessarily also involve many other actors taking decisions and allocating resources. Therefore while the unit is working on developing a rolling one-year Action Plan, it will need to develop different kinds of links with local interests. Rather than a broad and inclusive approach to networking (as institutionalized through the partnership), it will need fewer but stronger links with actors with decision-making responsibility and control over resources in order to achieve implementation.

One link that the partnership could build on is that with the Staffordshire Wildlife Trust mentioned above. The SWT already undertakes a range of activities in collaboration with and even on behalf of English Nature. This is not unusual in England. Local nature conservation is one area where NGOs often take on direct management functions. Research has shown that the incentive structures associated with this environmental issue actually favour collective action (Rydin and Pennington 2000; Pennington and Rydin 2000). Involvement in direct management is often intrinsically enjoyable for the members of such NGOs. In addition it fits with the values of the NGO membership and reinforces their identity as environmentalists. There are social or solidary benefits from associating with other like-minded people in these events. Unlike with many other forms of collective action, the benefits are often immediately and physically apparent. And these have a longer-term payback to the NGO members who may regularly use the local area involved for their recreational activities. For all these reasons, such collective action is easier to foster where management for nature conservation is concerned than with many other environmental issues.

Another route that the unit may take is to try and raise resources for implementation through putting together applications for funding. This may involve developing further, more specific partnerships for implementing particular parts of the plan. To date there have not been many partnership-based projects in the Chase but it seems likely that this will change in the future. The close links built within the partnership may then bear fruit in the form of smaller project-based partnership activity. Whether through such project-funding or releasing resources in other ways, there is a need to demonstrate the ability to achieve implementation. Otherwise the strong sense of cooperation built up through the partnership may be dissipated.

THE MUTUAL DEPENDENCE OF A NETWORK AND A POLICY CHAMPION

The story of the Cannock Chase AONB Management Plan is broadly a tale of successful networking to achieve a specific output. The AONB Partnership brought together key stakeholders in an open and inclusive way, within an overall management institution that was carefully structured to overcome collective action problems and maximize participation by a wide variety of stakeholders. The focus of the networking and collective work was clearly on developing a plan within a two-year period to meet locally recognized needs but also national requirements. There is evidence that a sense of reciprocity and mutual trust was built up within the network and that the finalized plan carried the agreement of all parties. These markers of reciprocity and trust suggest that social capital was an important element in the successful operation of the network and the institutionalization of agreement. However the emphasis in this case appears to be on bridging capital, the creation and strengthening of links between actors in different organizations. The partnership itself and the whole AONB management structure represents a particular form of institutionalized bridging capital.

Bonding capital seems to have been less important in this case. This may be because the main stakeholders that were involved were local authorities and government agencies, who were trying to find a way through the partnership to coordinate their statutory duties and responsibilities for the Chase. It is hardly necessary to invoke bonding capital to describe how representatives of these bodies relate to other members of their home organizations. The role of NGOs within the overall Partnership was less central than in say the New Forest case. The interests of dog walkers, horse riders and mountain-bikers were clear and in most cases there was no need to rely on bonding capital as a way of ensuring that the agreements reached within the partnership were binding on NGO members. The one exception to this was the mountain-bikers group, whose formation was important in getting the bikers to adhere to collectively agreed rules on biking within the Chase.

The existence of this group enabled others within the partnership to build bridging links out to the bikers, enabling two-way communication. But bonding capital within the bikers' group rendered this communication effective in terms of changing bikers' behaviour.

The key element that facilitated the creation of the essential bridging capital was the existence of the AONB Unit and the role played by its head. We have termed this the role of a policy champion in our discussion above. This has highlighted how institutional arrangements, however well structured, require activation through key personnel. Such individual agency is not a sufficient reason for success, but there are pivotal moments when such agency is necessary. Institutions tend to run on established lines, following daily routines and giving expression to embedded values and norms. The existing networks describe weaker and stronger ties between actors that reinforce these patterns of everyday behaviour. But if change is required or if, as in this case, a new network more or less has to be built from scratch, then specific individuals can be important in establishing these patterns of ties, the norms and values and the everyday routines. It is here that the AONB Unit and its leader appear to have been particularly influential.

The result of the work of the unit and the AONB Partnership over the first two years of its existence has been to create bridging ties, a sense of reciprocity, trust between parties and agreement between parties. The outstanding question though is how relevant these features will remain as the Management Plan process moves forward from formulation to implementation, and the focus of collective action becomes outcomes and impacts, not just outputs in the form of a plan. There has been some concern raised by the people interviewed that the management structure may be too complicated and time-consuming. Some restructuring may be needed, perhaps reducing the extent of some of the bridging ties. There will be a need to find and release resources to achieve specific objectives. This may require a different form of linkages. It has been suggested that more specific partnerships will need to be created with their own linkages and, perhaps, a greater contribution of bonding capital. There may be a greater reliance on the actions of outside organizations, such as the SWT discussed above, and again on the bonding capital that keeps such groups together. This may suggest a different combination of bridging and bonding among selected actors, along the lines implied by the concept of bracing capital.

And implementation may also require more knowledge resources to be invoked. To date the need for knowledge has not been a key issue in the deliberations of the partnership; the existing stakeholders have brought with them the required information and expertise. Knowledge claims have not been a site of contestation. Implementation may require more specific knowledge, including process and place-based knowledge, and ways of incorporating this into the network's operation will be needed (see also Ravenscroft et al. 2002). Implementation will begin with drawing up an action plan but will then be carried out through partnerships and projects. These will need to find their own ways of generating the necessary knowledge for successful implementation.

This case highlights the finding that institutions for resource management cannot be treated as static. The demands on such institutions change over time with changing circumstances. But they also change as the policy process shifts from phases when plan or strategy formulation dominates to phases when implementation of specific objectives is the focus, and then back again. An institution needs to be flexible enough to accommodate these different phases. Given the tendency for institutions to develop path-dependencies this can be difficult. The statutory requirement to develop a Management Plan was a strong impetus to setting up the network and creating a particular form of institution for plan development. The role of the AONB Unit and its leader as a policy champion during this stage has been emphasized. The question is whether the unit can steer a change in institutional arrangements to achieve the implementation of the plan; this may prove more challenging.

6.　The Rondane Region, Norway: common pool resource management through statutory planning

Hans Olav Bråtå

During the Ice Age, wild reindeer (*Rangifer tarandus tarandus*) were widely distributed throughout central and southern Europe. Today, the last remnants of this formerly so important species survive in the Norwegian mountains. International conventions give Norway a key role for the future of wild reindeer and in Norway wild reindeer symbolize the wilderness (Bråtå 2001; Andersen and Hustad 2005).

Nobody owns these herds of wild reindeer, but those who own or manage the land have a right to acquire hunting licences. Usually the licences are sold to the general public but locals often have preference. The primary landowners and managers are mountain boards, local communities and private individuals. Mountain boards, elected by municipal politicians, manage Crown land. The collective action problem is the reduction and fragmentation of the area used by wild reindeer. This is a collective action problem because wild reindeer depend on the entire range of land available in the region, whereas various impacts are decided on separately in each municipality and in different sectors. The consequences of minor and large-scale impact turn up later and can be difficult to relate to single impacts.

The Rondane Region is located in the eastern part of South Norway in the counties of Oppland (west) and Hedmark (east) (see Figure 6.1). The region is about 150 km long and in some areas no more than 20 km broad in an east–west direction. This chapter focuses on partial county plans as a means for ensuring collective action aimed at maintaining the wild reindeer habitats. To the north, the landscape in the Rondane Region is rugged with ten peaks higher than 2000 metres and huge U-shaped valleys with large tracts of barren land. To the south, the landscape is gentler and more forested. Annual precipitation is low in the north (especially the northeastern part), providing large areas of lichen and winter forage for wild reindeer. The southern and western parts have more precipitation and are

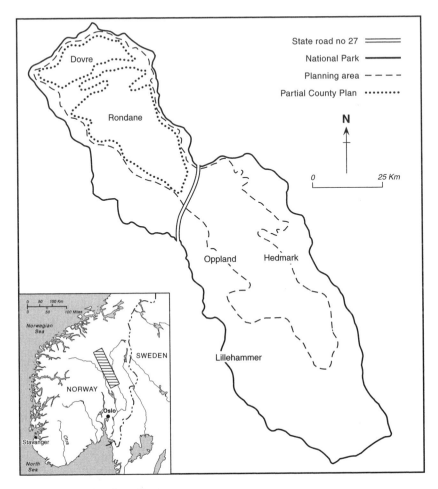

Figure 6.1   Rondane Region

better suited for summer pasture. The number of wild reindeer in the region is 4100 in the winter season. In the early 1990s, the wild reindeer in Rondane were documented as being genetically unique.

The total human population of the 12 municipalities in 2002 was 146 637, but few live in the mountainous area. Since the 1950s, the population of the northern parts has decreased whereas it has increased in the southern part, which includes the towns of Lillehammer and Hamar. The share of the population engaged in traditional agriculture has also decreased. Since the early 1900s, the Rondane Region has been a popular outdoor recreation area and consequently an attractive area for privately owned second homes. This trend has been most pronounced in the western part, and mostly in the Oppland County, but in recent decades the number of second homes has also increased in the eastern part. The last total computation of second homes is from 1991, when the number was estimated to be 11 000. In addition, 11 000 beds were estimated in hotels and other holiday venues. In summer, four roads cross the region in an east–west direction, whereas just one of these roads, State Road no. 27, is cleared of snow in winter.

The municipalities have a strong position in the hierarchy of Norwegian planning institutions and are responsible for spatial planning. At a regional level, two institutions exist: the county (based on political elections every four years) and the county governor (which represents the national government). The prime actors at the national level are the Ministry of Environment (MoE) and the Directorate for Nature Management (DN). Partial county plans are prepared to deal with specific areas or issues in one or more counties. They are based on instructions issued by the MoE, but the county usually influences the instructions. County plans are binding on a county's activities, but in principle only serve as guidelines for all other actors concerned. Still, such plans may justify objections from the county or county governor or comments regarding the local planning (which operates on a zoning principle). If an objection is put forward, the municipality may take corrective action in light of the objection or enter into negotiations with the concerned county level actors. Objections may be appealed to the MoE.

Ultimately the amount and type of land available to wild reindeer and the total number of wild reindeer are interrelated. Up to the early 1980s, spatial planning was carried out in an arena dominated by municipal planners and politicians. The concessionaires of wild reindeer hunting rights had little access to that arena, resulting in few evaluations of impacts in wild reindeer habitats. Because each of the 12 municipalities had great power over their planning and no knowledge on which to base their decisions or will to restrict their impacts, the suitability of the Rondane Region as a wild reindeer habitat was gradually reduced. Each municipality, in efforts to increase economic activity within the municipality, became a free rider on the overall wild reindeer habitat.

The challenge is to develop a land management strategy that acknowledges the need for a joint, regional perspective. Within the Rondane and Dovre national parks, the Nature Conservation Act ensures joint land management and conservation measures favourable to wild reindeer. Still, for large areas like the land surrounding protected areas, the legal framework is the Planning and Building Act (PBA) and the tools provided within that arena. The challenge is to develop spatial planning that realizes the municipalities' joint responsibility for wild reindeer habitats and spatial planning that avoids harmful impacts. That is complicated by the fact that an assessment of what constitutes a harmful impact is debatable. The PBA provides different means for joint regional planning. The question is which means are most appropriate, in a context of 12 powerful municipalities, two counties and a variety of sector interests.

THE INTRODUCTION AND DEVELOPMENT OF SPATIAL PLANNING

Much of the northern and central parts of the Rondane Region consist of Crown land, managed by mountain boards. Since the early 1950s, these boards and, later on, private landowners worked together on wild reindeer management, developed a network and established relationships of trust. This evolved into the Wild Reindeer Boards (WRBs), which are the concessionaires' voluntary and area-wide associations for wild reindeer management. These boards are focused on the management of the wild reindeer herds and have extensive knowledge of wild reindeer. Nevertheless their influence on maintaining wild reindeer habitats through spatial development processes was low due to their limited power in the arena of spatial planning. No joint, regional knowledge existed on current and planned physical development and the impacts on wild reindeer.

The establishment in 1982 of an environmental division at the county governor's offices improved the possibility of maintaining the wild reindeer habitats because the governors then had experts in wildlife, spatial planning and nature conservation at their disposal. The wildlife managers were powerful because they could object to municipal plans and had the financial resources to commission reports on wild reindeer and spatial planning. By means of this power, and good working relations with the WRBs, the wildlife managers in Oppland and Hedmark in 1984 commissioned a report on the use of the area by wild reindeer, human impacts and on spatial planning for the whole Rondane Region. This regional perspective marked a breakthrough in the regional assessment process.

The report 'Wild reindeer and impacts in the Rondane Region' (Bråtå 1985) provided a regional overview of the topics mentioned as well as spatial planning recommendations. Knowledge of the spatial range of wild reindeer was obtained by cooperating with municipal wildlife authorities and managers. The report was based on the managers' observations of wild reindeer and the managers' traditional knowledge of land-use patterns of wild reindeer, as well as reports and scientific knowledge. These two types of knowledge are respectively referred to as 'personal' and 'processed' knowledge

(Friedmann 1973; Rolf 1989; Bråtå 2001). Jointly accepted knowledge on status and trends was established. Several actors used the report as an argument against spatial development plans on the basis of their conflicting with the range of the wild reindeer.

INITIATING, PROCESSING AND APPROVING A JOINT PLAN

Still, the Rondane report was not a plan for the region. At the same time a controversial development plan was proposed. The development area was close to an important migration route and to the winter forage areas in the two municipalities in the middle of the region. The plan, the extent of existing impacts and the total situation documented in Bråtå (1985) caused the mayor in one of the two municipalities to contact other municipalities in Rondane in 1987. He wanted to establish a joint plan for preserving the wild reindeer habitat.

This mayor, representing Arbeiderpartiet (the Labour Party), was a former mountain ranger, and former leader of the Rondane South WRB. As a result, he was very familiar with the wild reindeer situation. As mayor, he was familiar with the rules of spatial planning and had an extensive political network. That network included mayors in many municipalities in both Hedmark and Oppland, and the county governor of Oppland, a former Arbeiderpartiet politician. Most of the other municipalities agreed to participate in a joint plan for the Rondane Region but some were quite reluctant.

This mayor – together with his fellow Arbeiderpartiet mayor across the border in Hedmark, and representatives of the two counties and the two county governors' environmental division – initiated the elaboration of a joint county plan. To some extent, bonding within the Arbeiderpartiet seems important to the origin of the partial county plan. A partial county plan was selected because the municipalities could accept it. One reason was that the partial county plan was not a conservation plan. The partial county plan was supposed to allow some development but its main goal was to preserve the range of wild reindeer. Another reason was that the municipalities could influence the joint management rules. It was anticipated that the municipalities and others would increase their commitment to the wild reindeer and the joint plan due to participation in the preparation process and voluntarily restrain from new harmful impacts.

During the national process of determining the scope and process of the plan, the Directorate for Nature Management (DN), wanted a strong national governmental influence. Despite these arguments, the Ministry of

Environment wrote that the local actors initiating the plan, especially the municipalities and counties, were supposed to decide on the composition of the steering committee, the process and the detailed guidelines. The preparation itself became a regional process. Moreover the ministry decided that the plan should cover the entire Rondane Region, forcing all municipalities into a joint planning process. In this process, the mayor originating the plan became a policy champion. He played an important part in putting the range of the wild reindeer on the spatial planning agenda where such issues were dealt with.

The initiators of the plan managed the planning process and tried to involve municipal politicians and planners, mountain boards, landowners and so on. The actual involvement of these actors seems quite limited however. Nonetheless the partial county plan was accepted by the 12 municipalities and was approved by the county councils of Hedmark and Oppland in November and December 1991.

The municipalities agreed on a 'planning area', equal to the range used by a wild reindeer herd of 4000–4500 animals. Basically, new developments were not supposed to be allowed but some could be accepted if the impacts did not conflict with the overall goal of preserving the wild reindeer habitat. A Planning Board was established. Its aim was to guide the implementation of the plan, including equal implementation across all borders and sectors. According to the mayor, another reason was to ensure that planning proposals were assessed within the 'political logics of spatial planning'. The Planning Board consisted of one representative from each of the county governors and counties, and two municipal politicians. The role as secretary and leader of the Planning Board was supposed to go by turns among the counties every second year. Later on, a coalition of NGOs (the Norwegian Mountain Touring Association, the Norwegian Association of Hunters and Anglers, and Friends of the Earth Norway) asked the Planning Board to be given one joint representative on the board. The board members refused the NGOs, arguing that the board should only consist of representatives from public bodies.

Partial county plans are supposed to be implemented by the municipalities through their binding spatial plans. Motorized activities such as driving snowmobiles also require permission from the municipalities. At the adoption of the plan in October 1992, the MoE decided that impacts outside the planning area should not be accepted if they caused a disturbance in the planning area (that is, the habitat of the wild reindeer). In principle this 'zone of influence' includes the entire area between the planning area and the limit of the partial county plan (that is, the bottom of the valleys) (see Figure 6.1). In this zone new development was more acceptable than in the planning area.

IMPLEMENTATION AND THE EFFECTS OF THE PARTIAL COUNTY PLAN

During the following years, few new developments within the planning area were proposed, probably due to the partial county plan. In the zone of influence, the municipalities proposed plans as before, often intending to increase the number of second homes. No joint commitment seemed to have been generated by the planning process. The factor primarily influencing the municipal planning during these years was the county governors' use of the partial county plan as a basis for making objections. The Planning Board judged the cases and was restrictive, causing the counties to raise objections more frequently. Still, the plan is supposed to allow for some impacts, especially within the zone of influence. A closer examination of which plans are harmful, and which are not, is especially important within that zone.

What about the overall picture, a decade after the first plan was approved? In terms of the planning area few new impacts have been accepted. In terms of the zone of influence, interviews and documents indicate an influence: some new development plans have been averted or reduced with regard to the total number of new second homes. New impacts are often located on the fringe of the region, at a greater distance from the wild reindeer. Still, the spatial planning processes leading up to this may be controversial when the municipalities try to locate new developments quite close to the planning area. Objections submitted, especially by the county governor, cause disputes on new proposed development plans. The network of marked ski trails and footpaths has been rerouted to some extent to steer people towards the fringe area, causing less disturbance to wild reindeer in the core areas. Such trails and paths are often an integral part of plans for new second homes and so on. In order to improve the research data on the Rondane Plan, a wide range of actors was surveyed. Generally, all groups, including municipal politicians, agree that the number of new adverse impacts in or close to the living area of wild reindeer has been substantially reduced, and the conditions for wild reindeer have improved. The improvement may to some extent be due to the rerouted network of marked trails, leading people away from the wild reindeer habitats.

A basic idea of the partial county plan was to establish coordinated planning for the entire region. According to mayors and other local politicians, the planning has become more coordinated. However as one mayor put it, 'We do not consider coordination across each single border.' What is important is a commitment to the best interests of wild reindeer. That commitment is generated by means of broader-scale processes and a generally increased awareness of the wild reindeer. There are still disagreements on how to assess different development proposals for the zone of influence. Generally speaking the respondents thought that development proposals had been considered quite equally and that the Planning Board has been important in achieving this.

The broader-scale processes mentioned above are the establishment of the new Dovre National Park and the enlargement of the existing Rondane National Park, as well as designation of protected landscapes in Rondane. This process started in 1993 and was completed in 2003, causing these interior parts of South Norway, including the Dovrefjell-Sunndalsfjella area, to encompass one of the largest concentrations of protected areas in Europe. The needs of wild reindeer were important to that initiative. In fact the habitat of wild reindeer demarcated the areas to be considered as a national park or protected landscape since the wild reindeer is the leading species of the high-mountain ecosystem. A recent climax in the increased focus on wild reindeer is the national consensus report on 'Wild reindeer and society' (Andersen and Hustad 2005).

REVISION OF THE PARTIAL COUNTY PLAN

As time passed, a revision of the partial county plan was needed, and demanded by the Planning and Building Act. Those preparing the plan were not satisfied with the existing guidelines. The municipalities demanded a more detailed background for its implementation in the zone of influence: it was not possible to treat development areas with a substantial amount of existing second homes in the same manner as mountain areas with no impacts. A revision would also put the plan and the reindeer back on the political agenda.

The revision started in 1997 and was managed by the Planning Board. During the revision process, each municipality was visited and meetings with top-level politicians and administrators were held. Meetings with NGOs, landowner associations, WRBs and the Wild Reindeer Committee (WRC) were also held. The WRC is a public committee covering the whole wild reindeer area, comprising one member from each municipality within the wild reindeer area. The WRC is supposed to supervise the WRBs on their herd management and it is the duty of the WRC to comment on spatial development plans. At the hearing most actors were satisfied with the partial county plan and the revised guidelines.

Some aspects were criticized, primarily by actors living in the southern areas and by private landowners, as well as by the leader of the WRC. Several actors, including the WRC, argued that the goal for the overall number of wild reindeer was questionable and probably should be reduced: it was not obvious that the primary goal was a herd comprising many individuals. Emphasizing the physical condition of the wild reindeer and a herd containing just enough individuals to provide a genetic pool could also be important goals. Actors criticized a proposed extension of the planning area and a new category of land: 'observation areas', that is, areas in which the land use by wild reindeer would be more closely monitored. According to the WRC, the knowledge justifying such areas had to be based on systematic registration. The planning area had to be limited to the areas regularly used by the wild reindeer. The extension of the 'zone of influence' was criticized because towns and areas of permanent settlement along the fringe, such as the town of Lillehammer, were formally included even though wild reindeer was not a relevant planning theme in those areas. Despite the criticism, the municipalities adopted the revised plan. In 1998, the County Council of Oppland adopted the revised plan.

Hedmark County postponed the adoption of the plan on several occasions. The delays in Hedmark became a problem for the county agencies, and the actors in Oppland pressured the politicians in Hedmark to make a decision. At the last voting in Hedmark in 1999, it was proposed that the revised plan should not be accepted due to an enlargement of the planning area and the observation areas. A joint plan was needed but the existing one was preferred. A proposal was made to disband the Planning Board and replace it by the WRC and the county governor's environmental divisions. The Høyre (Conservative Party) representative who put forward the proposal drew attention to the fact that his proposal was based on input from local stakeholders who had coordinated their interests. His arguments were shared by members of the Senterpartiet (Centre Party). The proposal was defeated by a vote of 23 to 19. The support of the Arbeiderpartiet, holding both the political leadership of Hedmark County and the leadership of the Planning Board, was essential for adopting the revised plan. They shared arguments put forward against the plan, such as the assertion that local communities had lost control over their natural resources, but they still considered the new plan to be an improvement because it would result in more balanced implementation and because a reduction of the extension of the zone of influence would be considered.

When the plan was approved in 2000, the MoE made it clear that the zone of influence had to be reduced. Individual guidelines for the planning area and the zone of influence were elaborated. Some 'municipal planning' areas, where more detailed management was to be considered, were marked out. Areas where the range of wild reindeer was uncertain were specified as 'observation areas'. The goal for the number of wild reindeer needed was changed from 4000–4500 in the first plan to 3000–4500 in the revised one.

NETWORKS, BRIDGING AND TRUST

Before 1982, strong regional bonding within the arena of herd control existed, but a bridge to the arena of spatial planning was lacking. An environmental division at the county governor's office was the first formal bridging (Hulgård 2004) concerning wild reindeer herds and their spatial needs. That bridging was important because the divisions were empowered to influence spatial planning throughout the entire region. At the municipal level, in the middle of the 1980s individuals who knew the two arenas from the 'inside' bridged across them. They tried to involve mountain boards and WRBs in the processes following the rules of the Planning and Building Act. The existence of the Rondane Plan is evidence of the bridging of the arenas. The overall goal of the plan, the general guidelines and the fact that the WRBs and the WRC are supposed to comment on spatial plans reflect this bridging (see Figure 6.2).

Prior to the introduction of environmental divisions in 1982, there were regional wildlife managers with some contact with the WRBs. From 1982 on, a network involving the WRBs in Rondane, the mountain boards and the wildlife managers evolved. This network became powerful enough to put wild reindeer and planning themes on the agenda. It is symptomatic that the idea of a report on 'Wild reindeer and impacts in the Rondane Region' was launched at an annual meeting of these parties, and that the WRBs financed parts of the report.

During the process of elaborating the Rondane Plan, the steering committee tried to involve a wider range of actors, such as top-level politicians and administrators in the municipalities, to foster commitment to the plan. Their efforts were not successful, because only a few of these actors participated at the meetings.

The Planning Board is a formalized network across administrative borders and levels. This type of coordinating board for the region did not exist prior to the Rondane Plan, despite the existence of spatial planning networks within each county. Such coordination, performed in the arena of spatial planning and based on its logic, is important. Still, this kind of network has caused some internal problems because the participants have different formal roles within the planning process. Generally though, the board members agree that the board has functioned well.

The interviews indicate that the core of the network concerned with wild reindeer and spatial planning are official actors such as municipalities, counties and county governors. These are all very important to the spatial planning process. Still, a wider range of actors exists and it is anticipated that the future of the plan depends on developing the networks further. The survey shows that in terms of spatial planning in Rondane, municipal

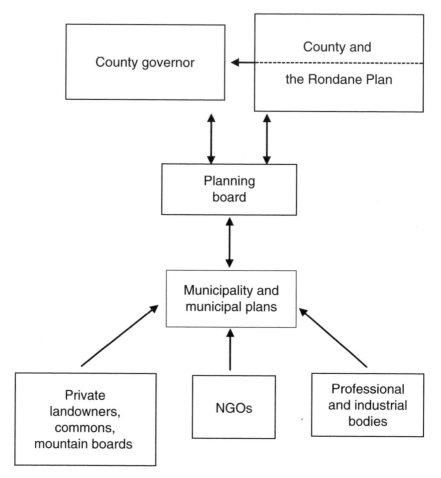

Figure 6.2   Actors and networks in the Rondane Region

politicians are mainly in contact with other politicians and the administration within their own municipality. They also have quite extensive contacts with those who own or manage the land in Rondane. County politicians are most frequently in contact with other county politicians and the county administration. Municipal and county contacts with the actors mentioned above have increased to some extent due to the introduction of the Rondane Plan, but municipal politicians have little contact across municipal and county borders.

A challenge to the partial county plan and the networks arises from the fact that new politicians may be elected every four years. People working within the administrations may get new jobs. In order to counteract this problem, as well as to stimulate cooperation, to inspire and foster trust, the Planning Board started the Rondane Conference in 1999. The conference focuses on the plan and wild reindeer, and it aims to spread knowledge and develop a forum where municipal representatives, landowners, NGOs, county-level actors and so on meet. The effort seems quite successful. Another measure for achieving the same purpose comprises visits by the Planning Board to the municipalities.

Trust is basic to common pool resource management because decisions and relationships cannot be based solely on rules and regulations. Hansen and Tjerbo (2003) suggest that trust is a substitute for immediate control. Somehow an actor such as a municipality has to trust that other actors will not act as free riders. The idea that the partial county plan should foster a joint commitment is based on developing trust. Another aspect of trust is that actors react as anticipated. In a formal situation, a municipality may trust the county governor's office for instance, despite its objections, because this is expected within the system. The informants pointed out that trust is very important to the functioning of the partial county plan. At the interviews the actors were ranked according to trust. Generally the actors mentioned trusted the spatial planning system and its official actors, such as the municipalities.

The survey shows that municipal politicians have a high level of trust in their own politicians and administration but also trust regional institutions such as the Planning Board, the WRC and the WRBs. As the Planning Board was founded as a result of the partial county plan, the municipal politicians' trust in that board has – not surprisingly – increased as a result of the partial county plan. The plan has also increased the trust in other wild reindeer institutions, the WRBs and the WRC. County politicians trust those with whom they have most contact but they also trust the polit-icians in their own municipality and the above-mentioned regional institu-tions. County politicians have increased their level of trust in each other and in their administration units.

The informants were key individuals in official positions. It is therefore not surprising that they were considered part of the primary network. Nevertheless the informants mentioned a wide variety of actors as their main contacts. To some, contact frequency was greatest with the WRBs and the WRC, to others it was with the municipalities. A good relationship with the county governor was mentioned as important. The informants often mentioned actors within their own county as those with whom they had greatest contact and in whom they had the most trust. Overall, the Planning Board seems to have a varied network ranging from wild reindeer author-ities and mountain rangers to high-ranking county officials. Networks within political parties seem to be important to the progress, survival and implementation of the partial county plan, both within and among the counties.

Knowledge concerning alternative or oppositional networks is limited but some such networks seem to exist. Studies of written material indicate that NGOs concerned with nature conservation and outdoor recreation, including hunting, cooperate to some extent and probably have a network. Documents also show that landowner organizations (private and co-owned land) cooperate with forestry and farming organizations. They often write joint statements and the arguments in their individual statements are quite similar. Earlier, these actors have used the existence of the partial county plan as an argument against 'even worse superior planning', namely establishing protected landscapes or national parks.

The comments put forward by Høyre's representative on behalf of stakeholders at the plan revision in Hedmark, reflect a network critical of some aspects of the Rondane Plan. This network seems to exist mainly in the county of Hedmark. An essential element is a general resistance to superior planning that restricts 'the development of the countryside'. Much of the recent criticism is related to the implementation of the plan, the inclusion of new areas in the planning area, and disagreement concerning the decisions of the Planning Board.

KNOWLEDGE RESOURCES AND THE LEVEL OF AGREEMENT

Jointly accepted, up-to-date knowledge is important to collective action (Ostrom 1990; Cars et al. 2002). Prior to the introduction of the county governor's environmental division in 1982, processed and personal knowledge about the range of the wild reindeer, activities in the area and some anticipation of the effect of the impacts existed. Still, the different kinds of knowledge were not systematically registered, processed or presented in a form suitable for aggregation and comparison across borders. The joint initiative for the 'Wild reindeer and impacts' report' was one way of solving the problem. Knowledge for the whole region was acquired, and personal knowledge was turned into processed knowledge. Due to the involvement of the mountain rangers, an important source of knowledge, a jointly accepted knowledge was established, much of it incorporated into the Rondane Plan.

Nevertheless, the implementation of the partial county plan is based on ad hoc assessments. Firstly, some new activities and development may be allowed, because the Rondane Plan is not a conservation plan but a plan in which proposals have to be assessed in each instance. This is especially pronounced for the zone of influence. There new development is supposed to be accepted to a greater extent than in the planning area. In the planning area new development is not supposed to be accepted. The second aspect, not explicitly defined, is that the county plan should be interpreted so that the municipalities continue to support it. Questions emerge on the context for those interpretations, and the relationship between processed knowledge and personal knowledge. Such matters may be difficult to examine and therefore a matter of conflict. The Planning Board is supposed to deal with such problems. These problems are also the basis of the third aspect, that is, the principle of the greatest degree possible of equal assessments across borders, across types of impacts and so on. The outcome of the Planning Board's assessments has been questioned, which has led to proposals to disband the board.

To reduce uncertainty and increase the level of common knowledge, the Planning Board ordered processed knowledge from a research institution on how the land is used by people staying in second homes. The report, Vorkinn (2003), is expected to be very useful in implementation of the Rondane Plan.

EXPLAINING COLLECTIVE ACTION IN THE RONDANE REGION

The original problem in Rondane was that individual actors, primarily the municipalities, acted as free riders in the absence of rules or norms for collective action that would have restricted them. A number of major and minor developments had negative impacts on wild reindeer. No bridging between the herd management and spatial planning arenas existed. The chain of reaction leading up to the partial county plan is rooted in some important actors' concern for wild reindeer habitats. The county governor's environmental division became important because environmental issues, as in Cannock Chase, acquired a structural bias (Schattschneider 1975). A powerful venue for linking the arenas was established. Nevertheless there was still insufficient knowledge with a regional perspective. Knowledge that is accepted by the majority of the actors is critical for developing and maintaining common pool resource management (Ostrom 1990; Bråtå 2001; Cars et al. 2002). A network involving the county governor's wildlife managers and the WRBs brought forward such knowledge. This knowledge became the foundation of the municipal plans and of the objections and protests against them. Still, no joint plan for the whole Rondane Region existed.

When selecting the means for planning, a dilemma arose between a *Leviathan* approach (Hobbes 1651/1998) and participation involving commitment to and trust of other actors. The Ministry of Environment's general support for partial county plans as a means of balancing development and preservation (Mørk 1990) helped to foster the Rondane Plan. The plan was also fostered by the fact that the initiatives emerged in the arena of spatial planning, which is the arena where the municipalities had the most power. Most important though was that a mayor with considerable political influence could link the arenas of wild reindeer management and spatial planning. As pointed out by Ostrom (1990), Bråtå (2001) and Stokke (in this volume) individuals are very important to breaking the 'shackles of the commons' and developing common pool resource management. The mayor had an extensive network, including wild reindeer authorities, mountain boards and a good relationship to fellow Arbeiderpartiet members, such as the county governor of Oppland. In difficult phases, the latter was an important influence in the process, the plan and its implementation. Considerable 'political capital' (Innes et al. 1994) was mobilized by this individual.

Despite efforts to establish commitment and trust, it was realized, as in other common pool resource management cases (Ostrom 1990; Eckerberg 1997; Bråtå 2001; Hovik 2001), that a system for punishing free riders is needed. In the case of partial county plans, this system is the ordinary planning system and the power designated to county agencies. For several years after the 1991 approval, the partial county plan had an effect mainly due to objections voiced by the county governor's environmental division and later also by virtue of the Planning Board and the counties. This was a pronounced feature within the planning area. Establishing this planning area emphasizes the core of the region and indicates where power may be exercised against development proposals. Stringently implemented planning rules seem to be accepted within this area, also by those critical to the implementation of the partial county plan. The frequent use of objections reflected a relatively low municipal commitment to the plan, probably because not all municipalities and actors wanted joint planning and because county plans were traditionally considered to be weak instruments.

A basic problem for migrating common pool resources is their changing land use and the fact that the whole area relevant to the resource – wild reindeer – ought to be controlled by joint rules (Ostrom 1990). By defining a zone of influence the plan incorporates such basic aspects. However since impacts are supposed to be more acceptable within that zone, the power of managing the zone is challenged. In another partial county plan regarding wild reindeer, the Hardangervidda Aust Plan (Buskerud and Telemark fylkeskommuner 1995), the main planning area is complemented by small areas for spatial development, outside the planning area (Bråtå 2005). Several areas formerly used by wild reindeer are not included in this partial county plan and those areas are therefore not protected by the power inherent in partial county plans. These areas are marginal to wild reindeer today, but marginal areas may be important in specific situations, such as early winter periods.

The Rondane Plan obviously includes some areas that are irrelevant, but it is unclear which. The problem is where to draw the line, because some impacts outside the planning area have a negative impact on wild reindeer. The Planning Board must assess which of the proposed impacts are potentially harmful and consider the mitigating efforts. An important aspect of long-enduring common pool resource institutions is that people perceive their proposals and actions to be considered equally (Ostrom 1990). The Planning Board is supposed to contribute to an equal assessment of development proposals, and the Planning Board seem to have performed this task quite well. The problem is that assessments are still questioned. Criticism has occurred, claiming that development is accepted in some municipalities and not in others, and that Hedmark suffers by contrast with the more developed areas of Oppland. Such experiences are probably important reasons for the oppositional network in Hedmark at the time of revision, which tried to disband the Planning Board. Conflicts with agricultural interests are another reason, as the area suffers from a declining population rate and few alternative investments in economic development. Arbeiderpartiet members in both counties seem to be important to the board's survival and to the adoption of a revised plan. As in earlier phases of criticism of wild reindeer management, processed knowledge was called upon to reduce the uncertainty and re-establish trust in the management (Bråtå 2001).

The actors' possibility of influencing the rules, which are supposed to guide their future activities, is important to their support of the plan. Revision is a formal procedure of influencing rules, and the actors did influence the rules. Despite that fact, the basic idea of the partial county plan is to achieve a management based on trust and commitment to the wild reindeer. Networks are one way of strengthening this. It is difficult to determine the extent of the network aimed at preserving the range of wild reindeer, but it may be too limited. This may be due to the fact that politicians and administrators come and go, making it difficult to develop stable networks and trust. The Rondane Conference and meetings in the municipalities are attempts to strengthen that aspect and increase knowledge of the plan and the region. Such efforts are important to establishing bridging networks (Granovetter 1973). The increased awareness of wild reindeer generally indicated in the interviews, and reflected in the comments at the time of revision, indicates that the management could to some extent be based on commitment and trust. Nevertheless it is dubious to base spatial planning and implementation on commitment in bridging networks alone. Too many actors may be tempted to propose new development plans. This may be caused by the temptation to act as a free rider but also because the plan allows for impacts, and because the effects of impacts are debatable. In common pool resource management, a general system for punishing free riders has to exist. A balance between commitment and trust and the exercise of power has to be achieved. Still, as mentioned in a document from an actor critical of the plan: the plan is a good means and it functions better than before.

CONCLUSIONS ON USING STATUTORY PLANNING

The absence of coordinated spatial planning aimed at preserving wild reindeer habitats is a threat to the long-term survival of the species. Partial county plans are a means for such planning, but for large areas, this may also allow for development. The question is how the plan is implemented. Ideally, implementation of partial county plans is based on commitment to the wild reindeer and on the trust that other actors will restrict their activities and avoid free-riding. Still, development is tempting. A system for punishing free-riding is therefore necessary based on the rules governing the arena of the Planning and Building Act. Public agencies have been important to bridge the arenas of wild reindeer management and spatial planning. Networks between official actors and WRBs have also been important.

Individuals have played a major part in linking the arenas of interest, in advancing planning and in keeping it on the agenda. Processed knowledge for the whole region has been very important and has played a part in uncertain situations. Wild reindeer cross many borders and the challenge is to assess planning proposals equally. A coordinating body, the Planning Board, has played a significant role here and as a continual reminder of the existence of the partial county plan. This board and the public bodies upon which the board is based are the core elements of the network and 'brace' the arenas (see Chapter 2). Still, a wider and probably weaker network bridges wild reindeer management with spatial planning. A commitment to the needs of wild reindeer seems to have exerted some influence on the development proposals within the region. Promoting this commitment is important, but a system for punishing potential free riders still has to be maintained.

7. Mafungautsi area, Zimbabwe: decentralized management of forests

Everisto Mapedza

Collective decision-making has always been a challenge confronting resource management in Zimbabwe (Murphree 1990). Within the forestry sector, the government's solution to the perceived degradation of forestry resources was to set aside forests through reservation which would 'protect the forests' from the people. This 'fortress conservation' strategy has not helped to solve the need to manage forestry resources, as peasant farmers have continued to illegally collect forestry products from Mafungautsi. The declining state resources have further undermined the capacity of the state to sustainably manage the reserved forests. The contestation of the 'reserved' forests has also meant there have been competing ideas on the strategy to manage the forest. The state, through the Forest Act of 1996, has the mandate to manage reserved forests but other local-level institutions have been contesting the state's legitimacy in managing the forest at the interface zones. There are various layers of authority, which are competing for the management of the forestry resources. These include the Forestry Commission (FC), the Rural District Council (RDC), ward and village-level institutions. This has forced the government to abandon the exclusive model of forest management and look at other options of collectively making the forest management decisions with the local communities. The success or failure of such a natural resource management strategy largely depends on the interaction and cooperation of various institutions.

BACKGROUND TO DEVOLVED FOREST MANAGEMENT IN THE MAFUNGAUTSI STATE FOREST

Mafungautsi State Forest Reserve, in west central Zimbabwe, is one of the 21 state forests falling under the control of the FC (Figure 7.1). Mafungautsi State Forest comprises some 82 100 hectares of forestland, which is almost

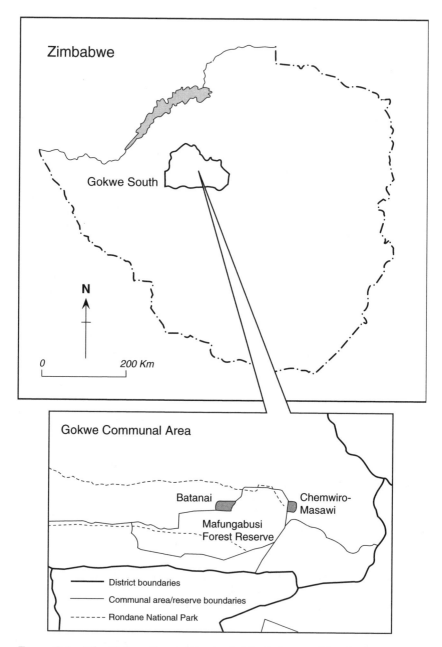

Figure 7.1   The Gokwe South District in Zimbabwe and Mafungautsi
            State Forest within the district

10 per cent of the national forest reserves of 827 200 hectares of indigenous forest reserves, mainly in the western parts of the country. Like most such state forests, Mafungautsi was created through the eviction of peasant communities originally residing in that area before it was placed under statutory designation in 1954. It is therefore characterized by tenurial and other conflicts between official state forest custodians and surrounding peasant communities. Reservation of forests, it was hoped, would help avoid the tragedy of the commons dilemma (Hardin 1968; Ostrom 1990; Saglie this volume).

The research reported here was conducted in two Resource Management Committee (RMC) areas, namely Batanai and Chemwiro-Masawi. These two cases were selected out of the 15 RMCs that have been formed in the Mafungautsi area of Gokwe South District in Zimbabwe. The initial selection criterion was to conduct research on one success story RMC (Batanai) and one failure (Chemwiro-Masawi), as the FC initially suggested to the researcher. Research revealed however that 'success' and 'failure' are not useful criteria, since success in the eyes of the FC might not have anything to do with the achievements of the RMC, but rather serves as a gauge of how amenable the RMC is to manipulation. The RMCs that stand their grounds are labelled 'failures'.

Nevertheless Batanai is a relevant case study. It is situated in an area that was formerly forestland, and some people within Batanai were evicted forest dwellers. This offers a contrast with Chemwiro-Masawi where few people used to reside in the forest area. Chemwiro-Masawi was also selected because it had commercial timber extraction, and this provided the opportunity to see how dividends were to be allocated in the context of the co-management arrangement. Differences in attitudes towards co-management were assessed in the two different contexts with different historical relationships with Mafungautsi Forest. Some comparative research was pursued in Sokwela, Chemusonde and other RMCs. These will be cited in the text, but they are minor research sites.

Over the years the boundaries of Mafungautsi have expanded and contracted, reflecting the difficulty that both the FC and the local peasant communities have in asserting effective and exclusive control over the forest reserve. The recognition that the conservation of the forest reserve could only be secured with the support and cooperation of neighbouring peasant communities dates back to the 1960s (Phillips et al. 1962). However over the years management formulations that have sought to involve local communities have mainly been structured to secure conservationist goals, and not to empower the communities. Such formulations came under a variety of fashionable populist-sounding terms including 'community development' in the 1960s (Mutizwa-Mangiza 1985), 'co-management' and 'resource sharing' in the early 1990s (Matzke 1993; Matzke and Mazambani 1993), and lately 'adaptive co-management'. For instance the Centre for International Forestry Research has commissioned an extended research project on adaptive co-management in Mafungautsi.

The transfer, through decentralization, of governance powers to units that are closer to the citizens is gaining increasing significance for governments in developing countries (Crook and Manor 1998; Mawhood 1983; Ribot 1999). The term 'decentralization' entails a process by which bundles of entrustments – including regulatory and executive powers, responsibility and authority in decision-making, institutional infrastructure and assets, and administrative capacity – are transferred to local groupings such as local governments or local communities. Entrustments can be defined as the responsibilities given to lower-level structures from above (Ribot 1999, 2001). In practice, decentralizations turn out to be disjointed and complex processes, having to operate within arenas characterized by the contestation and negotiation of interests between and within various levels of society (cf. Moore 1993; Peet and Watts 1996; Tsing 1999). This case study uses review and case-study approaches to examine critically the ambiguities and complexities of 'peasant empowerment' in a co-management arrangement from a Zimbabwean protected forest interface zone. The study questions benign-sounding presumptions of co-equal partnership status among co-managing actors that are often implicit in the designs of such projects. It argues instead that real-life co-management lies at the intersection of interests arrayed in particular sites, including states, international organizations, business and grassroots actors.

This study uses the Mafungautsi case to expose some of the ambiguities and complexities of 'peasant empowerment' under the devolved forestry initiative. It further explores the dynamics of collective decision-making in natural resource management. Co-management in Mafungautsi was viewed as an opportunity for enabling collective management decision-making (cf. Rydin this volume). The central thesis is that the state and other external actors have sought to mould seemingly local institutions and have tried to discipline these institutions towards the achievement of top-down conservation objectives. The case study shows that there is little scope for genuine local empowerment in partnerships in which the community or committees are currently being manipulated. This does not however imply that the communities are passive (cf. Scott 1985). The following section looks at the institutional complexity in the effort to collectively decide the management of Mafungautsi.

THE CRAFTING OF INSTITUTIONAL INFRASTRUCTURE FOR DEVOLVED FORESTRY MANAGEMENT

Resource Management Committees (RMCs) were introduced by the FC as part of the devolved forestry package. These new institutions were to bring in new dynamics within the Mafungautsi community as will be illustrated in the two case study areas of Batanai and Chemwiro-Masawi RMCs. The section below explores the introduction of these new institutions and how they contributed to the socio-political complexity in the Mafungautsi area of Gokwe. This section will also look at social capital and assess why the lack of bridging capital contributed to the lack of cooperation between different institutions (cf. Rydin this volume).

RESOURCE MANAGEMENT COMMITTEES

In order to create devolved forestry management through partnership that includes local communities, since 1995 the FC has been involved in the setting up of RMCs. An RMC is typically composed of seven members, namely chairperson, vice-chairperson, secretary, treasurer and three committee members. Committee members occupy offices through elections involving adult village suffrage – which is subject to manipulation. Electing RMCs is a confusing process with regard to popular participation, as it often does not generate much interest among the potential voters, who do not attach much significance to the elections. Lack of interest could also be attributed to the unresponsiveness of the FC to the people's needs. For instance at the 2000 pre-grass-cutting workshop at Shingai Training Centre, people requested to be permitted to collect fibre sustainably for construction purposes. The FC responded by saying that the peasants should buy ropes – the cost of which is beyond the reach of peasant farmers.

Popular participation is further compromised since FC wields rarely challenged advisory powers that determine who serves as members of the RMC subcommittees, particularly during the grass-cutting season, which spans June to October. Although this window of discretion enjoyed by the FC may be well intentioned, for example to reduce transaction costs of decision-making during a period of high labour demand, its overall effect is to subordinate democratic processes to bureaucratic fiat. The arrangement reinforces a top-down orientation of the committee.

RMCs in most instances cut across traditional villages or kraals. In some cases the RMCs were formed at a level equivalent to the *dunhu* which is headed by a headman. At the time when the first RMCs were formed in

1995, that was the time when traditional leaders had not been formally given back their powers through the Traditional Leaders Act of 1998. Effective implementation of this Act was after 2000. In Batanai, in 1996, three traditional village heads were requested to nominate people who would occupy the different posts in the RMC. It is important to note that in this instance the RMC covered three traditional villages. In cases where the RMC was formed at the then Village Development Committees (VIDCO) level the committees operated independently. Further, RMCs are constituted of individuals who have a grounding in other local institutions, adding to the ambiguities and complexity of the whole process as shown by Figure 7.2.

RMCs were introduced as part of decentralization within the co-management initiative. Decentralization of power and responsibilities were cited as one of the principles of co-management in Mafungautsi (Forestry Commission 1997). The RMCs were formed as subcommittees of the VIDCOs, but confusingly, some covered more than one village jurisdiction or even ward as illustrated in Figure 7.2. The bonding social capital seems to have been effective at village level but was very weak at higher levels. In Batanai the RMC struggled to bring different traditional villages together. One could almost observe the lack of bridging capital (Rydin this volume; Ostrom 1990). This resulted in some form of 'crisis of identity' for the RMC due to its confusing linkage to the existing institutions as shown by the simplified institutional organogram in Figure 7.2. RMCs are composed of seven members who are elected and are supposed to manage the forestry affairs on behalf of their communities. The operationalization of RMCs in practice will also be analysed below. The RMC activities are governed by a constitution, which was written by the FC and the then government department responsible for gender and cooperatives.

Residents in communal areas adjacent to Mafungautsi State Forest are members of VIDCOs or Ward Development Committees (WARDCOs), units created under a prime-ministerial directive in the immediate post-independence period, ostensibly to democratize the process of planning for local development (cf. Wekwete and de Valk 1990). The VIDCOs and wards were demographically defined administrative units that in principle were based on a system of popular representation. A VIDCO consisted of six members, four of whom were selected through an adult village suffrage. By default, all VIDCO members were members of the ruling party and there tended to be a very thin line between these institutions and the ruling party, with two posts being allocated to members of the ruling party's Women and Youth Leagues. The VIDCO was presided over by a chairperson elected by the members, and its job was to develop a local village development plan. Six such villages constituted a ward, which was headed by

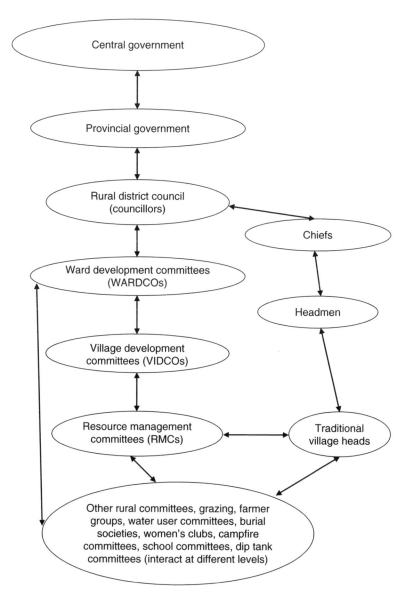

Figure 7.2   Institutional organogram of Zimbabwe's pre-2000 rural local governance system

a WARDCO, also having six members constituted on similar lines as the VIDCOs, but presided over by an elected councillor who represented the ward at the rural district council level. Although VIDCOs and WARDCOs in principle appeared democratic, in practice they were not effectively representative of local interests and aspirations as argued by some researchers (Mandondo 2000; Murombedzi 1991; Mapedza and Mandondo 2002). Decisions were effectively made at the district level with the technical advice of line ministry technocrats. These experts tend to make plans based on instructions coming from their head offices in Harare, rather than incorporate the input of the local communities, to whom they are not accountable. In Batanai RMC the councillor is not popular as he was accused of stifling development, especially on the issues of building a new school and a cattle-dipping tank. The people were further baffled when he was interviewed on the national radio saying that he had managed successfully to develop his ward since his election. In Chemwiro-Masawi the traditional village head said the councillor was not doing enough to convince the RDC that timber revenue had to be ploughed back into the communities. In one instance the village head attended a Gokwe South Rural District Council meeting in order to push through the request to get proceeds from commercial timber logging.

Moreover the VIDCOs and WARDCOs were not created in an institutional vacuum – they were superimposed on a 'traditional' system of social organization. It is important to note that 'traditional institutions' are dynamic and are always evolving with time. In this system the household (*musha*), under a patrilineal household head (*samusha*), comprises the smallest social unit. Several households constitute a village (*bhuku*) under the village head (*sabhuku*). Several villages constitute a *dunhu*, presided over by a headman (*sadunhu*), and these in turn constitute chiefdoms (*nyika*) under the chief (*mambo*). The current reforms under the Traditional Leaders Act of 1998 have resulted in the recognition of traditional villages, now called village assemblies (*dare* or *inkundla*), which have replaced the VIDCOs. Above the village assembly, there is now a ward assembly, which brings together all village heads, headmen and councillor of the ward. This is to be headed by the headmen. RMC boundaries do not coincide with the traditional institutions' boundaries. Related traditional institutions include spirit mediums, rainmakers and other holders of ritual office (Bourdillon 1991). This clearly demonstrates that organizational arrangements alone do not fully account for the dynamics and outcomes in environmental governance (cf. Rydin this volume).

The role of RMC chairpersons is made more difficult in that even their fellow committee members question their legitimacy compared to other local authorities. In an interview on 4 November 1999 with the Batanai

RMC chairperson on why they were not effectively mobilizing the people, he pointed out that he needed to mobilize the RMC itself before moving to the ordinary peasant farmer. Some reminded him that he was not the village head or the headman. An institutional ranking conducted by the researcher on 30 November 1999 rated the village head and traditional leaders highly with 69 points, with RMCs getting 11. Councillors and members of parliament each got zero points. The support for traditional leaders was even more resounding in Mutanhaurwa village where 216 people felt that the traditional leaders were the most appropriate institutions for rural development initiatives. VIDCOs got 48 with councillors getting 33. This institutional ranking used the criteria of responsiveness to local needs, feedback mechanism and accountability to the villagers. This seems to have glued villages together at a local level and made it almost impossible to cooperate with institutions at higher level.

The VIDCO–WARDCO and traditional systems of leadership rely on different systems of legitimization, which produces conflict between them. Each of the two systems relies on a unique corpus of regulation systems. Among other things, traditional regulatory mechanisms include explicit rules as well as implicit norms and taboos including a moral economy of rules that are written within the hearts of the people. Local censure mechanisms include payment of material fines, admonition and belief in the omnipotence of the spirits and spiritual censure (Mandondo 1997; Matowanyika 1991). The moral expectation that others will behave in a similar pattern has helped communities to internalize costs and hence make collective natural resource management decisions. Rather than a simple matter of 'top-down disciplining' for conservation objectives, the new organizations seem to be entangled with both bureaucratic politics (at multiple governmental levels) and local politics (cf. Ferguson 1990; Mapedza and Mandondo 2002). The Chemwiro-Masawi pre-grass-cutting workshop recommended that the RMCs should be a subcommittee reporting through the village head. Examples of traditional judiciary in natural resource issues include the judgements of Headman Ndhlalambi in Batanai on 29 June 2000 when nine people were ordered to pay Z$490 (about US$9 using the official exchange at that time) each for cutting down fruit trees for various purposes.

One must not over-romanticize the respect of traditional leaders, as their status is not fixed and they are being faced with new challenges. Some traditional leaders are even less democratic than the elected committees. In Batanai, a village head was assaulted for handing down a 'biased' ruling, according to the defendant. Manipulation of these leaders by government might result in traditional leaders who are even more autocratic than elected committees which are subjected periodically to electoral processes.

Traditional leaders are normally not subjected to such democratic processes. Village heads in both Batanai and Chemwiro-Masawi lamented the loss of control over their people as a result of challenges from new churches, mainly the Seventh Day Adventist church. The councillor for Batanai, in an interview with the researcher on 2 September 2000, argued that the RMCs were not going to succeed as they were hiving themselves off from him as the representative of the RDC by jointly organizing meetings with the FC without notifying him. He further argued that even the proposed school in Batanai would not materialize, as he would have to fight to assert his power over the traditional headman of the area. The councillor even tried to link the headman to the opposition party so that he would be forced out of office. In one instance a resignation letter, purportedly written by the headman, was sent to the chief. Further investigations showed that the headman's date stamp had been forged. The councillor wanted to take over from the headman in the wake of the introduction of the government's monthly allowances to traditional leaders. He likened the Batanai people to the grass bearing the brunt of two elephants fighting (himself and the headman).

Local government reforms, through the Traditional Leaders Act of 1998, have further conflated the above structures with a new system of village and ward assemblies. These are constituted through a curious mix of elected and nominated leaders and representatives. Membership of the village assembly is open to all adults in the village, but such bodies are presided over by hereditary traditional leaders, whose nominations and appointments are approved by chiefs and the minister – in accordance with local culture (Traditional Leaders Act of 1998). A ward council is composed of village heads of its constituent village assemblies, a councillor of the ward and a cohort of headmen nominated by chiefs and endorsed by the Minister of Local Government, Public Works and National Housing. The ward assembly is presided over by a headman elected by members of the assembly from among themselves. Village assemblies elect VIDCOs and supervise and approve plans from VIDCOs, whilst ward assemblies oversee all the roles and activities of their constituent VIDCOs. The superintendence of headmen and village heads over VIDCOs and WARDCOs elevate the system of nominee lineage leaders over elected representatives.

THE PRACTICAL POLITICAL ECONOMY OF DEVOLVED FOREST MANAGEMENT IN MAFUNGAUTSI

Resultant patterns of practical interaction in everyday social practice constitute what Li (1996) terms 'practical political economy', an analytical conception that reflects the contestation and negotiation of interest within and between stakeholders (Tsing 1999). Walker defines it as 'how human practices of resource use are shaped by social relations at multiple levels over time' (Walker 1995: 1). The new co-management initiatives have resulted in the different alignments of flows of benefits to people and groups within a society. New initiatives introduce new dynamics that see certain groups of people benefiting. The co-management aimed at reshaping the political economy and enabling the local communities to benefit. However the creation of upwardly accountable RMCs means that benefits are now accruing to an upwardly accountable committee. In Batanai, relatives of the village head were allocated positions in the RMC with business people hijacking a bee-keeping project in Chemwiro-Masawi.

The co-management has managed to glue the peasants together in their villages. Most villages, especially under the leadership of traditional leaders, have been united in order to fight back at the FC. This social capital is not easily displayed across villages. Villages getting more benefits from co-management than others were not willing to take drastic action such as invading the forests. There seems to be animosity across villages as there is no reciprocity. Villages in the same RMC tend to compete with villages in the other RMC. One of the reasons has to do with the assumed zero-sum permit areas allocation. The areas allocated for grass and broom grass are limited and these are allocated annually by the FC. There have been a number of instances where villagers in one RMC ended up harvesting areas under the control of another RMC rather than in their allocated areas. One reason was the existence of porous boundaries within traditional villages, which now had to cope with fixed boundaries under co-management (cf. Bruce et al. 1993). This pitted villages whose residents were evicted from the forest against those who have always been residing outside the forest over how co-management should proceed.

INDIGENOUS KNOWLEDGE

Local villagers claim to have a local indigenous knowledge of their ecosystem, which has been handed to them by their ancestors. This indigenous knowledge system, which is enforced through totems, taboos and traditional natural resource management, they argued, was important for the management of the Mafungautsi Forest. Natural resources were managed in the interest of the community. This type of management was based on customs, taboos, religion and clan name system (Schofelleers 1979; cf. Wilson 1986, 1989; Cavendish 1994). The traditional leader always had to consent to the harvesting of natural resources and the hunting or killing of wildlife (Sibanda 2001). Among the Shona people it became a tradition that when an elephant was killed, the tusk, which was closest to the ground, was to be given to the chief (*ishe*) or king (*mambo*). Sibanda (2001) and MacKenzie (1988) further point out that people could not kill animals which were part of their totems (cf. Beatie 1966; Mair 1974, 1984). Certain tree species were declared sacred. There were also traditional tree-harvesting controls and medicinal plant codes of conduct for collecting medicines and other tree products. These were, arguably, mechanisms for conserving different animal and plant species. The RDC and the FC on the other hand argued that they had scientific knowledge, which demanded that the forest should be managed in a particular way in order to protect biodiversity in the Mafungautsi Forest. It was also important to note that there was no regular ecological monitoring carried out in order to ascertain the impact of the current management strategy. One part of the forest was cleared in order to establish a eucalyptus plantation. Eucalyptus species have often been argued to be unsuitable for the semi-arid regions due to their high water uptake (cf. Calder et al. 1997). Indigenous knowledge was quickly dismissed as being irrelevant. One of the justifications for the designation of Mafungautsi was the need to protect the watershed for national electricity generation. This explanation did not appeal much to the local peasant farmers, as they had no electricity in their homesteads.

DEVOLUTION OUTCOMES

Decentralized forest management in the Mafungautsi forest has not produced positive ecological outcomes. It has also negatively impacted on the institutional dynamics in the Mafungautsi area. A closer analysis of the evolution of co-management in Mafungautsi shows that it could be one of many fashionable conservation–development initiatives having little to do with democratization of forest management. A variety of lobbies and interest groups have shaped the manner in which the co-management project specifically evolved (cf. Murphree 1990). A development lobby represented by the donors saw it as an opportunity for investing in the development of the institutional infrastructure for co-management between the FC and surrounding peasant communities (Roper and Maramba 2000). The donors provided generous funding, through the FC, for the creation of interface institutions to bridge communities and the FC in the new co-management partnership. A project coordination team seconded to the FC was created to facilitate the setting up of RMCs and to equip such committees with the requisite capacity in leadership, technical and other skills for the effective discharge of their new roles in the venture.

Recurrent expenditure including salaries, allowances and logistical requirements (like vehicles and tractors) of the coordination team and support and agency advisory staff took up a major proportion of the funding. Related infrastructural developments included the construction of a Resource Sharing Centre and accommodation including houses for the FC's members of the Forest Protection Unit (FPU). The original proposal had envisaged a diversified co-management initiative including ecotourism and wildlife management ventures. Massive funding was used to build chalets, which seem to be underutilized. Underutilization is a result of the poor tourist base, which has been further depleted by the invasion of the forest by communal farmers.

A conservation lobby including the FC exercises exclusive management over the state forests by restricting peasant settlement, cultivation and consumptive use of resources in the forest. Only those ventures considered to be environmentally benign have found support from this environmental lobby, and they are the only ones that have been included in the co-management set-up. These include cutting of thatching grass through a system of RMC-controlled permits for areas of the forest reserve allocated by the FC to various RMCs. Other areas of the forest reserve, particularly *vlei* (wetland areas with grass) areas like Lutope, where thatching grass is abundant, are still under FC control with the permits being issued directly by the FC. Those who need the grass can pay for the permits in cash either to the FC or to the relevant RMC. A system of payment using bundles of grass is used for collectors who cannot afford to pay for the grass permits in cash. For every five bundles of grass cut, the user is entitled to three with the remaining two being retained by the RMC or the FC for resale and the revenue accrues to them. Reeds for mats and grass for making brooms can also be extracted from the forest reserve through similar permits, but a single permit entitles the user to a day's equivalence of extraction of the resource with part of the revenue again accruing to the FC or the relevant RMC. This sounds like a neat and rational bureaucratic procedure, but practice in Mafungautsi does not work this way.

Collection of dead wood for fuel is only permitted under a stringent system of conditions including the requirement that extractors be in the company of the FC's members of the Forest Protection Unit. Peasant communities must not be accompanied by dogs and should not carry axes and matches or lighters on fuelwood collection excursions. These are seen as tools of those likely to be involved in nefarious activities like poaching (dogs), felling of trees (axes) and extraction of honey (matches and lighters) in the forest reserve. Peasant communities are also allowed to graze their livestock within the forest reserve but the no-dog policy still applies for herders entering the forest. Some respondents in Batanai manipulate the situation, illegally collecting products – including game – from Mafungautsi when the FPU is not in the vicinity. Peasants are innovative and find ways of circumventing the 'neat bureaucracy' in order to meet their own needs. Most peasants tend to hand over smaller bundles to the RMCs and retain bigger ones. The whole circumference of the 82 100 hectare forest cannot be effectively monitored all the time, hence some villagers sneak in and out of the forest without paying permit fees. The opportunity cost of transporting and selling the grass at Gokwe Centre has meant that no RMC member has been willing to sell brooms or thatching grass away from their villages. Broom and thatching grasses have simply been dumped at the homesteads of the RMC members, in most cases the treasurer or the chairperson. This has resulted in lots of bundles rotting. In Batanai 115 bundles of thatching grass were rotting at the treasurer's homestead in April 2001. The scenario was the same at the homestead of the Chemwiro-Masawi RMC chairman, where bundles could not be counted due to the advanced stage of rotting. Some informants argued that the RMC members were now using rotting of grass as an excuse for misrepresenting the actual bundles sold during audit-ing. Some RMC members were reported to be using the grass before it even begins to rot. This is a clear illustration of how the rationality of co-management and that of the people manipulating the rules may not neces-sarily coincide.

In Chemusonde RMC some villagers resorted to cutting thatching grass at the Lutope FC administered *vleis* as they felt that paying the RMC members would be a direct transfer of resources to the RMC members. Some respondents from Chemusonde interviewed at Lutope camp said however that they were coming to Lutope as it had better thatching grass than the area allocated to their RMC. In both Batanai and Chemwiro-Masawi there were unconfirmed incidences of non-payment of permit fees by the RMC members. In Batanai one RMC member was alleged to have harvested broom grass before the official opening in the pretext of moni-toring illegal broom grass collectors. In one instance, the research assistant successfully tracked cartwheel tracks from an area where broom grass had been poached to the RMC member's homestead. Some of the villagers have reacted by joining them in the illegal collection as indicated by issues raised at the Shingai Training Centre Workshop of 4 November 2000. This work-shop went further to recommend the use of incentives for those who assist in the apprehension of rule breakers. A similar arrangement has worked well in the Kana Grazing Scheme on the western parts of Mafungautsi – but not one of the main case study sites. People in Kana, through their own initiative, set aside some *vlei* areas within the communal area, for controlled thatching grass harvesting. They set up their own rules and a committee to manage the *vlei* was established. They have what they call 'Fibre Guards' as they do not have the conventional handcuffs. Anyone who grazes their livestock before the end of the grass-cutting period in the *vlei* will be fined Z$15, a third of which will go to the arresting guard. This project was initiated by the local people themselves as a way of securing supply of thatching grass. The negative ecological and institutional outcomes within co-management may be attributed to the fact that most decisions seem to be imposed from higher-level institutions with little local input. Co-management does not seem to abide by the subsidiarity principle (Ostrom 1990; Chitsike 2000).

The rights for grazing and grass extraction are used to leverage environmental protection goals. They are thought to reduce the fuel load and lessen the severity of burns in the event of outbreaks of forest or veld fires. Thus grazing and thatch grass extraction form the core components of the co-management scheme as it has come to operate in Mafungautsi today. Thatch-grass revenues accruing to RMCs belong to them, but the FC holds the power to approve the means of disposal of such revenues. The FC normally disapproves the use of such revenues on projects that are thought to be environmentally harmful. Such audits may enable well-intentioned monitoring and create supervisory tools; however by giving FC authority over a community's use of funds, this structure removes fiscal autonomy, which is an important incentive for the promotion of public participation and partnership

The FC favours a partnership that revolves around non-timber forest resources. But valuation studies conducted in interface zones have consistently demonstrated that peasant communities in such areas attach outstandingly higher values to the land and construction timber in the protected forest reserve than to minor forest products (Gwaai Working Group 1997; Matose 1994; Matzke and Mazambani 1993). From colonial to present times, state-enforced evictions have not effectively stopped peasants from settling and cultivating in the forest reserve. Evictions however have not completely quelled people's quest to be reunited with what they consider to be their land and resource heritage. For instance, soon after the Unity Accord of 1987, a peasant delegation from the Ndhlalambi area organized to meet the Minister of Local Government, Public Works and National Housing with whom they lobbied to return to the forest reserve. Their justification was that they had not supported dissidents and that the war was long over anyway, which according to them warranted their readmission into the forest reserve. The move was not successful. The minister explained that the forest reserve legally belonged to the FC, and that peasants could not settle on it since it was a protected area. Recently some peasants have started illegally constructing their huts in Gondoma *vlei* and close to the Lutope FPU Camp. This is being carried out in the context of the national land invasions, which are taking place in the commercial farms in Zimbabwe. This is a highly polarized issue and initial warnings by the FC have gone unheeded. The new settlers, about 49 households, with another 131 reported to have registered their intention to settle in the forest, have already established local branches of the ruling party.

CONCLUSION

Co-management in Mafungautsi thus appears to have very little to do with democratization of forest management in spite of presumptions implying co-equal partnership, co-ownership, co-use and co-management. RMCs for co-management were crafted from a multitude of bodies aligned with state and customary power bases, and were superimposed on local structures creating a complexity that counters the concept of co-ownership through co-management. A legislative environment that entrenches the centralization of natural resource governance whilst denying the privilege of legal mandate and fiscal autonomy to units closer to the citizens fundamentally contradicts notions of co-ownership and co-use. Co-management was supply-led. Like most top-down conceptions, it is practised on the terms and conditions of its authors and their allies, rather than those of the citizens whom it is ostensibly designed to empower.

RMCs, the institutional vehicle for co-management, are externally defined with respect to conception, formation, operation and legitimacy. These imposed structures form a new complex and fluid matrix when they interact with the existing power base. Further, their imposition on existing structures confounds relationships at the local level. There is therefore a need to ensure that the RMCs are more demand-driven, or at least more downwardly accountable with respect to their conception, formation and legitimization. Demand-driven and downwardly inclined approaches stand a greater chance of generating sufficient internal dialogue and debate, which can be the basis on which RMCs can become functional. Rather than generating fragmentation, they require the coalescence of complex and dynamic networks of interest and association. This further lends weight to the notion that downwardly accountable institutions are more likely to result in more positive social and environmental outcomes (Ribot 1999).

8. The Morsa River Basin, Norway: collective action for improving water quality

Knut Bjørn Stokke

This chapter highlights collective action in the Morsa River Basin through collaboration and networking, where the purpose is reduced pollution of the watercourse. The Morsa Project with its networks, established in 1999, provides the backdrop for the ensuing analysis of actors, networks, knowledge resources and collective action.

The Morsa River Basin is in the south-eastern corner of Norway, extending across two counties, Akershus and Østfold (see Figure 8.1). The entire basin covers 690 km² and includes eight municipalities. The Vansjø Lake, the basin's main water body, provides drinking water for more than 60 000 people in and around Moss, the largest town in the area. The lake is an important outdoor recreational area for the region and considered of national value to Norway. The greatest threat to the waters comes from nutrient input which has already caused widespread eutrophication. Pollution is worst in the lower and western areas of the lake. Here blooms of toxin-producing cyanobacteria (blue-green algae) prompted the authorities to close some of the bathing areas in recent years. The main impact of this pollution is that drinking water is threatened, together with recreational interests such as fishing and bathing.

Productive agrarian land borders the river basin, farming and forestry being the predominant pursuits. Most pollution is therefore from agriculture. Intensification and streamlining in the farming sector with many turning to grain production over the past decades adds to the gravity of the situation. Population concentration is relatively low, and there are no urbanized or industrial areas upstream of Vansjø. Housing in the basin area is relatively low density, and discharges here come second after agriculture as the main source of basin pollution (Solheim et al. 2001). Geographically the watercourse is more comparable in many ways with watercourses in Central Europe than other typical Norwegian watercourses, since it lies below the marine threshold (the highest sea level after the last Ice Age) and is therefore

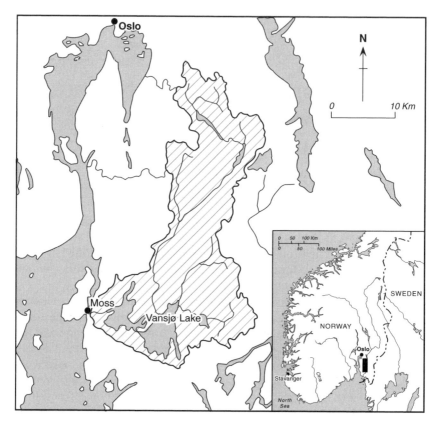

Figure 8.1   Morsa River Basin

naturally productive. Vansjø is additionally vulnerable to eutrophication because it is so shallow (with an average depth of 7.4 metres). Water quality has declined steadily since the 1980s.

The biggest impediment to collective action to improve water quality is the lack of a central management structure for the river basin. Responsibility for water quality straddles several government sectors and tiers, and responsibilities and powers have increasingly been decentralized to local authorities. Local responsibility is more likely to promote local agendas than those that take account of the river basin as a whole. This fragmented management structure is challenged by the EU's Water Framework Directive, which Norway is currently phasing in (Hovik et al. 2003). The many sources of pollution are additionally small and dispersed. The basin district contains about 450 farms and about 2300 sewage treatment plants for low-density habitation (ibid.). If farmers or households reduced their discharges individually, the impact would be too marginal to affect water quality substantially. It is the overall discharge volume that is the challenge. Such a situation gives a typical temptation for free-riding (see Chapters 1 and 2 in this volume). Many free-riders can whip the carpet from under collective action efforts, especially when implementation costs are substantial. In the farming sector, one would also have to rely on farmers' voluntary support for the proposed steps, since there are few legal sanctions available. In this perspective, Vansjø can be seen as a 'common sink resource' (see Chapter 1), and the collective action problem is to prevent free-riding on this resource.

THE MORSA PROJECT

The Morsa Project brought the eight local authorities in the Morsa basin district together with the affected county authorities and farmers' organizations in both counties in a voluntary organization. The Morsa Project was chiefly a response to the unabating decline in the quality of the water in the Vansjø Lake, but there were also central government incentives (in the shape of 'environmental area action') as part of the 1997 settlement between agriculture authorities and farming organizations. 'Environmental area action' applies agricultural policy mechanisms to particularly challenging issues related to water pollution and conservation of cultural landscapes. According to our informants, the idea came from the Østfold Director of Agriculture, and was a response to new opportunities arising from a wider environmental approach in farming policy. Increased information and awareness of farming's contribution to watercourse pollution also played a major role.

All parties stand on an equal footing as owners of the project. Being of an inter-municipal and cross-sectoral nature, formal decision-making is in the hands of the participating local and county authorities. A Governing Board (see Figure 8.2) heads the project. The board is responsible for overall management and acts as a general assembly. Sitting on the board are the mayors of the eight municipalities (with leaders of the opposition as deputies), farming representatives and representatives from each of the county councils and county governor's offices. In early 2003, in response to a perceived need to include consumer interests and more comprehensive management according to the Water Framework Directive, observer status was granted to the new members of the Governing Board. They were the inter-municipal water system company MOVAR, Østfold Nature Conservation Society and the Norwegian Water Resources and Energy Directorate.

The current management of the project is the responsibility of an Executive Committee (see Figure 8.2). The chair and vice-chair of the

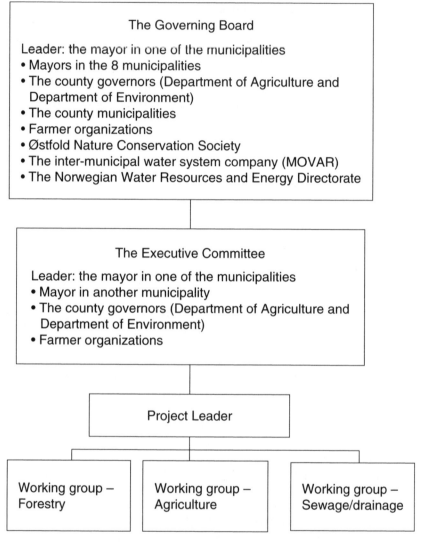

Figure 8.2   The Morsa network: actors and organization

Governing Board (to date municipal mayors) are also chair and vice-chair of the Executive Committee. The rest of the committee comprises the heads of departments of agriculture and environment at the office of Østfold county governor, the head of the department of agriculture at the offices of the county governors of Akershus, and a representative for the farming community. The project has a project leader in a full-time position. The project leader is also the project's administrative and technical head, and shares office space at the Østfold county governor's department of agriculture. Three working groups were appointed to oversee technical issues in three areas of responsibility: sewage/drainage, agriculture and forestry. They discuss and recommend steps to improve environmental standards within their areas of competence, promote inter-municipal collaboration and work to build competence and know-how. The working groups have civil servants and representatives of the farming community as members.

Project funding is shared by the local and county authorities along with grants from the environmental area action pot, supervised by the various county governors' agriculture departments. The Morsa Project was supposed to end by 1 February 2004, but was extended to the end of the year. From the beginning of 2005 the Morsa Project continues as a pilot project for the Norwegian implementation of the EU's Water Framework Directive.

THE MORSA PROJECT AS A BRIDGING NETWORK

The inability to reach consensus on the causes of pollution has led to finger-pointing and obstinacy. Parties were finding it difficult to work together, there was little policy coherence and collective action was impeded. Several informants suggested there was little mutual trust before the Morsa Project got off the ground. There were apparently splits between environmental and farming authorities, between upstream and downstream local authorities, between central and local authorities, and finally between the farming community and public authorities. The counties practised different management cultures, and little was done to ensure cross-county and inter-municipal harmonization. Given this state of affairs, much time and energy were spent at the start of the project to improve relations. It was particularly vital to ensure good working relations between the local authorities, and between the authorities and the farmers. After early discussions, a decision was taken to give farming organizations partner status, not least because action in the agricultural sector would depend on farming support, which is generally a voluntary matter.

The Morsa Project adopted a basically bottom-up approach, which meant involving and motivating farmers and local authorities, and impressing on them their responsibility for the environment. Information and training were key elements in the effort to change attitudes and practices. One important job was to 'translate' and simplify technical reports for the benefit of politicians, farmers and lay-people in general. Morsa's project manager succeeded in the crucial task of getting the different parties to work together. Several of our informants stressed how beneficial it had been to appoint someone from the 'outside' to the job, someone with an 'open mind' to lead the project. Old and entrenched conflicts and the pervasive sense of distrust would probably have persisted had it not been for the project manager's efforts, they insist. Several informants spoke of the leader's function as a general motivator, information disseminator and the 'glue' holding the network together. These sentiments are particularly evident in the responses to the survey of numerous public and private actors. The project manager was listed as the most contacted person in connection with watercourse management concerns. It was clear that the project manager enjoyed the highest level of confidence among survey respondents when it came to actually getting things done to improve water quality (Stokke, forthcoming). The importance of 'glue' individuals in heterogeneous networks is emphasized in the theory of bridging social capital. The role of policy champions in natural resource managing networks is also emphasized in Chapter 5 (on Cannock Chase) and Chapter 4 (Setesdal Vesthei-Ryfylkeheiane) in this book.

The organization of the Morsa Project has been important. While the Governing Board and the Executive Committee have contributed to the foundation of and a feeling of ownership to the project among the different organizations, the working groups have been important for the practical implementation. Many of the participants in these groups are street-level bureaucrats with responsibility for implementation of the proposed measures.

Although the Morsa Project basically represented an arena for the parties involved, it does foster the creation of other networks. First of all, the project brought public authorities and farmers and their organizations closer together. In this connection, the work put into preparing an environment plan for every farm clearly had a positive effect on the quality and frequency of contact between individual farmers and the authorities, mainly officials at the municipal departments of agriculture. The Morsa Project required environmental plans to be in place before funds could be disbursed to farmers for environmental action. Secondly, local authorities' water use planning also provided a much-needed opportunity to harmonize the work of municipal agencies and take action in the waste water sector. The plans are based by and large on the substance and objectives of the Morsa Policy Analysis (Solheim et al. 2001). Several informants emphasized the increased level of inter-municipal contact and cooperation brought about by the Morsa Project. Survey responses indicate growing inter-county contact and confidence (Stokke, forthcoming). Although we lack quantitative data prior to the Morsa Project, most informants nonetheless insist that relations were much improved, and have brought benefits in terms of increased harmonization and growth in confidence.

The political leaders of the Morsa Project engaged with their party colleagues in Cabinet and Parliament at the national level with a view to extracting more government money for the project. These connections resulted, according to our informants, in extra grants from the Ministries of Agriculture and Environment. Different government departments and the Norwegian State Housing Bank along with some private banks were also contacted to negotiate loans at reasonable rates for the property owners facing costs to improve their treatment facilities. These efforts culminated in the agricultural and waste water bodies issuing extraordinary grants. Many hold the view however that this government money is little more than the proverbial 'drop in the ocean' compared with what is needed to save the Vansjø Lake and river basin district.

OPPOSITION ACTORS AND NETWORKS

The deteriorating water quality in the lower and western parts of Vansjø Lake has attracted much attention. Networks critical of the failure to halt the process have sprung up. One such network is the 'People's Save the Vansjø Campaign', formed in 2003. These actors demand faster action to address private and public sewage discharges. But there is also disagreement concerning the right way of going about it and the best management strategies. Some calls are heard for harder penalties to enforce compliance by affected parties.

Some of those opposed to the Morsa Project seem to have bonded together in an unofficial network, partly independent of the People's Campaign. Its members live in the Moss area. Vansjø Sailing Club has made publicly known its criticism of the management of the watercourse in the local press. The club threatened to report the responsible authorities, that is, the municipal authorities and the county governor, to the police for aiding and abetting environmental crime if they failed immediately to act and put the measures in place required by the Pollution Control Act.

But the opposition has not spent their whole time criticizing the Morsa Project; they have offered some ideas as well. The first concerns even more dramatic changes in farming than originally envisioned, particularly aimed at encouraging some of the farmers to convert to livestock. A second idea concerns action in the shape of biomanipulation, in the form of fishing up much of the carp in Vansjø, which appears to be the current focus of scientific contention at the moment. But also the suggestion of changes in agricultural policy is disputed, and some experts point out that alteration to livestock will rather lead to a further deterioration of the situation.

KNOWLEDGE RESOURCES AND THE LEVEL OF AGREEMENT

There is a large number of scientific and technical reports on and measurements of various aspects of the Morsa watercourse. But scientific opinion has been divided, or at least unable to say with certainty why the watercourse is eutrophying, what needs to be done, and what the most cost-efficient procedures may be. This picture is complicated further by the presence of many minor players. The sources of pollution are widely dispersed and 'diffuse', and often therefore difficult to identify and quantify. In addition, the causal chain is complicated and there are major variations year on year, especially regarding the land-based pollution sources. In what follows, we concentrate on the 2001 Policy Analysis (Solheim et al. 2001). This report functions as the expert basis for the Morsa Project.

There was division about whether to initiate this expert policy analysis for the watercourse. Several felt that available information was adequate, and that what mattered was action. The Morsa project leader insisted however that consensus and backing for whatever steps might be necessary to meet set environmental targets must be based on the latest information and a neutral analysis. External consultants, led by the Norwegian Institute for Water Research (NIVA), were commissioned to do the study. It reviews current watercourse status in terms of pollution levels, suitability for various user interests and actors' contribution to pollution. The study recommends water environment targets. The final part of the study reviews methods to improve water quality and the likely costs.

Two pollution accounts were prepared, and the theoretical calculations showed that farming accounted for 57 per cent of total phosphorus input (11 000 kg per annum), dispersed drainage for 11 per cent, municipal drainage for 6 per cent, and background drainage and natural drainage 26 per cent. The analysis shows that the greatest volumes come from the upstream municipalities.

The Policy Analysis proposes two environmental targets (Solheim et al. 2001):

1. The watercourse shall be suitable for bathing, recreational fishing and for soil watering purposes (except certain parallel systems, where meeting fishing and watering standards suffice).
2. Vansjø-Storefjord shall meet drinking water standards.

The second target is the most important one. Targets were proposed on the basis of a controlled assessment of vital user interests, the natural state of the watercourse, present state and likely future state. One essential consideration when it came to target setting was that farming must remain a feasible activity in the area. The process of the Policy Analysis involved several public officials from the local authorities and the county governor agriculture departments. The working group on sewage and drainage was the reference group, and was an active and regular participant at meetings throughout the work on the analysis. The leaders of the farming associations were also involved.

There is little doubt that the actors involved in the Morsa Project willingly accept the information contained in the Policy Analysis. That information has gone on to inform many of the farming and drainage measures all the way through from design to implementation. The demonstration of causal chains was crucial and helped prevent a replay of the finger-pointing exercise of past years. Because the causal relationships described in the analyses were so widely accepted as accurate, it has eased the way for mechanisms to deal with dispersed drainage and agricultural contributions to pollution and to distribute the costs for cleaning up. Detailed and approved documentation through the Policy Analysis was considered vital to persuade local politicians, especially in the upstream municipalities, to agree to impose on their electorates expensive treatment requirements. We note that politicians involved in the Morsa Project made good use of the Policy Analysis to understand the problems and the steps required to solve them. The same can be said of farming-related measures. One informant, a farming representative on a Morsa Project body, said that he often showed 'Policy Analysis graphs and statistics' to other farmers to convince them of the necessity of the proposed measures. The analysis also informed municipal water use planning, environment plans for individual farms, and the action plan for Morsa. One of the mayors spoke of this consensus in the following way:

> For the first time, agreement was reached by the different parties, public bodies and expert groups concerning the way ahead, and which steps should be taken when. As we see it, it would be utterly indefensible to withdraw from the work at the present stage, and start over again each on his own little plot. (my translation)

The sense of understanding and consensus does not however appear to extend to actors outside the Morsa Project, especially when it comes to identifying necessary and sufficient steps, or timescale.

IMPLEMENTATION AND OUTCOMES

Farming-related Measures

One of the most effective farming-related mechanisms to reduce pollution of the watercourse entails cutting back on autumn ploughing, especially in areas vulnerable to erosion. While only about 20–30 per cent of farmland in the catchment area remained unploughed in 1999, this area had widened to 60 per cent in 2002. In the most sensitive erodible areas, the percentage is nearer 100, according to the Morsa Action Plan. There was a financial incentive behind this success, as farmers were paid not to plough. The Ministry of Agriculture released extraordinary funds from year to year in response to the particular challenges facing the watercourse. The environment plans, individually tailored for each farm, were also considered essential, since they provided an opportunity for 'trial and error', as one agriculture department official put it. Putting the environment plans into practice also favoured interaction between farmers and authorities – mainly agricultural authorities – and helped build confidence, both of which were considered important for the successful implementation of the measures.

As from 2001, farmers who continued to plough in the autumn in the areas most threatened by erosion could be penalized by cuts in their grants. According to our informants, refraining from ploughing costs the farmer both money and effort at the same time as it entails certain risks related to the spread of weeds and so on. The recent ability to penalize farmers created a certain amount of friction in some parts of the farming community, but calm was restored in the wake of negotiations and some give and take, and most have accepted the new situation.

Another form of action involves building catch dams to trap soil particles and nitrates that have ended up in the watercourse. After cuts in autumn ploughing, catch dams represent the easiest way of reducing phosphorus and soil particle content. While only four catch dams were built in 1999 along the watercourse, 32 came into being in 2003/2004, and ten new ones were on the drawing board. In 2002 around 100 km of vegetation zones were planted along the watercourse, divided among 50 farms. Vegetation acts as a buffer zone between the fields and watercourse. According to a log from the Morsa Project, nothing had been planted prior to 1999.

Drainage Mechanisms

In compliance with approved municipal water use plans and the Morsa Action Plan 2002–2005, all local authorities have worked together to approve directives on the treatment of sewage from dispersed discharge points. The most prominent step concerns upgrading pre-existing treatment plants, many of which are very ineffective. Most of the Morsa Project's municipalities have approved harmonized guidelines and regulations for minor drainage installations and municipal discharges. Harmonization here is part of the drive to apply a single standard for treatment installations throughout the river basin area. The Morsa Project has recently developed a common sanction policy directed towards those households that do not follow up the order. The daily penalty is 200 NOK (ca. 25 Euro).

The work involved in getting the private drainage systems through is time-consuming for Morsa council politicians. The local councils also decided to put more administrative resources into the effort, arranging public meetings and visiting and helping property owners instructed to improve their drainage systems. A lot of time has apparently been spent on assessing the situation in detail in each of the municipalities. All in all, 750 housing units have now installed treatment facilities. The average cost per installation is 100 000 NOK (ca. 12 500 Euro). Around 150 million NOK (ca. 19 million Euro) has been invested from 1999 to 2004, and the annual amount has been gradually increasing during these years.

CONDITIONS FOR COLLECTIVE ACTION

The ability of farmers and local councils in the Morsa River Basin to take action and reach targets over the past few years is an example of collective action in natural resource management. Collective action can be judged to have taken place when several independent actors act simultaneously for the same purpose. In this section it will be discussed how collective action obstacles were overcome in connection with the Morsa Project. In particular the relevance of theories of bridging social capital and institutional capacity to explanations of collective action will be explored (see Chapter 2). However to explain collective action in relation to the Morsa watercourse certain structural and contextual factors must also be taken into consideration.

BRIDGING SOCIAL CAPITAL

The theory of social capital is far from straightforward, but in the present connection the bridging social capital approach appears to offer the most promise. It differs from the communitarian approach to the concept, also known as 'bonding social capital' (Hulgård 2003). Bridging social capital is based on networks spanning different interest groups. The Morsa network is a voluntary pooling of resources across administrative and geographical divides, the purpose of which is to encourage different actors to take action for the common good. The study shows that the Morsa network, and its subsidiary networks, led to heightened contact and trust among the different actors in the river basin.

The terms 'trust', 'reciprocity' and 'reputation' are pivotal in the theory of social capital (Ostrom 1998, among others). Our findings suggest that working together on the Morsa Project boosted the trust of many actors in one another, replacing what used to be an often rather dim view. It is essential, we found, that actors are considered as equal partners in the project; this especially concerns the farmers. Active participation at an early stage in the watercourse planning process was essential to develop trust, as was also noted by Opedal and Thorèn (1996). Creating arenas where strategies can be hammered out and mechanisms discussed by participants in a face-to-face context appears to be a further prerequisite to build trust among different interest groups. Ostrom (1990: 184) suggests that when 'individuals repeatedly communicate and interact with one another in a localized physical setting . . . it is possible that they learn whom to trust . . . and how to organize themselves to gain benefits and avoid harms.' Successful bridge-building networks of the Morsa Project type seem to rely on a visible form of management that enjoys relatively widespread trust and is able to build bridges between the network's different members (Granovetter 1973). Bridging responsibilities in the Morsa Project rested in particular on the shoulders of the project leader and the chair of the Governing Board. The project leader succeeded in unravelling the conflicts between upstream and downstream municipalities by showing that downstream communities pollute as well, and that all would gain by sharing responsibility and pulling together as a team.

Trust is however a difficult concept, and allows for many interpretations. Its use as an analytical term has been criticized because, as a term in popular use, it fails to impart the necessary analytical distance to the social phenomena under consideration (Dulsrud 2002). Coleman (1990) aligns 'trust' with risk and uncertainty, suggesting that actors replace uncertainty with trust in situations where information is too sparse to allow them to gauge others' likely behaviour or actions. According to game theory, specifically the game of solidarity in uncertain situations, it might be 'rational' not to cooperate to implement measures as long as one does not know whether others intend to comply. In this game, somebody has to make the first move to get others to jump on board and get the job done (Bratt 1994). There needs to be a sense of trust that other network actors will act in compliance with the objectives and purpose of the network. As Hansen and Tjerbo

(2003) suggested, in that sense, trust acts by and large as a substitute for immediate control.

This approach to the term is largely in agreement with the other key social capital term, that is, reciprocity. We gained a marked impression during the study that reciprocity and mutual trust is decisive for collective action, especially in situations where the actors themselves have to pay large sums to execute the measures, in the shape of either financial outlays or increased risk. It was important therefore in the Morsa Project to demonstrate causal relations, which were widely perceived in the event to be accurate, and to target the measures at the biggest polluters in the catchment area. In this case they were farms and dispersed household discharges. It was essential to give each individual actor reasonable assurance that the other polluters would chip in. It was by means of collaboration and communication on common objectives that the Morsa Project succeeded in cultivating confidence among actors, not least between upstream and downstream actors. In his study of the Genevadsån watercourse in Sweden, Lundqvist (2001) showed that despite the fact that farms accounted for about two-thirds of the man-made discharges, insufficient numbers were willing to share the burden to reduce eutrophication of Laholm Bay. That others were not included in the clean-up strategy explains the failure of the project, and underlines how important it is to persuade other polluters to join in the effort to cut pollution. It was therefore a major step that the Morsa Project took when it looked at pollution from dispersed household discharges, not from agriculture alone.

Coming to the third key term in the theory of social capital, reputation, our data are too sparse to allow us to say with confidence how it affected collective action in the Morsa watercourse. Some informants told us that those farmers who continued to plough in the autumn met with disapproval. One said that farmers with second jobs are more likely to face social pressure to desist from autumn ploughing, than are full-time farmers. The municipalities in the network are also under pressure to implement the agreed efforts. The more municipalities implement measures, the more difficult is it for other municipalities to sit on the fence.

In the theory of bridging social capital, contact points among different actors and/or interest groups are considered an advantage by, among others, Granovetter (1973). The creation of contact points and collaboration among different actors and interest groups can spawn new opportunities for action through the dissemination of ideas and means across sectoral boundaries. There are indications that this occurred in the Morsa Project in the way the departments of environment and agriculture at the county governors' offices worked together, both playing central roles in the project. Environmental management appears to have adapted to agricultural management in terms of collaboration and service, rather than relying on long-established hierarchical procedures and directives. Farming management in turn appears to have adapted to environmental management in its deployment of penalties for non-compliance – in this case, the decision to withhold farmland grants from autumn-ploughing farmers. Readiness to penalize parties that fail to do their bit can in itself be an important mechanism to ensure that the willing actually deliver the goods (Ostrom 1990).

INSTITUTIONAL CAPACITY AND THE IMPACT OF SHARED KNOWLEDGE

The most important contribution of the theory of institutional capacity in explaining the collective action of the Morsa Project is the weight it puts on shared knowledge. Cars et al. (2002) suggest that developing shared knowledge is critical to collective action. This study can confirm the veracity of this essential point. The 2001 Policy Analysis for the Morsa watercourse helped provide the sense of shared information and common perception of reality, the causes of the pollution and the type of intervention required. Cars et al. (2002) and Healey et al. (1999) all use the term 'knowledge resources' which, in addition to the focus on the objective state of affairs, covers the ability of a network to acquire information, to learn from it and act on it. The way in which knowledge is received is a further important feature. Nenseth (1995) points out that environmental knowledge generation is neither linear nor hierarchical, and that it grows in breadth as much as in depth. Knowledge is thereby pluralized and politicized. It is therefore important to ensure that generated knowledge meets with a sympathetic process; it is not only the information in itself that is important.

The Morsa Project had the resources to hire NIVA and other reputable experts to conduct the policy analysis studies. Efforts were made to stress that the findings were produced by the best expertise in the area, and that the information and findings were objective and impartial. That the findings were so widely accepted as bona fide is doubtless due in no little part to these considerations. It was also important to involve local actors in the policy analysis studies, and allow members of the network to interpret, apply, distribute and 'translate' the information from the experts to lay people, be they politicians or farmers. This was an important job for the project leader. That key personnel were involved in the generation of knowledge also appear to be an important explanatory factor behind the success of the Policy Analysis and its impact on planning and intervention management. Knowledge resources are closely related to relational resources then, and both are vital to a shared perception of reality. While the actual knowledge in itself is important, the procedures involved in generating it and the manner in which it is translated for the benefit of non-experts are equally vital.

To improve collective action it was also essential to have actors with power and influence represented on the various bodies of the project. Examples are the mayors with their connections in local politics, and officials representing current expertise. Their presence meant that pre-existing resources and mechanisms could be brought into play in line with the intentions of the network. We can relate this point to what Innes et al. (1994, cited in Healey et al. 1999) call political capital, which they define as the capacity of the network to act collectively. Healey et al. (1999) and Cars et al. (2002) refer to the same thing in terms of mobilizing capacity, another key term in the theory of institutional capacity.

OTHER SIGNIFICANT VARIABLES

An explanation of the collective action engineered by the Morsa Project requires in addition other explanatory variables than those related to social capital and institutional capacity. These variables are associated with external forces, as described in Chapter 2. First, the pollution of the watercourse is visible and dramatic. This, over time, has caused politicians and local communities – especially downstream – to call for urgent, reparative action. This particular observation tallies with the studies of Pennington and Rydin (2000), which show that the extent and perception of a local environmental problem foster citizen involvement and collective action. The Morsa Project and the involved actors were – and are – under constant pressure of this nature.

Further, the reason so many mechanisms could be put into effect is due in large measure to the financial means that were made available. Although the active engagement of the farming community was considered essential to success, it was also said that it would have been impossible to succeed to the same extent without the financial incentives attached to the mechanisms. It was not possible to fund improvements to the drainage systems fully, but informants did say that government grants were the decisive 'carrot' to persuade local authorities and property owners to back the initiatives in sparsely populated areas.

Structural changes also help to explain the collective action to improve the Morsa watercourse. Without environmentally friendly changes in farming policy there would probably have been no Morsa Project at all. But in addition, it looks as if there have to be local actors in a position to enforce structural changes to promote community strategies and action. Such driving forces played an important part in putting the Morsa Project together, and informants point to the former head of the Østfold Agriculture Department and one local mayor as particularly worthy of mention in this connection.

CONCLUSION

Local foundations are one important criterion of success in the Morsa River Basin. Implementing agreed measures would be difficult without the establishment of mutual trust and reciprocity among the different actors in the river basin. In that connection, the Morsa Project has made an important contribution. Establishing shared knowledge has also been crucial, especially to reach consensus about the distribution of costs for the implementation of measures. Even though social capital and institutional capacity are not sufficient fully to explain the collective action, and may not be sufficient to save Vansjø, these elements have to be at the core of any attempt to achieve results. This is particularly important in this river basin with many dispersed sites of pollution, typical of many persistent environmental problems today (Koontz 2003; Weale 1992). At the same time, this study confirms other studies which show that it might be necessary to combine collaborative schemes with more potent mechanisms which reward participation and penalize non-participation (Hovik 2001; Eckerberg 1997).

Greater central government involvement and more financial means seem to be necessary to improve the water quality in the lower parts of the watercourse. Despite the implemented measures, the situation is getting worse and worse. Implementation of the 'polluter pays' principle has made it more complicated to get additional financial means from central government. Several of our informants argued that much of the blame for the pollution of the watercourse must be placed at the door of the central government and its agricultural policy. Since it is to blame, it should pay what it takes to repair the damage, they say. Another argument in favour of greater central government participation lies in the difference between who is doing the polluting and who is being damaged (Hallèn 1994).

This study shows that there is a limit to what local and regional actors and networks are able to achieve alone. The problems in Vansjø are so extensive and complicated that a more active central government involvement seems to be necessary.

9. The Lake District, England: participation in managing water abstraction

Yvonne Rydin and Tove Måtar

The Lake District is one of the most significant areas of open countryside in Britain. Covering some 2278 km^2, the Lake District encompasses, as its name implies, the major lakes of Windermere, Ullswater, Derwentwater and Coniston, together with numerous smaller lakes and tarns, all set in rolling countryside of hills and fells, rising up to 950 metres at Helvellyn, England's highest peak. This landscape holds a special place in British culture as the epitome of the Romantic ideal. Romanticism is a cultural movement that has had its expression in literature, painting and music and is a central thread running through much environmentalism (MacNaghten and Urry 1998).

The essence of Romanticism is that people gain a spiritual, even mystical experience from an encounter with nature. Nature is seen as the 'other' in an increasingly urbanized society but, within the Romantic worldview, the world beyond the city is no longer viewed as uncivilized, poor and frightening but rather as a source of a 'sublime' experience in which the individual is transformed through personal engagement with nature. The value of this 'sublime' encounter with nature was extolled in Romantic writings of the nineteenth century in Britain and North America (Herndl and Brown 1996), but also in other parts of Europe (Bramwell 1989). Many argue that this Romanticism not only gave birth to great art but also was a source of the environmental movement and that themes within Romantic thought can still be found in contemporary discussions concerning resource management, biodiversity and, above all, countryside use.

Romanticism has particular links with the Lake District. It was the birthplace and life-long home for the principal Romantic poet, William Wordsworth, and his presence there attracted other key figures of Romanticism such as Samuel Taylor Coleridge and J.M.W. Turner. Much of Wordsworth's poetry describes the beauty of the area and, in the context of Victorian society, this acted as a spur to the early growth of tourism in the area. Wordsworth himself was critical of this growth and, for example, resisted the construction of a railway line into the area westwards from Windermere, still the terminus of rail services. However the desire to enjoy the countryside, if not to experience the extremes of the sublime experience that the Romantics recommended, led to increasing numbers of people becoming Lake District tourists. Economic growth, continuing urbanization and greater mobility all contributed to considerable tourist development, mainly on the eastern edge of the Lake District, during the late nineteenth and turn of the twentieth centuries. This trend has continued through to this day and now the Lake District is the largest and most visited of Britain's 12 National Parks. The Lake District attracts a total of 12 million visitors per year, according to a 1994 All Parks Visitor Survey, with a third of the local residents being economically dependent on tourism.

National Parks are designated under the 1949 National Parks and Access to the Countryside Act and the Lake District was among the original set of designations in 1951. Such designations are undertaken with the aim of conserving the natural beauty, wildlife and cultural heritage of the area and promoting opportunities for the understanding and quiet enjoyment of its special qualities by the public. A mix of goals in terms of landscape protection, nature conservation, heritage conservation and recreation promotion is apparent. Trying to achieve this composite set of objectives involves handling a range of complex pressures and balancing many conflicts of interests. In addition to this list of objectives, there is also the need to consider the agricultural base of the area, which co-exists with the substantial tourist activity. Sheep, arable and dairy farming are the main agricultural activities, with some associated food processing. The sheep are particularly important in maintaining the landscape since they create the distinctive visual appearance of the fells through their constant grazing. But despite this synergy there are tensions between the farming and tourist industries over land use, the impact of tourism (including holiday cottages, second homes and retirees) on the local housing market and the detailed management of visitors in relation to farming activities. A variety of Countryside Agency schemes seek to negotiate these tensions. These tensions were particularly apparent during the outbreak of foot-and-mouth disease during 2001 when the tourist industry suffered huge losses as visitors were urged to stay away from the countryside and livestock.

MANAGING WATER RESOURCES

Planning for and management of the Lake District is highly complex. The focus in this chapter though is on one specific issue relating to water management. In addition to the agricultural and tourism roles of the area, the Lake District is the main source of water for the Greater Manchester area, a conurbation of some 2.5 million people, 130 km to the south. The western location of the Lake District in the context of prevailing westerly winds coming from the Atlantic and its relatively high peaks means that the climate exhibits high levels of rainfall. The rainfall collects in the reservoirs and lakes and makes the area of central importance to regional water management. Over half of the water supplies for the North West region come from the Lake District, North Wales or the Pennines.

Water supply in England has traditionally fallen to a mix of public sector organizations and private sector companies, with the public sector responsible for the larger share. In 1989 the then Conservative Government privatized the public sector water industry. Originally there were ten water service companies but the industry has been transformed since then by a series of takeovers and company restructurings. Water abstraction and supply is now the responsibility of a whole range of private companies, some large and some small, some British and some of overseas ownership, some focusing just on water and others undertaking a range of commercial activities. In the Lake District the main company handling water as a resource is United Utilities. United Utilities manages electricity, water and wastewater networks in the North West, servicing around 2.9 million customers.

Haweswater and Thirlmere are the main reservoirs in the Lake District used as a water resource for the Greater Manchester area. These reservoirs were both created through building dams and flooding villages: Haweswater in 1929 and Thirlmere in 1889. Together all the lakes and reservoirs in the Lake District create a delicate balancing system; minimum flows need to be guaranteed in order to allow everyday pumping of water. Windermere and Ullswater are used to secure the water resources in the main reservoirs and United Utilities currently has permission to pump up to 205 million litres per day from Lake Windermere and 363 million litres per day from Ullswater as long as minimum flow levels are maintained. During recent drought periods, United Utilities applied for permits to pump more water from these lakes in order to secure the water distribution to the Manchester area. These drought orders have been a more frequent occurrence since the late 1990s, which has caused some concerns to local stakeholders. Suggestions have been made that the current pattern of abstraction licenses should be revised and that alternative water resources should be considered.

The private water companies operate within a national framework of regulation, with the Environment Agency being the key regulator (discussed further below; see Blackmore et al. 2004 for a succinct history). The overall purpose of the regulatory framework is to ensure that water is managed sustainably and contributes to sustainable development more generally. This involves balancing demand and supply, ensuring that abstractions do not reach levels that would deplete the source other than temporarily. It also involves consideration of water quality and how abstraction patterns may create the circumstances for reduced water quality. Here, the water management functions of the Environment Agency overlap with its pollution control responsibilities.

There are two possible free-riding problems that can arise with regard to water management in the Lake Distrcit. The first concerns the impact of diffuse pollution from multiple sources; the Morsa case study in this volume concerns this kind of problem where many small farmers were generating pollution that resulted in the eutrophication of the main lake. This is not a major issue in the Lake District due to the nature of the farming and topography. The second concerns the possibility of many individual abstractions of water occurring, resulting in overall depletion of the source. This case study considers one form of institutional arrangements for preventing this second form of free-riding. It concerns a mix of regulation through licensing and participation by stakeholders in strategy development. These arrangements will be the focus of the following discussion. There are also some issues concerning recreation on the lakes including fishing, sailing and the contentious issue of motorized watersports; while this is not the primary focus of our analysis, these links between recreation and water management in the area are touched on below.

As emphasized in the other water management chapters in this volume, the national regulatory framework is currently being influenced by the implementation of the European Water Framework Directive (WFD). Again, the Environment Agency is the key actor involved in implementing the changes that the directive brings. The WFD will demand a River Basin Management Plan for every river basin district in the country and the Management Plans are to be reviewed on a six-year cycle. The overall aim of the WFD is 'to establish a legal framework within which to protect surface waters and groundwaters using a common management approach and following common objectives, principles and basic measures' (Environment Agency 2004b). The Ribble River Basin, south of the Lake District, is a site for the field-testing of European guidance on the implementation of this directive, as part of a wider project covering 15 river basins across Europe; this is being coordinated by the Environment Agency.

A NETWORK DOMINATED BY A FEW ACTORS

We begin by outlining the actors involved in water resource management, and water catchment abstraction in particular in the Lake District, before going on to examine the nature of the networks involved. As we will see, this is an area where a relatively limited number of actors dominate despite the large number of potential stakeholders.

As always, the elected local authorities are important stakeholders. There are numerous local authorities covering the Lake District. The county council is Cumbria County Council, whose boundaries extend from Carlisle in the north to Kendal in the south with a long coastline by the Irish Sea. Below this upper tier of local government are six different district councils: Allerdale Borough Council, Copeland Borough Council, Eden District Council, South Lakeland District Council, Barrow-in-Furness Borough Council and Carlisle City Council; the last two however do not have any territory within the boundaries of the National Park. While the local authorities within the National Park still retain a range of planning and other functions, where a National Park has been designated the roles and responsibilities of the local authorities are altered. This may explain in part why the local authorities have not directly engaged much in water management issues and have not been very involved in the networks concerning water abstraction.

Each National Park is managed by a National Park Authority (NPA), which in this case has two main responsibilities: 'To conserve and enhance the natural beauty, wildlife and cultural heritage of the Lake District' and 'to promote opportunities for the understanding and enjoyment of the special qualities of the National Park'. The NPA also has one duty: 'to foster the economic and social well being of local communities within the National Park'. The Lake District National Park Authority is made up of 26 members appointed by various bodies of which 14 are elected councillors appointed either by the county council or the district and borough councils. The other 12 members are appointed by the relevant Secretary of State: five of those are drawn from parish councillors representing parishes in the Lake District National Park.

Unlike in many countries, National Park designation in the UK does not alter the landownership of the area. The National Park Authority therefore needs to achieve its goals through engagement with the local landowners and other stakeholders. Such stakeholder engagement does take up much of the Lake District NPA's time. However water management as such does not figure prominently in the NPA's concerns, which are much more focused on how to handle tourism, generate economic prosperity for the area and manage the tensions with local farming. The NPA does not identify water management as an issue for which it needs to allocate a specific unit or individual; rather it deals with water issues as they affect its other activities.

The key governmental organization concerned with water management is the Environment Agency. The Environment Agency was formed from

Her Majesty's Inspectorate for Pollution (HMIP) and the National Rivers Authority in 1995 under the Environment Act. The Environment Agency (EA) has responsibilities in relation to flood defence, water management, pollution control and waste management. As part of those responsibilities it issues, monitors and inspect licences to make sure that environmental quality standards are being met. The Environment Agency states that 'it is our job to make sure that land, air and water are looked after by everyone in today's society, so that tomorrow's generation inherit a cleaner, healthier world' (Environment Agency 2004a). In relation to water resources, the EA is responsible for improving the water quality of fresh, marine, surface and underground water as well as securing the proper use of water resources in England and Wales. Under the 1991 Water Resources Act, all abstractions of water require an abstraction licence from the EA. This regulatory power gives the EA considerable significance within local water management. The Environment Agency is organized into regions and the relevant region covering the Lake District is the North West Region, which covers Cheshire in the south and in the north extends to the Scottish border. The EA also has a relationship with United Utilities through its role as a water regulator (see Gouldson and Murphy 1989 for further discussion of the relationship between regulator and regulated in such contexts). United Utilities is clearly also a key stakeholder in water management policy discussions in the Lake District.

There is a range of other local stakeholders with a potential interest in water management. Farmland forms most of the catchment areas surrounding the lakes and rivers in the Lake District and therefore catchment management affects the farming community. In some areas there have been problems with pollution from agricultural land; for example in 2000 sheep grazing near a North West Water reservoir in the Lake District were blamed for infecting drinking water with a potentially life-threatening parasite. Farmers also directly abstract some water for their own activities, but this does not amount to a significant quantity per catchment area. Other actors in the Lake District with an interest in water abstraction issues include hydropower generators, and small businesses which use water for their production activities, but most of these are again quite small in scale.

There are also nature conservation and recreational interests with some concerns over water management including abstraction. Anglers are largely concerned with water abstraction because of the impact on fish stocks. In some rivers the lack of efficient flows can lead to problems for the salmon population. However local representatives of national nature conservation and recreational NGOs do not seem to regard water management in the Lake District as a key issue, particularly compared to the other matters that take up their time, notably how to manage tourism so that recreation is promoted but not at the expense of important habitats or landscapes. It should be noted though that the governmental agency for nature conservation, English Nature, does recognize the relationship between water management and habitat protection and has been involved in relevant networks.

The main local NGO (apart from the angling groups) that is involved in water abstraction management is the Friends of the Lake District, a membership organization with supporters throughout Britain as well as locally in Cumbria. The Friends' goal is to make people recognize the special qualities of the landscape in the Lake District and Cumbria and to promote easy access for those who want to enjoy the countryside peacefully. The roots of the organization go back some 100 years when the Thirlmere dam was first built and the reservoir created; this was one of the Friends' earliest conservation battles. Today the Friends of the Lake District has 6790 members and is an entirely self-funded charity. Its current interest in water abstraction in the Lake District is linked to its overall goals concerning resource management in the area.

THE CATCHMENT ABSTRACTION MANAGEMENT STRATEGY PROCESS

So the stakeholders concerned with water management and more specifically with water abstraction (as opposed to the broader management of the Lake District) are quite limited. The key mover is the Environment Agency. It holds the main regulatory function and has instigated networks to assist in its strategy development. The stakeholder groups that have been formed for the purpose of developing CAMS – Catchment Abstraction Management Strategies – are the main networks that are examined in this chapter. Next we set out the principles behind the CAMS networks.

The system of licensing for abstraction was first introduced in the Water Resources Act 1963, but since then the details have changed and there has been a process of consolidation through more recent legislation, for example the Water Resources Act 1991, the Environment Act 1995 and the Water Act 2003. CAMS were first proposed in 1999 when the government published *Taking Water Responsibly*. In 2002 the Environment Agency published *Managing Water Abstraction: The Catchment Abstraction Management Strategy Process* which is the national document supporting the development of CAMS at a local level. It sets out the national policies and regulatory framework related to CAMS and guides the local process of developing a CAMS. CAMS are essentially strategies for the management of water resources at a local level. They make information on water resources and licensing practice publicly available and facilitate licence trading. The process by which they are developed is intended to allow a balance between the needs of abstractors, other water users and the aquatic environment to be struck in consultation with the local community and relevant stakeholders.

Each CAMS is based around the principle of defining a watershed or catchment area. This is a core principle of most contemporary water management and underpins the EU Water Framework Directive. English water management has also incorporated this principle since 1973 when the Water Act created ten regional water authorities, broadly defined on this basis (Rees, 1990). Although privatization of water supply meant that corporate structure now determines the scale of the organizations handling the operational side of water supply, the regulatory side remains structured around these predefined regions. The regional structure of the National Rivers Authority, set up at the insistence of the European Union when privatization took place, mimicked that of the RWAs and this then influenced the regional structure of the Environment Agency when the NRA was merged with Her Majesty's Inspectorate of Pollution to create the new agency. So watersheds are embedded into English water management.

However in practice the regional-scale watersheds amalgamated several smaller catchment areas together and so, when detailed planning of individual catchments occurs, there is a need for a more fine-grained focus. To set up the CAMS processes, these smaller catchment areas are mapped, each one defining an area where rainfall within the boundaries drains to a specific river and/or lake system. Nevertheless the advantage of history remains in that the regional structure of the Environment Agency does not cut across the detailed mapping of the boundaries of catchment areas. Rather, several small catchment areas can be identified within each agency region. There has been some criticism that the old boundaries were not always the most appropriate for developing River Basin Plans when geography, topography and water flows have been given detailed consideration, but these are adjustments at the margin that have to be made.

The purpose of identifying these catchment areas is that in each one a strategy, the CAMS, is drawn up to manage abstraction sustainably. Stakeholder involvement is a key principle of the CAMS process, so for each of these catchment areas the EA sets up stakeholder groups covering all the different and relevant stakeholders for that CAMS. These stakeholder groups represent the key networking around water abstraction in the area. Having established the intentions behind the institutional arrangements for this aspect of water management, we now explore the practice.

PARTICIPATION IN PRACTICE

There were three CAMS in preparation in the Lake District at the time of our research, each at rather a different stage of development. What each of these CAMS processes reveals is the exercise of consultative processes at the behest of the Environment Agency; this is an interesting contrast to more extensive governance arrangements discussed in the other chapters. The agency decides on the stakeholder group and sets out clear rules on how the process should proceed (see Figure 9.1). The focus of the discussions on developing a catchment abstraction strategy was emphasized, so that actors were discouraged from straying off into other issues, even if these were seen by a stakeholder as related and concerned core interests of that stakeholder.

The first CAMS process undertaken was that for the Leven and Crake area. The Leven and Crake area extends from Grasmere in the north to the Leven Estuary and Morecambe Bay in the south. The River Crake drains Coniston Water, an area of 92 km². It includes the biggest natural lake in England, Lake Windermere. The River Leven is the only river to flow out of Windermere and drains an area of 254 km². There was some concern expressed by the stakeholder group in the development of the CAMS that the boundaries for the Leven and Crake CAMS catchment do not take all flows into Windermere into consideration, limiting the full picture for the area and thus making it harder to monitor outcomes. The lake levels in the Leven and Crake area are currently monitored at Coniston Water and Windermere by the Environment Agency. Average annual rainfall in the catchment ranges from 1300 mm in the lowland areas to 3400 mm in the High Fells. Hydroelectric power generation is the largest abstractor in this catchment with 84.8 per cent of all abstraction. Public water supply is the second-largest abstractor group with 10.4 per cent.

The Leven and Crake CAMS was finalized in 2002 (see Figure 9.2). The stakeholder group set up by the EA consisted of ten representatives covering environmental, agricultural, industrial and angling interests, along with the water company and those from outside the area but with an interest in this catchment. In line with the identification of the stakeholder group as a 'task and finish' exercise, since the completion of the strategy none of the actors involved has remained in contact with each other through an ongoing network. The network was a one-off and time-limited exercise in consultation rather than a way of institutionalizing governance. There was some broader consultation during the development of the strategy, trying to engage some of the wider public by distributing awareness-raising leaflets and trying to get people engaged that way, but the results of this consultation exercise were considered by some interviewees to be poor.

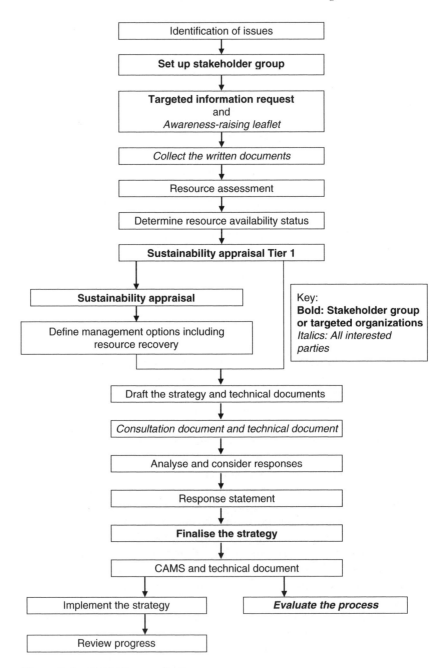

Figure 9.1   CAMS consultation process

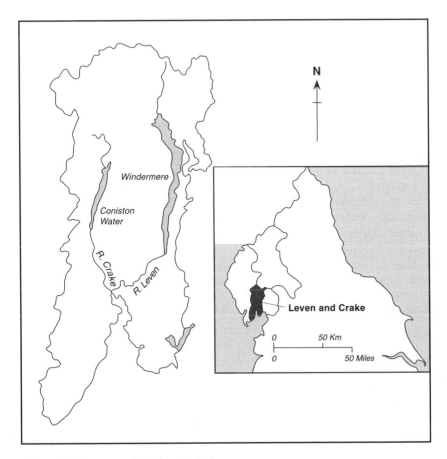

Figure 9.2 Leven and Crake CAMS

The involvement of the different stakeholders during the CAMS process did not focus around significant conflicts. Water management seems to have been regarded as neither a particularly salient issue nor a conflictual one, certainly not compared to some of the other issues that these various organizations were involved with in other forums and contexts in the Lake District. There was some discussion of maintaining water levels, especially during critical seasons, in order to ensure sustainable fish stocks; the angling associations were particularly concerned with this issue. Pollution was not a concern given that the surface water quality in this area was generally considered satisfactory; the General Quality Assessment of watercourses in the area revealed that 57 per cent by length were 'good' and 43 per cent were 'fair'. It is notable though that ambitions did not extend to moving watercourses into the 'very good' category. There was an annual update on the Leven and Crake CAMS at the beginning of 2004 when it was established that as there had been no changes in the availability of water resources in the catchment area, there was therefore no need for any changes in licensing strategy.

The Environment Agency recognized that there were some limitations in how it handled consultation in the Leven and Crake case and sought to remedy these in later CAMS processes. They hoped that this would result in more participation and interest in these processes. The Kent CAMS was completed in 2004 and is considered by the Environment Agency to have been more successful than the Leven and Crake case (see Figure 9.3). The Kent area covers some 550 km². in the south-eastern corner of the Lake District draining into Morecambe Bay. Other than the River Kent, it includes the rivers Sprint, Mint, Gowan, Winster, Gilpin and Bela, together with several small reservoirs (Dubbs, Kentmere, Fisher Tarn and Killington reservoirs). There is also an old canal, the Lancaster Canal, that has its origins within the catchment. The water quality in this area is particularly good, with 79 per cent of the length of watercourses classified as 'very good', 13 per cent as 'good' and 8 per cent as 'fair'.

The biggest abstraction in the Kent catchment is by industry at 47 per cent, followed by energy generation with 31 per cent, amenity and water supply with 8 per cent each and agriculture with 6 per cent. This pattern of abstraction is reflected in the stakeholder group with hydropower generation, agriculture, industrial, angling and environmental interests, alongside rural landowners, rural businesses owners and the local authority all represented. In addition, the Environment Agency at an early stage published an awareness-raising leaflet for distribution to the wider public, with comments invited. The involvement of the stakeholder group contributed to a CAMS published in 2004, but concerns about inclusiveness remain despite the enhanced participation efforts. It was generally felt that some issues were not given enough emphasis; as in the Leven and Crake CAMS, the EA made it clear at the beginning of the process that only certain issues were up for discussion. For some of the stakeholders the material provided and the terms of the process tended to be too technical to follow easily. Similarly the poor results of the wider public engagement were also thought to be due to the material being inappropriate for the audience. Finally, as with the Leven and Crake catchment area, the work on the strategy did not result in any continuity of the stakeholder group. Both the stakeholders and EA believe that a new stakeholder group with different members will need to be put together for the revision of the Kent CAMS in around 2010.

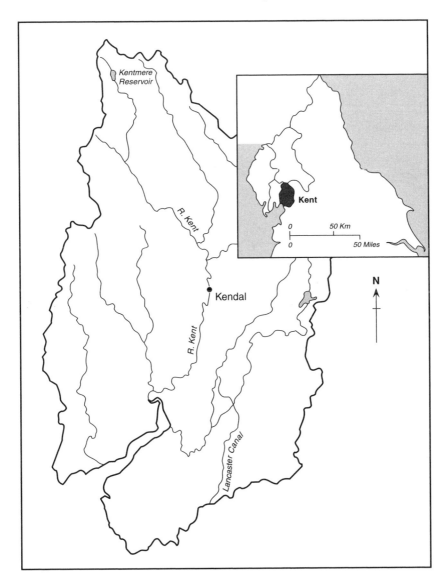

Figure 9.3   Kent CAMS

The CAMS for the Eden and Esk area had just begun at the time of the research (see Figure 9.4). This area includes a north-eastern part of the Lake District, along with the important settlements of Penrith and Carlisle that lie outside the National Park. The Eden and Esk catchment area includes

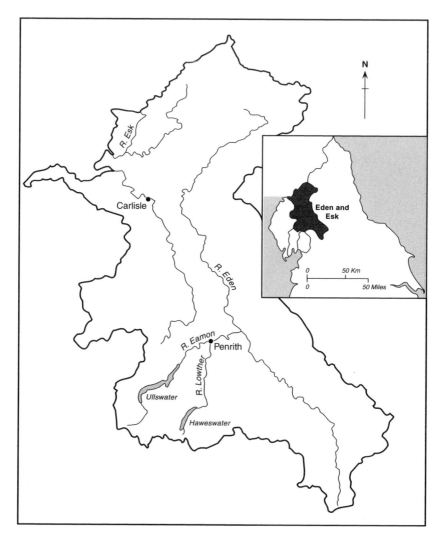

Figure 9.4   Eden and Esk CAMS

both Ullswater and Haweswater, plus the river basins of the rivers Eden and Esk. The River Eden rises on the northern edge of Hogwill Fells and runs through the Eden valley; its major tributaries include the rivers Irthing, Caldew, Eamont and Lowther. The River Esk rises near Eskdalemuir in Dumfries and Galloway (within Scotland) with the River Lyne and Liddle Water as major tributaries; these also form part of the border between England and Scotland.

At the time of our research, an awareness-raising leaflet for the Eden and Esk CAMS had already been published and the Environment Agency had put together a stakeholder group. However this had only met a couple of times when the whole process was put on hold due to a lack of available data and a need to clarify some issues. These principally concerned the adequacy of hydrology measurements for assessing river flows. This hold-up has caused an estimated delay of 12 months and the CAMS that was due to be finished in Spring 2006 will now be finalized in 2007. It remains to be seen whether the lessons of the previous two CAMS processes will alter the pattern of networking in this case. Already there had been some questioning of the adequacy of the stakeholder group given the location of the CAMS in relation to the Scottish border and the absence of Scottish interests within the group.

Overall the networking associated with these three CAMS processes has much in common with 'government' as compared to 'governance' models. There is an involvement of stakeholders but this is restricted rather than wide-ranging. Control over this involvement is retained by the Environment Agency, which decides who should be recruited into the network. The agency argues that it does not have the internal resources to include more than a limited number of actors in the process. A wider stakeholder group and wider public consultation would have taken time and personnel resources that the EA says it does not have. But as a result, some stakeholders have felt left out and the wider public consultation (involving awareness-raising leaflets at the beginning of the processes) has not been seen as an adequate means of engaging with such actors. On the other hand, not all local organizations felt a need to be fully involved within the CAMS process. For example the Friends of the Lake District, a key NGO, was not invited to participate in any of the CAMS stakeholder groups, but rather was consulted and invited to comment and this proved quite satisfactory.

The agency's basis for choosing actors for inclusion in the CAMS stakeholder groups has also been a matter for local comment. The EA decided to identify key interests in the catchment areas and thereafter identify the key stakeholder within that interest group. These persons were then individually invited to participate in the CAMS stakeholder group. So for the business and industry interests, the EA did not contact a group and ask them to send a representative; rather it contacted individuals who it knew to be active in a certain area. This meant that such individuals were not always clear whether they were acting in their own capacity or representing a specific organization. Most of the representatives in the stakeholder groups interviewed made sure that they reported back to their own organizations and were usually quite involved in their own networks. But this handpicking technique was one of the most widely criticized issues throughout the CAMS processes, and it may have affected the quality of the bridging capital within the CAMS network (see below).

Despite the concerns of some local actors over the consultation in these CAMS, there appears to have been general agreement over the directions taken by the strategies themselves. This went with a general acceptance that the Environment Agency was the appropriate lead actor in water abstraction management and that they should retain ultimate ownership of the strategies. There does not seem to have been a desire for ownership and responsibility for management to be dispersed among stakeholders in the way suggested by discussions of governance approaches.

There is some logic to this position. All stakeholder involvement incurs costs and in a situation of concentrated regulatory powers that appear to be being exercised appropriately, then government rather than governance may be the better institutional arrangement. This conclusion does rest though on the assumption that abstraction is being appropriately managed. This leads onto another question: How would the network cope if some conflicts arose? The current patterns of interaction have not developed any internal institutional capacity for handling conflict. It may be that the underlying pattern of resource use in this case supports a centralized approach, with a dominant Environment Agency largely dealing bilaterally with abstractors. Government may be the right institutional fit for the local circumstances concerning water resources. However if this essentially bilateral arrangement is disrupted, then the CAMS system, as currently operationalized, may not be able to cope. There is some limited evidence that conflicts are already being threatened due to the increased frequency of droughts in the area, itself a result of changing patterns of rainfall. In 2003, the Environment Agency had to issue three drought orders allowing United Utilities to pump more water from lakes Windermere and Ullswater in order to protect supplies to consumers. The Friends of the Lake District expressed some concern about the impact of these increased abstraction levels on wildlife, particularly fish.

The Environment Agency argues that the drought orders included special measures to protect wildlife but the Friends remain concerned about the increased frequency with which such orders have been sought since the late 1990s. Some interviewees raised the question of whether water companies should not be looking for alternative sources of water or alternative means of controlling demand rather than resorting to such drought orders. The pattern of abstraction licensing and issuing drought orders, although not happening every year, is potentially creating routines of decision-making that encourage path-dependencies. As the Friends point out, 'the frequency of drought powers being sought and the threat posed by climate change to aggravate the situation further is a cause for concern'.

Several other interviewees echoed this, seeing it as a potential problem for the area.

There is a certain amount of regional networking occurring in the North West over the possible impacts of climate change. The national UK Climate Impacts Programme (www.ukcip.org.uk) has sought to promote such regional partnerships in order to undertake more local assessments of how climate change will affect local economies and communities. The Lake District is covered by the North West Climate Change Group, established in 1997 following a regional colloquium on the issue. The group brings a range of regional stakeholders, including government agencies, research institutes, the regional assembly and business organizations, and is managed by a Local Agenda 21 organization, Sustainability Northwest (www.snw.org.uk). The Environment Agency and United Utilities have both joined in meetings and discussions. The first result of the group was the 1998 report detailing climate impacts in the region, followed by a regional inventory of greenhouse gas emissions and a number of projects including ones on renewable energy and the future of the tourist industry. Another significant project was REGIS, which looks at the impacts of climate change in two regions, the North West and East Anglia; water resources are a specific aspect of this project but it does not appear that the deliberations of this climate change group are feeding directly into the stakeholder activities under the CAMS processes.

Some interviewees pointed to the possibility of the new European water management framework altering these patterns of networking. Hopes were expressed that the implementation of the directive might usher in a new era of more inclusive management of water resources since one of the core requirements of the directive is public participation. The Ribble project mentioned earlier, piloting implementation of the WFD, has considered how to enhance participation and has tested different methods of stakeholder engagement. The Environment Agency also sees lessons learned during implementation of the CAMS as helping towards the implementation of the WFD in England and Wales and the EA is considering how the CAMS can be incorporated into the river basin plans under the WFD, bearing in mind that the WFD covers more water bodies than those assessed by CAMS, including lakes, artificial water bodies, transitional waters, coastal waters and minor aquifers. There is certainly scope for the EU directive to change practice on CAMS since these abstraction strategies also operate on a six-year review cycle, so that future strategies may be developed differently in the future. Whether this results in more inclusionary policy-making is a matter for future research.

LIMITED OPPORTUNITIES FOR BUILDING SOCIAL CAPITAL

CAMS stakeholder groups were designed as a time-limited exercise in consultation on the Environment Agency's CAMS. They should not be judged against the expectations of governance structures. But they provide an interesting contrast to the governance initiatives explored in other chapters. In particular, they provide a benchmark for the development of social capital and the handling of knowledge in non-governance contexts. While the stakeholder groups involved putting the formal infrastructure of a network in place, they lacked social capital. The bridging capital was weak, with links being formalistic as well as formal. There was agreement on the final strategy but this was largely because no difficult or contentious issues were handled. There was less agreement that the working of the network had been entirely satisfactory due to the limited and controlled nature of the participation by many local stakeholders. The reliance on the regulatory powers of the Environment Agency in ultimately implementing the strategies rendered the issue of collective action on the part of the stakeholders to achieve implementation largely irrelevant. In this context there was no need to use the stakeholder network to identify, release or activate resources. Neither did interviewees draw attention to the use of sanctions or blame or a shared culture of reciprocity and trust between stakeholders as a significant factor in achieving either agreement on the strategy or the implementation of that strategy.

There was some evidence of bonding capital within the individual organizations of the networks. This enabled the different organizations to act as effective representatives of their broader membership. Indeed the Environment Agency relied on this to give legitimacy to their CAMS networks although this was somewhat undermined by their identification of key individuals they were aware of for inclusion in the network, rather than asking the various stakeholder organizations themselves to identify such individuals. Furthermore there is little harnessing of this bonding capital to the work of the networks, as might be suggested by the concept of bracing capital and has been found in some other cases, such as the New Forest Committee. Such cases have shown that governance is fostered by building both bonding capital within organizations and bridging capital between organizations, and making full use of both types of capital to achieve legitimacy for and implementation of a joint strategy.

The lesson to be drawn from this case study of the stakeholder groups developed in order to produce CAMS is that networks do not always equate with governance, as envisaged in the academic or policy literature. These cases are much closer to government than governance. This could be criticized in terms of inadequate participation by stakeholders, whether due to a lack of commitment on the part of the Environment Agency (the principal criticism made by interviewees) or a reluctance to be involved on the part of the stakeholders. However it could also be argued that in this case a governmental approach is adequate and indeed appropriate. The costs of collective action in terms of participation in these networks would exceed any benefits, and the locus of monopoly regulatory powers with the Environment Agency justifies a more centralized approach. This would be true as long as water management was indeed sustainable under these conditions. It has been suggested that such an approach may be less robust in the face of conflicts over water use, as are increasingly likely to arise in conditions of climate change and reduced certainty of rainfall. The pattern of social capital associated with this governmental approach – weak bridging ties and limited bonding capital that is not tied into the policy process – may ultimately be inadequate for sustainable water management.

THE ROLE OF KNOWLEDGE RESOURCES

The institutional capacity framework draws our attention to factors beyond the building of social capital, notably the importance of knowledge resources. These were clearly an issue in this case. The efficacy of the government style of networking assumed that the agency held sufficient resources for effective management, including appropriate knowledge. However some interviewees raised doubts about whether the agency did have sufficient knowledge.

The Eden and Esk CAMS process was effectively put on hold while new data was collated, while the Environment Agency itself questioned the adequacy of its knowledge resources in the Leven and Crake case. The first annual update on this CAMS monitored the implementation of the strategy and concluded that the CAMS process 'highlights where we would benefit from additional knowledge and provides a framework for addressing this. As a result, new monitoring sites are being developed throughout the Leven and Crake catchment. The data from these will increase our knowledge and confidence for the next cycle of the Leven and Crake CAMS which will be published in 2009' (Environment Agency 2004c). Indeed the Environment Agency argued in this document that this identification of knowledge gaps was one of the benefits of the whole CAMS process; that is, it met the internal needs of the agency in terms of planning and management.

This approach could be critiqued as failing to take advantage of the ability of governance networks to release knowledge resources. Advocates of governance patterns claim that they release a variety of knowledge resources from a range of actors, all of which can contribute to policy-making and implementation. According to this view, the pattern of networking involved in the CAMS limited this potential and, in time, this may impact back on future water management. However it could also be argued in the case of water abstraction planning that the main knowledge required is technical in kind and not likely to be vested in the local or experiential knowledge of local stakeholders. This was certainly the Environment Agency's own view. They felt that the consultation with stakeholders had given them sufficient access to local knowledge and that technical knowledge is best generated within government rather than governance structures, as this can create knowledge through simple commissioning from other expert bodies. For example the agency has invested in a project on Catchment Hydrology and Sustainable Management (CHASM) concerning the Eden River, which is being undertaken by the University of Newcastle-upon-Tyne. This is testing new gauges that will improve the quality of data on water flows needed for the management of abstraction. There is no obvious reason why governance networks would be better at generating or utilizing such technical knowledge.

However the limited involvement of a breadth of stakeholders within the CAMS networks meant that this pattern of knowledge resources was not fully tested out or open to challenge. This may prove to be a weakness in the strategy development and implementation process in the future as conditions change. In a similar case study, looking at the Tweed River Basin, Collins (2004: 17) notes that the Environment Agency and its Scottish equivalent did not always acknowledge the scientific uncertainties and gaps in their knowledge, nor allow for this in their regulatory decision-making. Collins also found in his case that some local stakeholders did make claims for the importance of local knowledge, particularly in relation to historical and experiential knowledge of flooding events. However while the local networking arrangements were both broader and deeper than in the Lake District (see below for further comparison), this did not result in any critical assessment of the different kinds of knowledge and how they interrelate. There seem to be some significant limitations on the potential of networking arrangements to handle different knowledge resources and requirements in the context of water management. Yet knowledge resources will be an increasingly important issue as the impacts of climate change place a premium on the incorporation of new knowledge in order to develop effective strategies.

THE LESSONS FOR NETWORKING

Our Lake District case study has shown the impact of a controlled exercise in stakeholder participation over one aspect of water management. It has highlighted the limited bridging social capital that results, the weak nature of the link between members of such a network, and the resultant lack of connection between the main network of stakeholders and the other 'home' networks that the stakeholders belong to, partly because of the way that particular individuals were recruited to the main network. This is the case even where there is strong bonding capital within the organizations repre-sented in the bridging network. The stakeholder networks were successful in developing and agreeing strategies, but this was largely because of the lack of overt conflicts in a situation where water supply was currently seen as adequate. In this case, there was no history of conflicts that had sensi-tized stakeholders to the need to be more involved in strategy development and implementation. While the Environment Agency may be characterized as controlling rather than facilitating in relation to stakeholder involvement (to follow Ostrom's categories, 1990), it is only fair to note that there was no significant demand for greater and more meaningful involvement. The lack of continued relations of the Environment Agency with stakeholders and between stakeholders after the CAMS processes were completed is further evidence of this. This means that bottom-up pressures for network-ing were largely absent. It would suggest that such pressures are a prereq-uisite for the dense and reciprocal relations characterized by social capital to develop.

In support of this argument, we can refer again to Collins's study of the Tweed river basin. This area lies across the Scottish–English border and Collins identifies an example of networking in the form of the Tweed Forum. This was set up as 'a loose network of concerned individuals and organisations' (2004: 12) in response to a specific event involving a mechan-ical digger and disruption to the salmon spawning areas. From this it devel-oped its agenda to address poor management practices among riparian managers, and formally constituted itself as a company limited by guaran-tee in 1998. The forum subsequently went on to achieve significant funding in 1999 and 2001, resulting in it taking a leading role in the development of the Catchment Management Plan in the period up to 2003. Collins makes it clear that the success of the forum lies in its roots among stakeholders' con-cerns and their perception that the forum could play an important role in resolving conflicts, which were already apparent on the ground (Collins 2004: 13). Another key feature of the network was the recognition of inter-dependencies between members of the forum, a key element of social capital (Collins 2004: 14). On this basis the forum has been able to be proactive over new issues, such as river access and the release of water from reservoirs, and to develop a catchment-wide perspective.

So the River Tweed case suggests that denser networks can be built around water management in the English context. However they require some kind of prior conflict to energize the parties into networking and to convince them of their reciprocity in relation to each other. It also requires the key governmental bodies to act in a facilitating manner. This raises particular difficulties in cases where water management problems may be anticipated rather than currently experienced. The impact of climate change on water supplies is an important example of such an anticipated problem. Stakeholder involvement in an effective network may only arise once a water crisis as a result of changed climatic conditions has already arisen. It seems difficult to generate such collective action in anticipation of problems.

This throws the onus back on government bodies – whether departments, agencies or elected authorities – to handle such anticipated problems; government rather than governance may be the more appropriate policy mode. Such bodies can then set the framework for other actors to generate sustainable outcomes. However while such a reliance on state bodies may be inevitable given the limited ability of networks to operate in a precautionary way, there are also problems with this approach. Such bodies may lack the flexibility and creativity to respond to anticipated problems; in particular, they may tend to follow path-dependencies. We saw some evidence of this in the handling of knowledge resources in our case and in Collins's work (2004). Here there was a reliance on a specific type of technical knowledge and a tendency to overemphasize its certainty. Other forms of knowledge were not always recognized nor integrated into policy-making alongside more technical assessments. Thus while the limitations of networking in handling new and emergent situations must be recognized, the path-dependencies of governmental bodies can also be a significant constraint on a sustainable response arising.

10. Castilla-La Mancha, Spain: collective action and inaction in groundwater management

Elena Lopez-Gunn

Lack of collective action in groundwater management can turn a potentially renewable resource into a non-renewable one. Therefore groundwater is a classic example of a common pool resource that can particularly benefit from developing strong institutional frameworks that favour self-governance and mutually beneficial collective action.

This chapter will address the problems inherent in developing strong institutional networks in Spain, by comparing three aquifers located in the same geographic region, La Mancha, an arid region located in central Spain where water is a particularly scarce resource and has considerably added value. It will be discussed how the three aquifers have fared very differently in addressing the logic of collective action; since many physical, socio-economic and cultural parameters are very similar, it provides a particularly fertile ground to show how institutional frameworks have provided the key to their different success in terms of collective action.

The chapter is structured in the following way; in the first section, the case study areas are briefly introduced, and their specifics in terms of collective action problems discussed. The case studies are then set in the context of the key characteristic of common pool resources, applied to groundwater. The second section undertakes a brief network analysis of the organizational structure of the case study areas and the main actors and networks. Norms and values compared to the regulatory framework, social capital, the role of knowledge, external events and dominant discourses are then analysed in order to address the question of collective action, its development and implementation.

INTRODUCTION TO THE CASE STUDY AREAS

Water in Spain is an emotional issue. It is also highly politicized. This is due to its scarcity, a limiting factor for development in many Spanish regions, including Castilla-La Mancha where the case studies are located. In contemporary Spanish political history, promises of increasing water availability have been a constant.

Yet until the 1970s, groundwater was a largely unknown and underused resource, generally surrounded by mystery and associated with a rural past, when villages and individual houses had to supply their own water. However since the 1970s groundwater has became a passport to development, turning Spanish agriculture, which was generally subject to the whims of weather, into a much more reliable and profitable enterprise. This has had enormous socio-economic benefits in areas where this resource was available and tapped. It also led in many cases to unsustainable rates of use (MIMAM 1998). The three case studies analysed here are examples of this phenomenon: quick development, huge short-term economic profits and possible long-term consequences.

The region where the case studies are located – La Mancha – has undergone dramatic socio-economic changes since the 1970s. Groundwater exploitation halted a massive process of rural migration to the cities that was taking place between 1950 and 1980. The pervading paradigm of the Spanish Hydraulic Mission meant irrigation equalled development (Swyngedouw 1999b), and this paradigm was pervasive in Castilla-La Mancha. In an interview, a senior civil servant stated:

> [The] region was extremely poor . . . The region depopulates . . . then they discover groundwater and the opportunity to irrigate. This becomes a true driving force for development that is how we defined it. Wells are opened everywhere and traditional wells (norias) are abandoned. Yet, everything irrational has a limit and the development was so strong that there started to be problems. There was a drop in water levels, from the norias at 10–15 metres to the 100 metres from submergible pumps.

THE WESTERN MANCHA AQUIFER

The Western Mancha aquifer is the main aquifer in the Upper Guadiana Basin in terms of size, capacity and socio-economic importance due to the large population living within its perimeter (estimated at 300 000). The aquifer occupies an area of 5500 km^2, over the provinces of Cuenca, Ciudad Real and Albacete. Renewable water resources fluctuate between 200 Mm^3/yr (in dry periods) and 500 Mm^3/yr (in wet periods) (Llamas et al. 2000; Cruces et al. 1997). Recharge is highly variable, depending on the area and year, although it is estimated that a renewable extraction rate could be 300 Mm^3/yr (EFEDA 1997; Llamas et al. 2000).

The first wells were drilled to tap the groundwater resources, which had been previously inaccessible through lack of knowledge and technology. The first wells were legalized, replacing a traditional, extensive dry-land Mediterranean agriculture of olives, vines and wheat with irrigated maize, sugar beet and barley. From 30 000 irrigated hectares in 1973, there was an increase to 130 000 hectares by 1989. The consequence of intensive groundwater use was felt from the mid- to late-1980s as a result of dry years coinciding with the expansion of irrigated land. The drop in aquifer levels reached 40 and 50 metres in some areas. Many wells dried up and farmers deepened wells (the so-called 'pumping war'). Abstraction had risen from 150 million m³/yr for the period 1960 to 1976, to 600–700 million m³/yr in the late 1980s, to drop to 300 million m³/yr in the mid-1990s (Llamas et al. 2000). In recent years the water levels have recovered slightly, which can be attributed to a reduction in water abstractions, a wet sequence (1996–98) and an EU Agri-environment Programme designed to reduce water abstractions, which are now threatened by aquifer overuse.

In the case of the Western Mancha aquifer, the conflict has been mainly one of competition between agriculture's intensive use of the resource and the impact this had on the natural environment (in particular wetlands). Despite the aridity of the area, due to low relief, the definition of surface watercourses and the geological characteristics of the area, groundwater has produced wetlands like the Tablas de Daimiel National Park (Llamas et al. 2000).

THE CAMPO DE MONTIEL AQUIFER

Our second case study, the Campo de Montiel, has an area of 2700 km², located between the provinces of Albacete and Ciudad Real. It is an aquifer, recharged mainly through rainfall, discharging almost exclusively to the Western Mancha aquifer. Its water levels are very sensitive to rainfall variability: water levels go up in wet years and go down in dry periods (Cruces de Abia et al. 1998). Thus its storage capacity is limited. Closely related to the aquifer is the Lagunas de Ruidera Natural Park, which stands at the point where the Campo de Montiel drains into the Western Mancha. This is a series of interconnected lagoons, unique in Western Europe. The Lagunas de Ruidera was designated in 1979 as a Natural Park. It includes 15 lagoons, which drain into the Peñarroya reservoir. The lagoons' value is not so much ecological, as landscape and geo-morphological (LRNP, pers. comm). Once again it was water projects that marked part of the damage to the Lagunas, with the construction of the Peñarroya reservoir in 1959, in order to transform the *vega* of Argamasilla de Alba, in line with the 'hydraulic project' then in vogue (Swyngedouw 1999b). Irrigation expanded rapidly in the 1980s, from 200 hectares in 1981 to 8000 eight years later (1988).

The case in the Campo de Montiel has similarities and differences to the Western Mancha. The main similarity is that the year of biggest aquifer abstractions was also in the mid-1980s, when in 1987, 33 Mm^3 were abstracted to irrigate 5225 hectares. The expansion of irrigation coincided with a dry period that started at the end of the 1980s, and led to the drying of some of the lagoons, and the lowering of water levels in the Peñarroya reservoir (discharge of the aquifer) and its associated irrigated land. The lowering of water levels also affected a spring providing water supply to the neighbouring villages. Conflict exploded in the late 1980s, and the issue was quickly transformed into a battle between the authorities and some large landowners over damage to the Lagunas, the village wells and lack of groundwater drainage into the Peñarroya reservoir (and therefore preventing surface water irrigation for small farmers from the reservoir).

The estimates over the renewable resources of the Campo de Montiel are 130 Mm^3/yr (MIMAM 2000). In view of this figure the aquifer is not overused, since at the peak of abstractions only 33 Mm^3/yr were taken out. However what is contested is how irrigation can affect particular sectors of the aquifer (Cortina, pers. comm). When there are a large number of hectares under irrigation this can affect both the Lagunas de Ruidera and natural springs that supply water to villages, since irrigated land, springs and the Lagunas rely on the same groundwater source.

THE EASTERN MANCHA AQUIFER

The Eastern Mancha aquifer has an area of 8500 km^2 over the provinces of Albacete and Cuenca (see Figure 10.1). It is located mainly in the Júcar catchment and for management purposes it has been divided into 11 areas, some of which have been used much more intensively than others. The recharge of the eastern aquifer is mainly through rainwater (325 Mm^3/yr) and groundwater contributions from other aquifers (15 Mm^3/yr). Like the Campo de Montiel, water figures for the Eastern Mancha are heavily contested. Different figures are found in reports and papers. However in the Júcar River Basin Plan, although 400 Mm^3/yr are allocated for use in the Eastern Mancha, only 320 Mm^3/yr are allocated from groundwater resources. The rest has to be made up through transfers originating in the now cancelled National Water Plan (JCRMO 1999; JCRMO 2001). The Ministry of Environment had estimated that net abstractions were between 300 and 350 Mm^3/yr (MIMAM 1997). This would mean there is a yearly deficit of 115 Mm^3/yr (JCRMO 2001). Similar to the Western Mancha, the

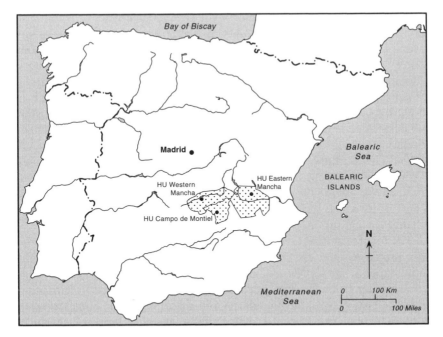

Figure 10.1   Castilla-La Mancha

development in the use of groundwater for public water supply and irrigation started in the mid-1970s. However a marked difference with the
Western Mancha and the Campo de Montiel is that the number of hectares
irrigated has shown a continued steady increase, with the peak of 98 000
hectares currently under irrigation.

In the Eastern Mancha aquifer, intensive groundwater use has affected
the surface water flow of the River Júcar. Downstream users like the
aquifer's drainage into the Alarcón reservoir and irrigation in the Valencia
area have been affected and have complained on the basis of prior use –
'first in time, first in right' (Getches 1990). Under the Water Act older,
established water rights like farmers from the Acequia Real del Júcar and
the hydroelectric company Union Fenosa have preferential use.

COMMON POOL RESOURCES AND GROUNDWATER

The section above has identified a problem with heavy groundwater
abstraction in the three case study areas. This section discusses the peculiar
characteristics of groundwater as a common pool resource.

As already identified in Chapter 1, the key characteristics of a common pool resource is its 'non-excludability' and 'subtractability'. There are many examples of common pool resource discussed in other chapters of this book, yet one of the most often cited in the literature is that of aquifers. Blomquist (1994: 284) notes in relation to aquifers in southern California: 'The exclusion of multiple pumpers is difficult and costly . . . Consumption is rival. As water withdrawals from the basin exceed the amount replenished (due to any combination of more pumpers, greater withdrawals by each, or declining replenishment), pumpers visit appropriation externalities on each other.' This 'pump war' process occurred in the three case studies, examined in this chapter. Yet according to the Institutional Analysis and Development Framework, there is a possible third way, neither privatization nor state control, in which networks resolve collective action problems through changes in institutional arrangements (Ostrom et al. 1994).

The first factor that favours collective action is a clear definition of who can use a resource. As Ostrom (1992: 90) states, this refers to 'both the boundaries of the service area and the individuals or household with rights to use water from an irrigation system area clearly defined'. Therefore it refers to both geographic boundaries and a clear definition of water rights. Common pool resources are defined vis-à-vis other types of resources (public goods, private goods and toll goods) because of the key characteristic of non-excludability. The aim therefore is to turn an open access resource into a common pool resource, by turning non-excludability into excludability. According to Ostrom (Getches 1990; Bassets 1992) the most important factor to solve common pool resource problems is to ensure excludability of some water users through the development of strong internal norms.

In our three case studies geographic boundaries were clearly defined by the particular aquifer. Boundaries are defined by the state, and in cases of overuse, instituted by Act. The situation is not so clear in relation to water rights. It will be discussed below that whereas there are thousands of illegal water users in Western Mancha, with implicit farmer consent, this has effectively been prevented in Eastern Mancha. The question is: Why is there such a clear difference between Eastern Mancha and Campo de Montiel on the one hand, and the Western Mancha on the other? How did they succeed where Western Mancha failed? The rest of this chapter will attempt to answer this question by looking at different factors discussed in the introductory chapters of this book, since both cases show opposite ends in the spectrum of collective action: clear failure in the Western Mancha and halting steps in Eastern Mancha towards strong institutional designs that foster long-term collective action. The next section introduces the first factor identified as key to the resolution of collective management of groundwater: the design of the networks themselves and whether they are inclusive or exclusive.

FROM ISSUE NETWORKS TO POLICY COMMUNITIES

This section will argue that in the current shift from government to governance, institutional networks are key to deliver mutually beneficial collective action. The policy network perspective explicitly states that it concentrates mainly on the meso level, not the macro (state–civil society) or micro level (individuals). A policy network according to Bomberg (1998: 167) would include a set of public and private actors who depend on one another for resources such as information, expertise, access and legitimacy. Most networks develop around functions (implementation, regulation) or around specific policy sectors (in our case groundwater management).

According to the so-called 'Rhodes model' networks are relatively autonomous (for example interests not directly involved are excluded), relatively stable and the actors are resource dependent on each other (for example for legitimacy and access to the network itself) (Rhodes 1997). Policy networks can be classified along a continuum from tight policy communities to loose issue networks, where the institutional structures in terms of power distribution affect the operation of the network. Our three case studies provide examples on how policy networks have evolved from loose 'issue networks' towards tighter 'policy communities'.

For our case studies, the Western Mancha aquifer policy network started to develop in the mid- to late-1980s as a loose issue network, and a section of the loose issue network (namely the Irrigation Communities, the main farming union and the regional government) matured into a policy community in the early 1990s. Meanwhile the Campo de Montiel was and remains a loose issue network. By contrast the Eastern Mancha network, although it started to develop later (in the early 1990s) it quickly transformed into a close policy community including – most importantly as will be seen below for collective action – not only the regulated (farmers) but also the regulators, that is, the regional government and the water authority. In contrast to the Western Mancha it excluded the main farming union to prevent capture of water users by lobbying interests.

The set of actors in the Western Mancha policy community and the Campo de Montiel issue network were identified through a network approach (Sabatier and Jenkins-Smith 1988). Both networks developed over time, and organized as advocacy coalitions, as a result of dissatisfaction with existing policies for example on the one hand those worried over plans to drain the local wetlands or impact on existing wetlands and on the other those worried over threats to agriculture if strict regulations were enforced.

The policy networks in both aquifers overlap to a large extent in relation to public authorities and environmental groups (see Figure 10.2). The

Policy networks		Western Mancha	Campo de Montiel	Eastern Mancha
National authorities (administrative agency, 1998)		Ministry of Environment ITGE		
Regional authority (administrative agency, 1998)		Castilla-La Mancha Regional Government (JCCMM)		
Water authority (administrative agency, 1998)		Guadiana Water Authority		Júcar Water Authority (CHJ)
Irrigation community (material group, 1998)		General Irrigation Community (and 20 Individual Irrigation Communities)	General Irrigation Community	General Irrigation Community (JCRMO)
Environmental NGOs (purposive group, 1998)	**Reg.**	AEDA 23		Salicor
	Nat.	Birdlife International WWF Spain		
Protected sites (administrative agency, 1998)		Tablas de Daimiel National Park	Ruidera Natural Park	
Journalists				
Academics and scientists		Castilla-La Mancha University, Madrid University, Autonomous University of Barcelona, Expert Committee		

Note: Indicates strong 'permeability' or 'informal contacts' between actors.

Figure 10.2   Comparison of the Western Mancha, Campo de Montiel and Eastern Mancha policy networks

regional government is a key actor in relation to potential coalitions, as the main 'sovereign' in the area. The other key institution is the water authority. In Spain water management has been organized since 1926 on a catchment basis, with the creation of water authorities. These water authorities are formally ascribed to the Ministry of Environment, except in the case when the catchment does not cross regional administrative boundaries. In this case, the regional government itself becomes responsible for water management. In our case however, all three cases cross regional boundaries and therefore water authorities are responsible for their management.

Both the Western Mancha and the Campo de Montiel are located in the Upper Guadiana Basin. Therefore both are under the aegis of the Confederación Hidrográfica del Guadiana (or Guadiana Water Authority). However within the Guadiana Water Authority there are officials responsible for particular geographical areas. Meanwhile the Eastern Mancha is part of the Júcar Basin and therefore falls under the responsibility of the Júcar Water Authority. This is an important difference because the institutional cultures of both water authorities are very different. The Júcar Water Authority has had the longest experience in Spain of irrigation and in dealing with some of the oldest Irrigation Communities worldwide.

Equally, environmental groups are shared across the region. International NGOs like the World Wide Fund for Nature (WWF) Spain and Birdlife Spain have focused on specific campaigns on the Tablas de Daimiel and Lagunas de Ruidera. In addition to these national environmental NGOs, specific local and aquifer-specific groups have developed, like AEDA (Asociación en Defensa del Acuífero 23) and Salicor. Environmental groups have been proactive and vociferous in the Western Mancha and Campo de Montiel. Groups have campaigned actively for the protection of the Tablas de Daimiel National Park, and the Lagunas de Ruidera. Equally active in the case study areas has been the *bête noire* of NGOs, the main farming union, ASAJA (Asociación Agraria de Jóvenes Agricultores). However what is highly relevant is the slow but certain co-option of Irrigation Communities in the Western Mancha by the main farming union, which has created a tight policy community where the regional government, in a classic case of political horse-trading, has traded electoral support in exchange for agri-environment subsidies (as will be discussed below). This however has been at the expense of the relationship with the Guadiana Water Authority, which remains an outsider of this tight policy community.

NORMS AND VALUES AND THE REGULATORY REGIME IN SPANISH GROUNDWATER MANAGEMENT

This section will introduce the norms and values that operate in the three aquifers, framed by the main regulatory framework of the 1985 Water Act. Despite the same regulatory framework, this section emphasizes how in the Western Mancha illegal has in effect become 'legal' in terms of norms and values as an accepted type of behaviour, whereas in Eastern Mancha it has become morally unacceptable among the farming community to open illegal wells. First, a short introduction is given on the development of a complex regulatory framework.

Groundwater was considered *res nullius* under Roman law, until the Water Act of 1985 (that is, a resource that had no owner and therefore could be appropriated by whoever drilled it first). The Old Hydraulic Paradigm never really dealt with groundwater. It was an 'invisible resource', not really included in the Big Hydraulic mission that Spain had embarked upon. Yet groundwater sources were strategically important since the whole population's water supply depended on them. Up to the 1970s their close connection with surface water was not appreciated. This was partly due to the technology available and the low level of abstraction, which gave no indication of possible third-party effects of small wells, abstracting water from the same aquifer. Therefore a separate system dealt with groundwater rights, under the 1878 Water Act. Groundwater users had only to document their use if they so wished, in the Springs and Wells Registry of the Mining Department. Under the 1878 Water Act, any landowner had the right to abstract water from their land. Groundwater pre-1985 was a private resource, to be used by private landowners since it belonged to the landowner once they had abstracted it, according to Article 18 (Garcia-Vizcaino 2003). Usage was only limited by the cost of investment and to the (vague) principle that other water users should not be affected.

Under the 1985 Water Act groundwater became subject to 'the general interest' (or *interés general*). In other words, it was publicly owned by the state. Such a change, in its political context, was bold on the part of legislators and politicians. It was only ten years before that Spain had started its life as a young democracy and not too long before this debate there had been an attempt at a *coup de état* (1981). In 1982 a new socialist government won the elections with a comfortable majority. However 'nationalization' was a sensitive issue, given a contemporary history of civil war. There was always the risk that the Act would be declared 'unconstitutional', since no compensation was provided for private groundwater owners. The strong opposition to drastic change made the threat of legal cases high. A compromise was reached, in the development of legal transitional measures (*disposiciones transitorias*). The transitional measures included in the 1985 Water Act were an acknowledgment and recognition that there were groundwater users in existence and no economic compensation had been granted. A Water Register for public water and a Private Water Catalogue for private water replaced the old Registro de Aguas Públicas. There was an uneasy coexistence within the same regulatory system of both public and private water property regimes. The legislators had to look for arguments as to why this change to public, rather than private ownership (without compensation), was justified. The arguments were legitimized by references to the Old Hydraulic Paradigm, on the role of the state, overseeing and protecting groundwater resources, via permits since permit holders would be protected by the state.

Therefore the regulatory framework in Spain around groundwater is highly complex, with the coexistence of private and state rights. However this complex regulatory framework only comes to life when analysed in specific contexts. It is only when one applies this formal regulatory framework to our case studies that the difficulties in implementing this regulatory framework and the ensuing problem of collective action can be appreciated.

In the case of the Western Mancha it is estimated that there are thousands of illegal wells, opened after the 1985 Water Act expressly forbade it. This is a glaring example of lack of collective action. Furthermore the dominant norms and values in the Western Mancha excuse illegality, with farmers, mayors and the main farming union marching publicly to stop the closure of illegal wells. This is in marked contrast with the case of the Eastern Mancha where farmers have actively collaborated with the water authority to close illegal wells. The question was posed before: What can explain these differences, taking into account the similarity in physical, historical and socio-cultural factors and the application of the same formal rules or regulatory framework? The structure of networks was already identified as a key factor, and whether networks are inclusive or exclusive of regulated and regulator. Yet this institutional 'scaffolding' has to be imbued with an understanding of social capital enveloping it (or not, as the case may be) and the role knowledge and external factors can play. The last sections analyse these factors as key to understanding collective action on groundwater management.

SOCIAL CAPITAL: THE KEY INGREDIENT FOR COLLECTIVE ACTION IN GROUNDWATER MANAGEMENT

The key concept underpinning social capital is 'trust', a critical element in social cohesion. The question that remains is whether social capital can be encouraged through processes that encourage trust, for example, through learning as:

> Interactive processes that contribute to change . . . processes whereby people interact with each other . . . to lead to changes. These changes may involve knowledge or skills acquisition, or result in a capacity to take on new values and attitudes, which in turn help in the adoption of different roles. Learning is the mechanism, which has the potential to facilitate development and change of individuals, work, organizations and institutions in response to the need for interaction between economic policies and their social and political context. (Falk and Kilpatrick 2000: 91)

Therefore social capital is considered as an outcome, and interactive learning as the process that leads to the outcome. Similarly Svendsen and Svendsen (2000) draw an analogy in their conception that social capital can be built up or eroded.

Social capital can be analysed in three main ways: first, its bonding aspect; second, as bridging social capital; and third, through the catalyst provided by leadership. What can be learnt from the analysis of our case study areas is that organizational and institutional design can help create or erode all types of social capital.

In the case of bonding social capital, the three aquifers have had to organize irrigation communities to manage groundwater, required to do so under the Water Act since they are classified as aquifers in overdraft. Yet the three case study Irrigation Communities have very different internal institutional set-ups. The Western Mancha has a main irrigation community, and 20 individual village irrigation communities. This could build on the strong thick trust that exists internally in each village irrigation community. However, in practice this situation operates against the collective good of the aquifer, due to strong *localismo* (Pitt-Rivers 1971) wherein villages are traditionally and historically distrustful of other villages and this distrust has infected irrigation communities. Internally within each irrigation community, cognitive social capital is very strong; however the structural or organizational set-up has hampered collective action and collaboration between irrigation communities. In effect it has fostered the dark side of social capital, where villages are trustful of their own but heavily suspicious of the activities of other villages, which in the case of the successful collective management of an aquifer of 5500 km² is essential.

The case of Campo de Montiel is different because here there is only one Irrigation Community for the whole aquifer. Here the key issue was to develop trust between a small group of farmers (101). A key difference between farmers lay in the size of their properties, with a clear dichotomy between small (<3 hectares) and large (>50 hectares) farmers. Here the leadership skills of the Irrigation Community president have succeeded in bonding these dichotomous farmers and their interests. However this type of leadership is vulnerable to change since it is a transformational (or charismatic) type of leadership, which does not necessarily ensure easy succession (Purdue 2001). This is in contrast with the Eastern Mancha.

The Eastern Mancha Irrigation Community has a federal–decentralized–structure, like the Western Mancha (Subramanian, Jagannathan et al. 1997); however it is not based along geographical village boundaries but along functional lines: that is, for different types of water user, like individual farmers, Irrigation Communities, municipalities and industries. The social capital here is thin (Newton 1999), but it is more flexible and inclusive towards external organizations and the development of both bonding and bridging social capital (Montgomery 2000; Rothstein 2000). In addition it has built on existing thick trust and social capital in older, traditional institutions like other irrigation communities that have joined it, and other neighbouring institutions to the east. The type of leadership found is different for Western Mancha and Campo de Montiel. There was no evidence of rivalry as found in Western Mancha and there was evidence of succession (contrary to the case in Campo de Montiel). Therefore the leadership is transformational as opposed to charismatic. This points to a stock of potential leaders that can succeed one another, and learn from one another, and to a more even distribution of power.

Finally social capital was analysed as bridging social capital. As was discussed before, Western Mancha and Campo de Montiel stand out when compared to Eastern Mancha. The relationship between the Irrigation Communities and the Guadiana Water Authority has generally been very antagonistic and there is mutual distrust. Meanwhile Eastern Mancha and the Júcar Water Authority are slowly building a high level of trust, which can be seen in the increased number of agreements on the management of the aquifer. In recent times actions have been jointly taken in areas where traditionally Irrigation Communities have been reluctant to tread, because of unpopularity with their own farmers, like the allocation of water rights and sanctioning. Eastern Mancha shows a high level of third-party trust (Falk and Kilpatrick 2000) with many other institutions, and these institutions themselves encouraged the bottom-up formation of the Irrigation Community. In contrast, both the Western Mancha and the Campo de Montiel were formed top-down and in the case of the Campo de Montiel even this proved difficult since for more than ten years the Guadiana Water Authority queried the Statutes of the Campo de Montiel Irrigation Community.

This section has focused on the analysis of social capital as demonstrated through bonding and its structural bridging aspect, as highlighted by the

Irrigation Community structure. This analysis also emphasized the key role of leadership as a catalyst for both communal and collaborative social capital and how in Western Mancha the main Irrigation Community leadership has acted as a gatekeeper for traditional farming interests, as voiced by the main farming union. A point of relevance in this regard is Fox and Gershman's (2000: 183) comment on how social capital can often threaten vested interests, so conflict can be expected in the possible redistribution of power ensuing from potential institutional reforms. The Irrigation Community in Western Mancha opted to side with vested interests, rather than build bridging trust (understood as trust in political and societal institutions). This is in stark contrast with Eastern Mancha where horizontal and vertical capital have been created, and imbued with a positive collective memory. Self-esteem is high in Eastern Mancha and so is self-determination, to the extent that Eastern Mancha is now successfully moving towards achieving factors that foster self-management (as described by Ostrom 1992).

Therefore social capital is the missing piece in the factors that lead to collective action. Yet it is a difficult enterprise, which as Foley and Edwards (1999: 155) summarize, requires a careful list of ingredients like social networks, existing organizations and enterprising individuals.

KNOWLEDGE, ARGUMENTS AND THE 'DEVIL SHIFT'

This section will assess a key element of institutional capacity, knowledge and the ability to activate knowledge to generate collective action. According to Rydin (see Chapter 2 in this book) analysing Healey et al., knowledge is understood as a relational concept, with an emphasis in interactive learning, rather than on knowledge as an asset owned by actors; therefore the emphasis is on knowledge as socially constructed and on what knowledge is recognized as legitimate for example by the different actors. In this chapter we will assess knowledge in two ways, as an interrelational concept, as suggested by Rydin, and in view of the scientific nature of the debate, the view on scientific knowledge and experts as holders of knowledge. It will be seen that both cannot be separated, since for example the view in Western Mancha (see below) on experts and scientists is coloured by the pragmatic use of knowledge in legitimizing (or eroding) the claims of different stakeholders.

This section is structured in the following way: firstly, an analysis is undertaken of who is considered to hold accredited knowledge claims, and unpacking the knowledge frames which give meaning to the relevant information. Secondly, the emphasis is on how knowledge is transferred in and between networks. Most importantly in the context of collective action is evaluating the openness of the network to learning and absorbing new knowledge, and what is considered possible and/or desirable, which would then help provide opportunity for change.

Krale (1996: 41) states: 'The conception of knowledge as a mirror of reality is replaced by a conception of the "social construction of reality", where the focus is on the interpretation and negotiation of the meaning of the social world . . . the multiplicity of meanings in local contexts; knowledge is perspectival, dependent on the viewpoint and values of the investigator.' This interpretivist approach links with postmodern approaches to knowledge, which questions the belief in one true and objective reality (Krale 1996). In our case studies it was clear that information (for example technical and/or scientific) was used in an 'argumentative' manner, to bolster the debate, and try to persuade. Time and resources were spent collecting information that would be used in an 'advocacy fashion', trying to convince other actors as to the validity of their position (Majone 1989). However actors belonging to opposing coalitions were suspicious of information from opponents, more so in high-conflict situations, when the 'devil shift' is more pronounced, where opposing sides assume a siege mentality in which all evidence put forward by the opposition is regarded as suspicious (Sabatier 1993). Knowledge does not suddenly appear and become accepted and incorporated into governmental programmes. Rather, findings emerge gradually, can be heavily contested particularly by those who see their interest challenged and thus give rise to dynamic analytical debates (Sabatier 1993: 219).

In high-conflict situations, the policy champion can play a key role. The concept of 'policy champion' (or broker) is similar to an extent to the actions played by 'policy entrepreneurs' in the study of agenda-setting by Kingdon (1984). Fischer (1993: 22) comments how governance is dominated by technically trained knowledge elites. Their function is to replace or control democratic deliberation and decision-making processes (based on conflicting interests) with a more technocratically informed discourse (based on scientific decision-making techniques). The result is the transformation of political issues into technically defined ends that can be pursued via administrative means.

In all our case studies experts undertook the role of policy champions and farmers saw a valuable role in experts. Yet their attitude was heavily pragmatic and advocacy-based. For example the participation of a particular professor, well known in both Western Mancha and Campo de Montiel, was welcomed since he had played a policy champion role in attempts to bridge the gap between the administration and the farming community, finding compromises and trying to reduce conflict. However the farming community probably accepts this academic because reports carried out have generally been supportive of views held by farmer communities, which question official data. Farmers in an argumentative policy style have relied on expert opinion as an instrumental tool. Yet Western Mancha and Campo de Montiel have employed their own hydrogeologists and have commissioned hydrogeological reports to confront the authorities on scientific grounds, emphasizing the key role knowledge plays in collective action (CIDESPA 1988; Llamas 1991).

So the view on scientific knowledge and participation by experts is heavily instrumental, where scientific data is used in an advocacy fashion to buttress farmers' arguments and build the farming coalition's case. Those experts that issue reports or studies that are sympathetic to the farming cause are valued and trusted. Yet other experts, who had expressed more critical evaluations of the current situation, are ignored, disregarded or actively disliked. Yet increasingly the view on scientists and their knowledge is that, as Berglund states: 'Scientists . . . are thoroughly embedded in social and cultural systems' (2001: 836). Indeed different stakeholders have a clear perception on how scientists' core values permeate their work. Experts and scientists are no longer considered as 'neutral', 'objective' bystanders; instead they are part of the 'social construction' of reality (or realities).

Indigenous knowledge is also relevant. In the case of the Western Mancha, local knowledge due to poor bridging social capital is highly distrusted by the authorities; this contrasts with Eastern Mancha where scientific and local knowledge are being merged through the initiative of the main irrigation community, acting as a bridge between the water authority and farmers.

Most importantly in the context of collective action is evaluating the openness of the network to learning and absorbing new knowledge, and what is considered possible and/or desirable, which would then help provide opportunity for change. In the three case studies analysed here the main conclusion is that knowledge in itself would not be capable of generating policy change. It is only when knowledge claims are accompanied by the other factors identified above, namely a favourable network structure, which for example is inclusive of regulators and regulated and bolstered by strong bonding and bridging capital, that the potential for knowledge to provide opportunity for change can actually occur. In the case of the Western Mancha rival knowledge claims turned evidence of aquifer overuse into rival claims of whether this was caused by farmers' actions, as claimed by the regulator and environmental NGOs, or by climate change as argued by the farming coalition of irrigation communities and the main farming union. Meanwhile in the case of Eastern Mancha knowledge on the extent of aquifer overuse collected jointly by regulator and regulated has resulted in initial steps to address collective action by farmers to prevent aquifer overuse (for example introducing monitoring and sanctioning of aquifer overabstraction).

EXTERNAL EVENTS PROVIDING 'WINDOWS OF OPPORTUNITY' FOR CHANGING INSTITUTIONAL NORMS

Finally, the chapter concludes with an analysis on the role external events can play in effectively creating 'windows of opportunity' for change, for example to help collective action (Kingdon 1984). It will argue that in our case studies at least, these external events were translated in accordance with the dominant institutional norms in the case study areas, and this heavily conditioned the extent to which these windows of opportunity could be maximized. This section will concentrate only on the Western Mancha since it is the case where collective action has so far proved difficult as a result of internal initiatives, and where external events could trigger or be the catalyst for changes towards collective action. This is compared to Eastern Mancha where internal initiatives alone can help explain policy change toward collective action.

The external event analysed here is an agri-environment programme that was introduced in 1993 by the regional government, which was used as an opportunity to bring funds to the region. A window of opportunity opened when the problem (aquifer overuse) coincided with a policy stream: at the European level the price drop for Common Agricultural Policy (CAP) surplus crops, the introduction of 'accompanying measures', and at the national level, the introduction of a tough and unpopular regime to control aquifer abstractions by the Water Authority which could mean economic losses for the region. This coincided with the political stream, a marriage of convenience between the regional government and the main farming union. Whilst the regional government got farmer support for the coming elections, the introduction of this programme fed on the rent-seeking behaviour of farmers, inhibiting any opportunity for collective action. Indeed the agri-environment programme had the perverse effect of raising farmer expectations to expect subsidies for reducing water use, thus crowding out farmer-level initiatives to deal with the problem of aquifer overuse (see also Varela-Ortega and Sumpsi 1998). An external event, in this case access to external subsidies, possibly prevented an opportunity for social learning, since farmers were cushioned from the economic cost of their own lack of collective action to reverse aquifer drawdown.

This takes us to the last analysis of a key element: the development of institutional norms which become dominant. From the mid-1990s, after the introduction of agri-environment subsidies, the dominant institutional norm was that the problem of aquifer overuse was due to climate change and lack of rainfall, not due to farmer action. In some of our case studies 'climate' (in this case lack of rainfall) became a useful scapegoat, a myth to explain water scarcity. However it is absolutely crucial to differentiate the dominant institutional norms and frames, and the biophysical world. This is based on a contextual analysis of social construction. As Mehta states:

> Hence it might be useful to distinguish between 'real' and 'manufactured' scarcity. Real scarcity is a biophysical phenomenon with biological and social dimensions . . . This complexity is 'obscured' by 'manufactured' scarcity, which is a discursive construct. Scarcity is made out to be 'natural', thus ignoring the anthropogenic areas of culpability. The manufactured nature of scarcity allows controversial schemes . . . to continue to be legitimised. Largely powerful actors benefit from the manufacture. (Mehta 2001: 20, 38)

A concise analysis of the dry and wet climate series for the Upper Guadiana basin shows no dramatic change in climate in recent times (since at least the 1930s). It can be clearly seen that although the period 1980 to 1995 was dry, there was an equally dry period between 1941 and 1959, when rainfall in specific years like 1950 was even lower than in 1995. Note however that the climate series is too short to be able to give scientific opinions on the possibility of climate change. Yet farmers move comfortably between 'real' and 'manufactured' scarcity. Farmers comment positively on the recovery of aquifer levels in recent years, which they attribute to a series of generous rainfall years and the agri-environment plan. This mention of the agri-environment plan indicates a degree of inconsistency in the farmers' institutional norms, since this programme meant farmer abstractions were reduced.

In this case relying on 'natural science' institutional norms serves the farmers' interests in continued aquifer abstractions, without the need to accept responsibility for the situation: rather blame 'the climate'. The farmers' construction of the problem is in marked contrast with other actors in the network on the severity of aquifer overuse. Although a partial recovery of aquifer levels is acknowledged in Western Mancha for recent years, views are still pessimistic. This recovery is seen as ephemeral since it is dependent on the continued supply of subsidies to compensate farmers not to abstract water.

The use of scientific data in the argumentative turn on aquifer overuse cannot be underestimated. In our study it is not hydrological data per se, in terms of water levels or abstraction that is relevant but the use (or misuse or underuse) of hydrological data in arguments and dominant institutional norms between different stakeholders. Western Mancha is the most problematic of the three aquifers studied in terms of overuse and potential to solve this problem. The general perception is that water levels are still going down, because of farmer abstractions. The farmers contest this, and blame drought – the *pertinaz sequia* used by Franco as an integral part of the Old Hydraulic Paradigm. Water level data therefore are like the glass that is 'half full or half empty'; for the farmers the drop in water levels in the mid-1990s was due to drought, for the authorities, as was discussed above, it was due to a peak in illegal abstractions. This dominant institutional norm of manufactured scarcity, together with the co-option of irrigation communities by lobbying organizations like farming unions, have thus halted collective action and instead generated a very successful free-riding on European subsidies, at the expense of social learning concerning the cost of collective inaction.

CONCLUSION

This chapter has sought to analyse the problem of collective action in the case of three aquifers in Spain located in similar socio-economic circumstances, with a complex regulatory framework and similar organizational arrangements. Yet outcomes have been very diverse.

In the case of Western Mancha, actions to halt aquifer overuse have been guaranteed, not through development of self-governance and mutually beneficial collective action by farmers, but rather through subsidies effectively paying for farmer compliance, and in the process crowding out self-initiative and eliminating any potential for social learning on the potential real costs (in terms of increased pumping costs) of continued over-abstraction. Therefore although the substantive outcome has been to halt the drop in aquifer levels, an opportunity has been missed to generate collective action and social learning. Instead farmers have adapted to free-riding on public subsidies to prevent further externalities. This is in stark contrast with Eastern Mancha where collective action by farmers, supported by the water authority and the regional government, has addressed the problem of aquifer overuse by jointly developing strong institutional norms and structures to collectively manage groundwater resources through farmers' action, including sanctions for non-compliance. Campo de Montiel, our third case study, is perhaps exemplary on how, despite the uneasy relationship with the regulator, collective action and self-governance by farmers themselves has been the 'key' ingredient to trigger actions to address groundwater use and self-restraint in water use.

The emphasis in this chapter has been on unpacking the key institutional variables that have in the case of Eastern Mancha favoured collective action; namely the appropriate network strengthened by strong social capital (bonding and bridging), which has then been able to capitalize on knowledge resources both scientific and local to help deliver collective action. Meanwhile this is in marked contrast with the case of Western Mancha where collective action has so far proved impossible and action to solve aquifer over-use, for example in the shape of subsidies, if anything has possibly crowded out any opportunity for self-regulation. Furthermore the way the network has developed has, if anything, strengthened the potential for conflict and hindered the development of social capital, except for enhancing its dark side. In this context knowledge (both scientific and local) becomes a weapon to be used in establishing a dominant institutional norm through a power struggle to dictate what is the 'right' story. Sadly, the winning argument at the moment is collective inaction, since the mismanagement of the aquifer is excused under the dominant cloak of climate change.

ACKNOWLEDGEMENTS

The author would like to gratefully acknowledge the support of the Botín Foundation, who funded the Groundwater Project directed by Professor Ramon Llamas. It was under this project that all information in this chapter was collected and analysed.

11.   The Rönne and Em rivers, Sweden: resilience, networks and bargaining power in water management

Victor Galaz

Consider two river areas plagued by the impacts of institutional fragmentation. Both areas have rather serious water-related environmental problems, such as chemical pollution, eutrophication and the degeneration of biological diversity. In one area however, key actors manage to create networks that overcome this fragmentation, and realize several ambitious water improvement projects. In the second area on the other hand, the networks are far from being able to achieve the joint action needed to tackle water related environmental problems. More interestingly, the two areas do not differ significantly in aspects such as the number or type of actors involved, the political setting, or geophysical features. So the question is: What might explain this difference?

Despite the importance networks might play in natural resource management, many aspects remain theoretically underdeveloped (Scharpf 1993; Macy and Flache 1995; Mizruchi 1994; Dowding 1995). This chapter addresses one such issue, that is, how distributional conflict and differences in bargaining power among actors affect the function and emergence of these networks. I use two strategically selected cases of existing water management networks in southern Sweden, the Rönne and the Em River, to discuss and elaborate not only how differences in bargaining resources affect the joint actions assumed by actors involved in networks, but also how the institutional context of Swedish water management structures this interaction (see Figure 11.1).

NETWORKS, RESILIENCE AND DISTRIBUTIONAL CONFLICT

As will be described further in the next section, Swedish water policy is notably affected by the plague of institutional fragmentation. One important

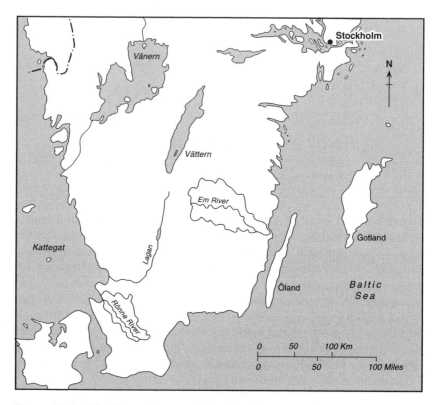

Figure 11.1   The Rönne River and the Em River areas

reason for this fragmentation is the well-recognized lack of congruence between ecological (that is, the catchment area) and administrative boundaries. The fact that water resources more often than not are shared by a number of actors across administrative boundaries forces stakeholders to build networks and create water management common pool resources (CPR)-institutions (cf. Ostrom 1990).

Networks might not only bridge over institutional fragmentation in Swedish water management, but might also have the ability to reduce vulnerability and enhance the resilience of social and ecological systems. Sudden flooding, unexpected nutrient leakage and algae bloom, or unanticipated high levels of toxic pollutants in groundwater resources all indicate the complexity and surprises inherent in hydrological systems (Wilson 2002; Levin 1999). Under certain circumstances, networks in natural resource management are able to tackle and learn from these surprises and provide users with arenas to reduce vulnerability to environmental change (for example climate change) and surprises (for example floods, technological innovations). The reason for this is that they might enhance the capacity of local groups to self-organize, learn and actively adapt to ecological surprises and crises by connecting institutions and organizations across levels and scales, and by facilitating information flows (Olsson et al. 2004).

Network analysis has gained an increasing number of adherents since the 1980s, especially in the field of natural resource management. How often, and under what circumstances, these networks actually contribute to sustainable natural resource management is however a theoretical and empirical issue. Recent work on institutional analysis and institutional change begins to provide a solid theoretical foundation for understanding the conditions needed for individuals to craft their own institutions and enforce these institutions themselves (for example Ostrom et al. 2002).

TAKING DISTRIBUTIONAL CONFLICT SERIOUSLY

Far too often however these social relations and networks are understood as evolving from mutually profitable resource or information transfers (Macy and Flache 1995: 75), or are treated simply as labels or classification schemes with limited explanatory power (Dowding 1995). While parallel aspects such as the role of leadership and economic heterogeneity have been discussed in important later publications in the field, aspects of distributional conflict seem to be both theoretically and empirically underdeveloped (Galaz forthcoming; Ostrom 1990: 188, 213; Ostrom 1998: 15; Hardin 1982: 67–89; Ostrom et al. 2002). This 'blind spot of collective action' is most obvious in cases in related fields of research where institutional emergence and change in the commons is studied as an evolutionary process (Richerson et al. 2002), or using conceptual tools borrowed from immunology and linguistics and hence as self-organizing complex adaptive systems (Janssen 2002).

The difference that differing distributional outcomes make for the possibilities of cooperation has nonetheless received attention from scholars of political institutions, mainly in international and comparative politics. As an example, Fearon (1998) discusses the fact that international cooperation can take various forms and that before states can cooperate and enforce an agreement, they must bargain to decide which one to implement. International cooperation can hence include both a bargaining problem, and an enforcement problem. One important implication from this analysis is not only that though a 'long shadow of the future' might make the enforcement of an agreement easier, it might also give states an incentive to bargain harder, hence making cooperation more difficult to achieve. Frank

Alcock's analysis of the emergence of formalized property rights in fisheries (Alcock 2002) highlights the fact that there are an infinite number of possible distributive outcomes along the Pareto frontier. Hence arguing that actors cooperate and create institutions in an effort to move from status quo situations to the Pareto frontier begs the question of trajectory as possible agreements differ in their distributional consequences (see also Keohane 2001; Knight 1992; Krasner 1991; Heckathorn and Maser 1987).

Though the theoretical arguments in these two examples are based on examples from international and comparative politics, they can be applied to regional or local networks created to overcome institutional fragmentation in natural resource management.

Consider two cities A and B, trying to coordinate their joint use of a common aquifer. While both agree on the fact that networks defining rules of extraction prefer the existing 'open access' situation, they differ on which agreement to reach. That is, while city A prefers an agreement that guarantees its key industries unlimited amounts of water during dry months of the year at the expense of city B, or an agreement that excludes jointly implemented rules to cut down on environmental pollutants leaking into the aquifer, city B prefers the opposite. That is, B prefers an agreement that guarantees its key industries unlimited amounts of water during the dry months of the year at the expense of city A, or an agreement that includes jointly implemented rules to cut down on environmental pollutants leaking into the aquifer. That is, not only do the players have to coordinate their actions to achieve an agreement, but they differ on which of the agreements to choose due to their differing distributional consequences. This might provide a serious obstacle for collective action, and hence the creation of networks (Raiffa 1982; Miller 1992: 36–57).

What if the players have unequal stakes at risk in a possible breakdown of negotiations? Or if they differ in other ways that systematically gives a type of player a distributional advantage in the creation of networks? Once we introduce these aspects, attributes referring to the actors' bargaining power, such as credibility and reputation, become fundamental (Baland and Platteau 1996: 85ff; Knight 1992). Consider a case where one of the cities in the example above (say B), also has access to a large lake that might be exploited as a freshwater source. This fact could be used as a bargaining advantage as the city can credibly commit to withdraw from existing networks if its demands are not met. Representatives from city A might prefer the existence of a network to overcome the present destructive 'open access' situation, even if the distributional consequence is to their disadvantage.

Differently put, even if shared norms of reciprocity might develop between natural resource users creating networks, they might be skewed to the advantage of certain 'stronger' actors (Calvert 1989; Galaz forthcoming). This skewness is possible if (1) cooperation with different distributional conse-quences is possible, and (2) one of the actors is able to credibly commit to their preferred strategy (cf. Knight 1992).

Though the argument might sound like a theoretical artefact, this phe-nomenon is nonetheless potentially present when natural resource users differ in both social and economical power. It is not difficult to find real-world examples in which poorer segments of the population have a vital interest in the preservation of common properties, while the rich do not have that concern because they have exit options available (Baland and Platteau 1996: 86; Galaz 2004; Dayton-Johnson 2000; Varughese and Ostrom 2001).

The words 'may', 'could' and 'under certain circumstances' are import-ant here. Though differences in bargaining power might affect the emer-gence and function of networks, the argument should not be understood as a deterministic one. Stokke's chapter in this book is one example of how collective action can be achieved despite unequal distribution of costs and benefits. Specifying under what circumstances social and economical het-erogeneity negatively affects the function of important natural resource management networks is a major and important research task. What this implies for the networks created in Swedish water management is the subject of the next part of this chapter.

INSTITUTIONAL FRAGMENTATION IN SWEDISH WATER MANAGEMENT

As mentioned above, Swedish water policy is notably affected by the plague of institutional fragmentation. One important reason for this is the obvious and well-recognized lack of congruence between ecological (that is, the catchment area) and administrative boundaries. The fact that water resources more often than not are shared by a number of these actors across administrative boundaries forces stakeholders to cooperate to build net-works and create water management CPR institutions (cf. Ostrom 1990). Hence despite detailed state regulation and formal central control at national, regional and local level, Swedish water politics is profoundly dependent on the voluntary contribution and cooperation of water users such as municipalities, county administrations, industry and other stake-holders to monitor and to deal with concrete quantity and quality problems. This remains a fact despite the present implementation of the European Water Framework Directive (Galaz 2005).

One typical problem that arises from this fragmented institutional setting is nitrogen and phosphorous leakage from agriculture, industry and airborne pollutants. This leakage creates costly water quality problems especially in southern parts of Sweden with resulting eutrophication (that is, algae bloom), massive death of bottom fauna, too high concentrations of nitrate in groundwater and a continuous threat of a complete death of the bay's marine life (Wittgren et al. 2000).

ACTORS AND NETWORKS

The type and number of actors involved in managing Swedish water resources is impressive. The reason is that the sources of pollution stem from various activities such as municipally owned water treatment plants, industry, farming activities and other diffuse polluters such as individual households. The number of actors increases drastically if we add non-polluters with an interest in the resource such as fishing organizations, recreational interests, environmental NGOs, municipalities, universities and others. Empirical studies do however give a clear picture of the main actors in the networks: municipalities, county administrations (Länsstyrelse in Swedish), farmer organizations, environmental NGOs, industrial interests and fishing organizations (Gustafsson 1996).

Some players however are more important than others. In Sweden there is a long history of local governance which makes the municipalities the key actors in Swedish water politics (Dobers 1997; Burström 2000). These actors have a constitutional responsibility to attend to the common interest of their residents, and are vested with tax power for this purpose. Since the 1990s the Swedish state has transferred an increasingly heavy burden of responsibilities for implementing national policies, water management issues in particular (Lundqvist 2004a: 29f; Dobers 1997; Burström 2000: 42f). Municipalities are hence key players in Swedish water networks.

Other key players are the county administrations which have the authority to issue environmental permits to large-sized plants and facilities, thus having important supervisory responsibilities (Lundqvist 2004a: 30). These governmental bodies at regional and local level do not possess sufficient authority, resources and knowledge to effect the achievement of water policy intentions (Lundqvist 2004a; cf. Bresser et al. 1994). This is why the range of actors involved in creating water management institutions includes more than governmental bodies.

These voluntary created water management networks often interact within self-maintained CPR institutions (in Swedish: *vattenkommittéer*, *vattenvårdsförbund*, *vattendragsgrupper* and so on). These are considered as important actors by Swedish authorities (SOU 2002: 105; SOU 1997: 155) and hence could easily be added to the number of case studies that pay a tribute to the creation of sustainable CPR institutions (cf. Ostrom 1990). By 1993 there were over 50 associations, varying in size from managing big lakes and large rivers, to small catchments in southern Sweden (Lundqvist 2004a: 36; Gustafsson 1996).

DISTRIBUTIONAL CONFLICT IN SWEDISH WATER MANAGEMENT

Even though cooperation is required to manage the institutional fragmentation inherent in water resource management, there are issues of distributional conflict that water users in Sweden simply cannot ignore. The issue at hand is the scope of water management CPR institutions, that is, how ambitious cooperation between the actors should be. The scope of these institutions varies considerably in Sweden, the lowest scope implying CPR institutions designed with the sole purpose of monitoring water quality, and the highest including various sorts of water management projects, pilot initiatives such as promoting cooperation projects among farmers, and costly monitoring initiatives including Geographic Information Systems (GIS) technology.

Choosing the proper scope is however far from an uncomplicated task and the reason for this is quite straightforward. While the costs of creating and maintaining CPR institutions in general are paid by water users themselves without government support according to the 'polluter pays' principle, the benefits are distributed differently. Take eutrophication: while high-polluting upstream municipalities and industry tend to be the actors with the highest financial burden in creating water management institutions, they receive only limited benefits from any attempt to tackle nutrient flows. The opposite applies to water users such as existing fishing associations, environmental NGOs and downstream low-polluting municipalities.

Consider the choice facing a representative (usually an environmental chief inspector) from an upstream farming-intensive high-polluting municipality when it is time to decide how ambitious cooperation should be. If we assume that actors are rational and self-interested, the answer is obvious: as low as possible. The reason is that the costs for this municipality will be high (according to the 'polluter pays' principle) but the benefits low due to the municipality's geographical location in the catchment area. The opposite applies to actors such as environmental NGOs that face a different choice situation with high benefits but low costs. This results in two different coalitions of water users in Swedish water networks, with diverging preferences over institutional choice. The first coalition prefers

Water user		Expected benefits of institutional change	Expected costs of institutional change	Preference order institutional scope
Upstream municipality	High-polluting	Low	High	Low > High
Upstream municipality	Low-polluting	Low	Low	High > Low
Downstream municipality	High-polluting	High	High	High > Low
Downstream municipality	Low-polluting	High	Low	n.a.
Industry		Low	High	Low > High
Farmer's organization		Low	High	Low > High
County administration		High	Low	High > Low
Fishing organizations		High	Low	High > Low
Environmental NGOs		High	Low	High > Low

Figure 11.2   Institutional choice and preferences among actors regarding the Rönne River

a less costly (that is, ambitious) scope of the existing CPR regime, and the second a more ambitious one. While the argument might sound far too theoretical and at worst cynical, this conflict of preferences over scope is confirmed by interviews and documents collected in the Rönne River case during 2001 and 2004 (to be described below).

Figure 11.2 summarizes the findings from interviews, documents and meeting proceedings. The table illustrates the preferences for institutional scope in the Rönne catchment area for a selected number of stakeholders. Expected benefits and costs are rough theoretical estimates of the benefits and costs of the change of existing CPR institutions. As an example, the reason fishing organizations receive a high benefit is that their members would benefit substantially from improvement of the quality of water. The group is however not a high polluter, which implies that its costs according to the 'polluter pays' principle are low. The preference order found empirically is High > Low, where > means 'preferred to'.

As can be seen in Figure 11.2, there is indeed a difference in what the different parties want to achieve within their commonly created network. The consequences of this difference are the subject of the next section.

KEEPING AMBITION DOWN: THE CASES

As discussed earlier, two strategically selected cases of existing water management networks in southern Sweden, the Rönne and the Em rivers, will be used to discuss and elaborate how differences in bargaining resources affect the joint actions assumed by actors involved in networks (from Galaz forthcoming). The Rönne River catchment is the second-largest catchment in Skåne, the most southern region of Sweden. The catchment covers 1900 km² and drains westwards through the Rönne River, with its tributaries, into the bay of Skälderviken in the North Sea near the city of Ängelholm. Fourteen municipalities are more or less within the catchment, of which Klippan and Ängelholm are the largest. Eight municipalities, one county administration, a number of industries, the Farmers' Union and NGOs cooperate in this watershed.

Since the 1990s the Rönne River has experienced several water-related environmental problems: flooding, periods of drought, acidification, eutrophication, pesticide and metal pollution, and threats to biodiversity along the streams, to mention the most important ones. Eutrophication is one of the more serious problems in the area compared to other parts of Sweden (Miljömålsrådet 2004: 38ff). The sources of pollution are several, and in general are the result of human activity such as diffuse pollution from agriculture and point-source pollution from municipal and industrial activities.

The scope of the only existing CPR regime that could tackle these problems is, despite serious environmental problems, remarkably low. The only activity assumed by the Rönne River Committee (RRC) – created as early as in the 1970s – is monitoring water quality (see Figure 11.3). More precisely, CPR institutions are designed to organize and distribute the costs of a joint measurement programme, which is the lowest level of ambition required by law (Gustafsson 1996). According to the interviewees, what drives cooperation in the RRC is the interest to reap the financial benefits of coordinating a joint monitoring programme, instead of realizing monitoring activities individually as required by law. The total cost of such a programme is approximately 400 000 Swedish kronor (~40 000 Euro) yearly. The sum is low compared to the measures needed to halt the degradation of valuable water resources in the area (71 million Swedish kronor according to a report). Put differently, the parties involved in the creation

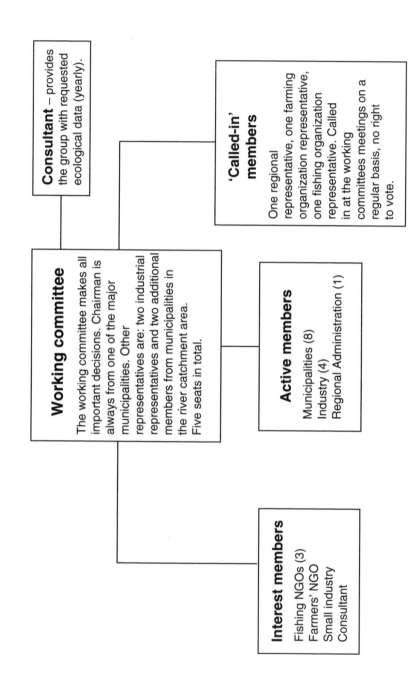

Consultant – provides the group with requested ecological data (yearly).

Working committee

The working committee makes all important decisions. Chairman is always from one of the major municipalities. Other representatives are: two industrial representatives and two additional members from municipalities in the river catchment area. Five seats in total.

'Called-in' members

One regional representative, one farming organization representative, one fishing organization representative. Called in at the working committees meetings on a regular basis, no right to vote.

Active members

Municipalities (8)
Industry (4)
Regional Administration (1)

Interest members

Fishing NGOs (3)
Farmers' NGO
Small industry
Consultant

Figure 11.3   The Rönne River Committee

of the CPR regime have decided to limit their joint activity at the lowest possible level, thereby halting the possible protection of the resource.

A comparison with another similar committee in southern Sweden, the Em River Project (ERP) created in 1997, reveals the obvious lack of adaptive response from the RRC (see Figure 11.4). The Em River is in the southeast of the country, and the catchment area is 4500 km² and the river system, including the tributaries, is about 800 km in length. The mouth of the river is at sea level in the Baltic. Eight municipalities, two county administrative boards, the Farmers' Union, NGOs, fishing water owners, angling organizations and local history associations cooperate in this watershed (Liedberg-Jönsson 2004). The ERP does not only realize monitoring activities, but has also implemented various investigations and projects to tackle eutrophication, metal pollution and floods such as a water flow management plan, inventories of natural areas and cultural history, and support to farmer-governed 'watercourse groups' to reduce nutrient leakage. What is interesting here is hence that while water users in the ERP have managed to create institutions to monitor and manage practically the same environmental crises such as flooding, metal pollution and eutrophication, the RRC still focuses exclusively on monitoring activities.

It is important to note that both these two committees have repeated working group meetings – including municipalities, county authorities and industrial representatives – and yearly public meetings, which indicates the existence of active water management networks. One important difference exists however. Though both committees have continuous contact with non-governmental organizations such as environmental NGOs, farmers' organizations and fishing interests, the participation of these groups is far more formalized and extensive in the case of the Em River. More precisely, unlike the RRC, these groups are an active part of the work assumed in the board and the working groups within the ERP (Galaz forthcoming).

Why do these networks look so different, despite the fact that they are facing similar problems within a similar institutional setting? As discussed in the following sections, the fact that the joint action needed embeds distributional conflict provides an important explanation.

BLOCKING CHANGE

Interestingly enough, several attempts have been made to change the scope chosen by the participants in the Rönne River Committee. According to interviewees with stakeholders in the Rönne River area – and this is the only subject that has led to disagreement among the parties – there have been a number of attempts to change the institutional solution chosen by the

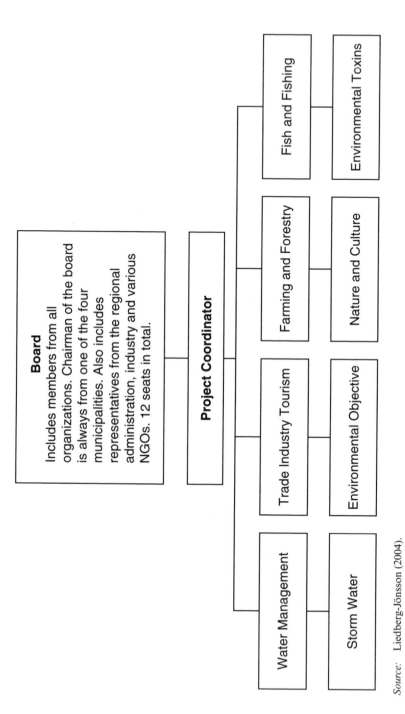

Board

Includes members from all organizations. Chairman of the board is always from one of the four municipalities. Also includes representatives from the regional administration, industry and various NGOs. 12 seats in total.

Project Coordinator

Water Management

Trade Industry Tourism

Farming and Forestry

Fish and Fishing

Storm Water

Environmental Objective

Nature and Culture

Environmental Toxins

Source: Liedberg-Jönsson (2004).

Figure 11.4 The Em River Basin Stakeholder Association with eight task groups

participants in the Rönne River Committee (RRC). This is confirmed by records of meeting proceedings that show that this has happened on at least three occasions in the 1990s. The most important attempt was in 1993 when the environmental NGO in the area, at one of the yearly public meetings of the committee, suggested a more ambitious cooperation along the river. This attempt resulted in one report that included a description of the status of water-related environmental problems in the area, but also a concrete proposal of measures to achieve an improvement of the resource. This report was presented in 1995. The RRC also put together a working group (henceforth WG) of representatives from a small number of key municipalities in the area, and one representative from the agricultural sector. The purpose of this group – that existed for a couple of years in the mid-1990s – was to coordinate their actions and find the financial resources necessary to fund the measures suggested by the report. This goal was never realized.

The intriguing issue at this point is why the several attempts to change the scope of the CPR institutions were not successful. There are several reasons why this is puzzling. Firstly, water resources in the area were clearly deteriorating – a fact that municipal decision-makers and other users clearly were aware of. Secondly, a proposal on how to deal with the problem and execute the necessary measures based on solid data was on the table. The cost to be distributed was 6 million Swedish kronor over a period of 12 years. Thirdly, everybody in the WG agreed on the necessity to implement measures, but worried about how to finance the project. Fourthly and lastly, as the documents show, a full organizational structure was set up, including a political board, and a working group including consultants and cooperation with other water management groups to secure valuable input.

Interviews with the participants in the WG does not give us a clear picture of why the initiative to change the scope of the CPR institutions lost momentum. While some of the interviewees point out that the reason the WG failed to change the scope of cooperation was the lack of an organizational action plan, others point out that the municipalities involved lacked the political will and financial resources to realize such ambitious cooperation. Others claim not to remember why coordination eventually failed in the WG.

IDENTIFYING KEY PLAYERS IN NETWORKS

The picture presented by the actors involved is hence ambiguous. An analysis based on our earlier discussion on distributional conflict and bargaining power does however help us to push the analysis further. Thinking in terms of actor constellations, it is interesting to note that industrial representatives never took part in the discussions of the WG, despite the fact that the group not only is an important user of water resources, but also is one of the most important polluters of water resources in the area. Why this group was not represented has a simple answer: not only did they not want to, but the other participants knew it. The question is how this might have affected the only serious attempt to change the scope of the RRC.

From a bargaining perspective, the expected refusal to participate in the WG indicates that industry has sent a clear signal to the other actors in the area that it refuses to participate on issues that imply an increased scope (and costs) of cooperation. That this signal is understood by the rest of the actors in the network is not only confirmed by interviews with industrial representatives, and an impressive number of other actors in the RRC such as chief environmental inspectors in municipalities in the area, but also by records of meeting proceedings that date back to the very emergence of the CPR institutions. As is clearly stated in the first meeting when the constitution of the RRC was discussed in the end of the 1970s:

> § 6. A constitution draft for the committee was presented. The following changes were decided upon: Fifth section, 4 § cut out – and non-profit organizations . . . The scope of the undertakings of the committee was discussed. B Stone [Company B] wanted a note to the protocol that no responsibility in addition to those presented in the draft, ought to be prescribed.
> (Protocol 1, 1977 from Galaz forthcoming)

Hence industrial interests have credibly committed to their most preferred institutional solution. The implications should not be underestimated. Actors with an interest in mobilizing existing networks to enhance the scope of the CPR institution are simply discouraged from doing so. The reason is that these actors are likely to prefer a low-ambition CPR institution to a non-existing one.

While this does not seem to apply to NGOs in the area, it certainly seems to apply to two important chief environmental inspectors. As becomes clear in the interviews, not only do chief environmental inspectors want to do more, but they are unable to do so given the limitations in the CPR institution. Industry again is of main interest here. As the chief environmental inspector in Municipality B puts it:

> Q: What is your opinion; could these companies lower their pollution level further? Or have they reached the limit . . .
> S5: They should be able to lower it further, yes, that is my opinion . . . What I find most unpleasant though, personally, are all those substances that we don't know anything about.
> Q: What kind of substances do you mean?

S5: Sometimes you can tell there is something in the water, but you don't have a clue what it is all about. I think that is the unpleasant thing. Measuring nutrients and phosphor and temperature, that is pretty easy. But stable organic compounds are created, and we are not certain of what happens. Industry B has very complex water, and what happens when you mix A with B, what is the result C, and what is C?

Q: Is it possible to see any effects in the ecology directly, or is it just . . .

S5: There are things you just don't know why. That I think is the most troublesome thing.

(Interview, Municipality B)

Discussing the same issue, another chief environmental inspector discusses water pollution problems related to industrial activities in Municipality B:

Q: Your municipality receives a large amount of pollution from upstream industrial activity . . . Is that a big problem?

S9: No, not in the way you think it is, but it's there. It's a large industry with an extensive activity that deals with a lot of chemicals, and has always done so. Sewage treatment plants are nowadays being constructed, and larger and larger security measures to deal with that as well. And there are a lot of old debts in dams, in the mud and in the lakes surrounding the R-stream, and in the dams on the outskirts of Municipality B. It is not a problem that you think of on a daily basis. But if you look at the results [in reports], you can see an obvious effect.

Q: Could industrial interests upstream do more to lower their pollution levels?

S9: My spontaneous reaction when it comes to Industry A1 is, do we really have a clue about all the chemicals they deal with, and all the chemical compounds that could be part of it, what do we really know about this? It is such a complex technology that is used there, that frightens me, since it is a chemical industry.

(S9, Municipality A)

As the interviews show, both chief environmental inspectors in the two municipalities that host industrial activities are worried about the impacts of chemical pollution on the river basin. The issue here is not that this pollution is illegal – because it is not – but rather a recognition that the RRC could and should jointly and proactively try to get a better grip of its diffusion and possible ecological impacts. This however has never been an issue discussed seriously among the cooperating parties in the RRC.

As discussed earlier, working together within natural resource management networks can be a highly strategic enterprise. If the actors know that institutional change depends on participation from a number of actors clearly signalling that any institutional change to their disadvantage is unacceptable, this could efficiently block any attempt to change the activities assumed by the participants of the network. As discussed above, this is indicated by interviews and documents in the two case study areas.

EXCLUDING POSSIBLE EXPLANATIONS

But there could be other reasons to why these two networks differ so much. The arguments and the evidence presented so far might seem to be determined by the model and the theoretical assumptions presented at the outset. A closer analysis does however indicate that key factors relating to both social and ecological features in the areas do not differ significantly.

First of all, the constellation of actors involved in the two cases does not differ in number, or in type. The only difference in the constellation among the parties cooperating in the studied river basins is that the Em River includes two central agencies instead of one, and only one industrial representative. This representative however represents an organization that totals around 50 small and large companies.

Another important aspect that might seriously affect the incentives actors face to achieve a higher level of ambition is of course the seriousness of water-related environmental problems. A serious crisis in the ecological system might trigger institutional innovation and change as natural resource users attempt to adapt to a changed ecological reality (for example Folke et al. 2003). To achieve this potentially complicated comparison in a simple and comprehensive way, a survey was sent out to the county administration in charge of environmental monitoring in the respective areas. The two officials in charge were asked to grade the existence and seriousness of several water-related environmental problems. The survey shows that the problems in the Rönne River are considered – in most cases – more serious by responsible authorities than they are in the Em River. This is the case for problems such as eutrophication, groundwater pollution by pesticides, threats to aquatic biodiversity, extreme oxygen deficit, and temporary water dry-outs (Galaz forthcoming).

Furthermore the differences in water use do not differ in such a way as to explain the difference in scope between the two cases. A heavy dependence on water resources for domestic use – just as an example – might provide strong incentives for municipalities to protect and drive institutional change to a higher ambition level. Another advantage in comparing the distribution of water use is that it provides an indicator of the importance of different sectors in the various municipalities (that is, industrial vs. agricultural activities). The reason is that diffuse pollution from the agricultural sector is more complicated to tackle, which might affect the incentives actors face in the two areas. If we study the mean value in water use, the differences between the municipalities is minor. The only difference seems to be that municipalities in the RRC use a slightly larger share of their water resources in agricultural activities (19.8 per cent), compared to municipalities in the Em River (14.4 per cent).

Another important difference between municipalities could be how much they contribute to pollution. A group of actors that are more homogenous in terms of pollution level might have a better chance of achieving collective action, and hence creating CPR institutions with a more ambitious scope (cf. Baland and Platteau 1996: 160f). This is not the case in the Em River. Just as in the Rönne river, the Em River has a constellation of actors which contribute very differently to pollution levels in the river (from 3 to 29 per cent in the Rönne River and from 1 to 34 per cent in the Em River).

The third alternative explanation deals with the financial strains facing the different municipalities. The 'common sense' argument from stakeholders themselves and water politics experts in Sweden (for example Gustafsson 1995) is that municipalities with financial problems probably are less interested in creating ambitious CPR institutions to protect water resources. Three indicators of municipal financial strain have been used in Galaz (forthcoming). The first – the average municipal tax – gives an indication of the economic potential of the municipality. A high percentage in municipal tax indicates a less wealthy municipality, just like the second indicator – the unemployment rate. A high rate implies a more pressured financial situation. The third indicator – that is, average taxable income for municipal inhabitants – also gives an estimate of the financial situation in the municipality. The higher the income, the better the municipal economy. The three indicators are often used to describe the financial situation of Swedish municipalities (for example SOU 2002: 88, 53, 72, 355), and are possible to analyse on a longer term thanks to official data presented by Statistics Sweden (Statistiska centralbyrån). As shown in Galaz (forthcoming) the average municipal tax is in fact lower, and the average taxable income slightly higher for the municipalities in the Rönne River compared to the Em River case. This indicates that the financial situation is better in the case of the Rönne River, compared to the Em River area.

COMPARING AND SUMMING UP

Distributional conflict and bargaining power seemingly make an important difference to the creation and maintenance of natural resource management networks and to the institutions designed by actors intended to create and maintain trust. This seems to be the reason why actors in the Rönne case do not manage to achieve cooperation to tackle the water environmental problems in the area. To summarize, the reasons why bargaining power seems to matter are the following (from Galaz forthcoming).

Firstly, the county administration and all but one of the municipalities agree that the scope of existing CPR institutions is far too limited considering the problems facing water resources in the catchment area. Secondly, a vast majority of the water users identify three industries in the catchment area as key water users needed to make cooperation in the catchment area efficient. Industrial representatives themselves do acknowledge their crucial role in catchment cooperation, which gives them a bargaining advantage compared to other users such as environmental NGOs.

Thirdly, industrial interests repeatedly signal that any costly change to the scope of existing CPR institutions is unacceptable. As one representative puts it: 'Are we really supposed to pay to prevent discharges from completely other sources? We do what we can and none of the industries are stingy, we think that it is up to other actors, but we are ready to take part of the discussions.' This unwillingness among key actors to change the scope of CPR institutions is a well-known fact among practically all water users in the area.

Moreover data from all existing and voluntarily created Swedish water management CPR institutions indicate that this mechanism might be at work at a national level. The scope and ambition of water management institutions in Sweden differ substantially with the kind of parties involved in water management networks. The commitment of industrial interests not to accept participation in too ambitious CPR institutions seems to block the institutional change needed to achieve a more adaptive response to water resource problems (Galaz forthcoming).

Interestingly enough, this is not the case in the Em River case. Firstly, as interviews show, industrial representatives are less important for cooperation than in the Rönne River case. That the Em River area is characterized by a high number of both small and medium-sized industries, instead of a few large ones as in the Rönne River case, is one probable reason. Second, the preference order (Low scope > High scope) seems to be the reverse for the large water-consuming papermill industry in the Em River as it benefits substantially from some of the projects assumed collectively by the ERP. The reason is not only that this industry is downstream (and hence dependent on the cooperation and goodwill of upstream users) but also that it is required by law to shut down the papermill if water flows are too low in the Em River. These facts make a non-learning strategy from this large industry non-credible as it benefits substantially from cooperating with upstream users, compared to the Rönne River where industrial representatives can pull out from cooperation without great losses.

CONCLUSIONS

Networks are important for natural resource management. This is even truer in countries and policy areas defined by the problems that follow from institutional fragmentation such as Swedish water management. The main thrust of the argument in this chapter has been the following: despite the important role that networks play in mitigating the problem of opportunism involved in single exchanges, they may at the same time reflect the asymmetrical bargaining power relations between the natural resource users involved.

The two presented case studies seem to be a good example of how differences in bargaining power can seriously affect the emergence and function of natural resource management networks. Networks facing a degradation of the natural resource they are supposed to manage might be too rigid to adapt to environmental change due to distributional conflict and differences in bargaining power. As discussed above, industrial interests can credibly commit to withdraw from existing networks if the scope is changed to their disadvantage. Representatives from key municipalities wanting to do more about water-related environmental problems seem to prefer the existence of a low-ambition network, to the alternative of no network at all, even if the distributional consequence is to their disadvantage. Hence though shared norms have developed among water actors in this particular area, they are skewed to the advantage of actors with a strong bargaining position.

Hence the answer to our original question of why two seemingly similar settings produced networks with such different functions is, in short: asymmetrical bargaining power. But this answer is only partial if we exclude the important role the institutional setting plays in structuring the interaction of water actors. As discussed earlier, the institutional fragmentation of Swedish water politics creates serious collective action problems that eventually result in networks that are far too unmotivated to tackle sometimes serious water environmental problems.

As discussed in this chapter, the fact that institutional change embeds distributional conflict results in networks that are unable to achieve the institutional change needed to tackle a complex and uncertain hydrological system. The present vulnerability and the increasing stress from human activities and climate change on scarce water resources around the world guarantees that this will remain an issue of great importance in the future.

ACKNOWLEDGEMENTS

This study was performed within the Swedish Water Management Research Program (VASTRA), which is financed by the Swedish Foundation for

Strategic Environmental Research (MISTRA). The author is grateful to various researchers in VASTRA, the Department of Political Science, Göteborg University the Centre for Transdisciplinary Environmental Research (CTM), Stockholm University and to the editors of this book for comments on earlier drafts.

12. Conclusion

Yvonne Rydin

This book has presented nine case studies of institutional arrangements for natural resource management, five of them broadly dealing with landscape and nature conservation and four concerning various aspects of water management. They are diverse in their locations, with three British cases, three Norwegian cases and three others from Sweden, Spain and Zimbabwe. However they have in common a concern with analysing natural resource management from the perspective of the involvement of stakeholders in networks and with understanding those networks in terms of not only the linkages between actors but also the cultural aspects, such as norms, values, agreements and everyday routines of practices. We have been particularly interested in how relationships of trust, reciprocity and mutuality – captured in the concept of social capital – may be helpful in explaining the effectiveness of the institutional arrangements for natural resource management in these cases. We have also sought to explore the role that knowledge resources have played as well as the impact of factors external to the network, two key aspects that the institutional capacity framework highlights.

In this chapter we bring together our conclusions on the nine case studies and what they reveal for our understanding of natural resource management and the appropriate institutional structures for facilitating sustainable management. We begin by summarizing the findings of our case studies in terms of the kinds of networks we found in our fieldwork, and how effectively these networks fostered collective action. We also address the question of what makes these networks effective (or not), in terms of both strategy development and implementation of such strategies. Then we return to themes raised in Chapters 1 and 2 and address the key issues of policy integration, the persistence of fragmentation and the democratic challenge involved in natural resource management.

VARIETIES OF NETWORKS

Our case studies had been selected on the basis that there was some *a priori* evidence of networking activity to try and manage natural resources and prevent free-riding. Therefore it is not surprising that in each case there was indeed a form of network in place. These networks broadly sought to bring together actors across boundaries of scale, level, territory and function. They generally involved both resource users (often through representation of users) and those with policy or regulatory authority for the resource. Links were made from local to central government, often through governmental agencies. Local representation was a key factor in all cases, generally through formally elected local government but also through other forms of community representation, particularly in more rural and in developing country contexts. Above all, the networks sought to handle the complex challenges of the multiple interests inherent in use, enjoyment and hence management of natural resources.

However a broad acknowledgement of the existence of networks in each case disguises the variety involved in these cases and in the outcomes of network-building. For example the scale of inclusion and the depth of involvement varied considerably from relatively low-level consultation in the Lake District CAMS processes and tokenistic reference to local communities in Mafungautsi, through to situations where engagement was in-depth and involved devolved power over strategy development, as with the New Forest Committee and SVR. In some cases, structures were fairly simple with all stakeholders involved in a main committee, while in others there were complex structures to manage the involvement of the different actors in ways appropriate to their interests and capacities (as in Cannock Chase). Where the formal structure was quite simple, this often hid a complexity in informal networks (as in SVR), whereas other cases showed little evidence of informal networks beyond these formal structures. And, as we discuss below, there was great variety in the role that formal political actors played, with elected politicians such as mayors being highly significant in all our Norwegian cases (Setesdal Vesthei-Ryfylkeheiane, Morsa and Rondane) whereas officials played a much more prominent role in most British cases.

There was a somewhat imperfect distinction between those cases where the focus of networking was to develop a strategy for resource management and those where the ambitions of the network went beyond document production to immediate changes in behaviour of resource users. The water management networks in particular saw considerable involvement of direct water users, whether many small farming interests (as in Morsa and Castilla-La Mancha) or quasi-monopoly water utilities and industrial interests (as in the Lake District and Southern Swedish cases). This raises the issue of how far the networks directly resulted in changed behaviour by such users. In most of the landscape and nature conservation cases (except perhaps in Mafungautsi), the networks' engagement with direct users was more indirect, through representatives or via bodies who themselves managed or influenced such users. This raises the rather different issue of how networks were able to influence these bodies' decision-making and hence indirectly the behaviour of resource users. As we will discuss further below, the links between the activities of networks and implementation are complex.

Our main concern in studying such networks though is to understand how they foster collective action. We are particularly interested in the relationships between the nature of these networks and the level of collective action. We have examined this in the different cases but to help bring our results together, it is useful to provide an overview of how our cases fit along a spectrum of collective action. Figure 12.1 illustrates this approach, plotting our cases along this spectrum. At one end, there is a denial of the need for collective action due to free-riding. This may be due to the fact that free-riding is not yet impacting on stakeholders, so that the need for collective action is only predicted as arising in the future. Any collective action in such cases would need to be anticipatory. Or the need for collective action may be actively suppressed by certain interests, particularly powerful interests already active within networks. Further along the spectrum lie cases where there is overt conflict over resource use. As one moves towards greater collective action, this conflict is recognized as an issue, as a problem in itself. Further down the spectrum, collective action takes the form of agreeing and even committing to a common problem frame for resource management and, finally, to a common policy frame for action on such management. As Figure 12.1 shows, our case studies lie at several points along this spectrum. The next question is then to understand the various factors that generate this pattern of response to collective action problems.

NETWORKS, COLLECTIVE ACTION AND SOCIAL CAPITAL

Our starting point for developing a framework to understand networking for collective action was to consider the nature of the linkages in terms of different kinds of social capital. In particular, the social capital literature encourages us to distinguish between bonding and bridging capital, with a more recent emphasis on considering specific combinations of these as another distinct form, bracing capital (see Chapter 2). Considering the pattern set out in Figure 12.1 against the evidence we have of bridging and bonding capital suggests some clear patterns.

The over-riding importance of bridging capital in creating such networks was immediately apparent. Among our cases, the ones which demonstrated weak (Lake District and Rönne River) or absent (Mafungautsi) bridging capital were also those at the end of the spectrum furthest away from

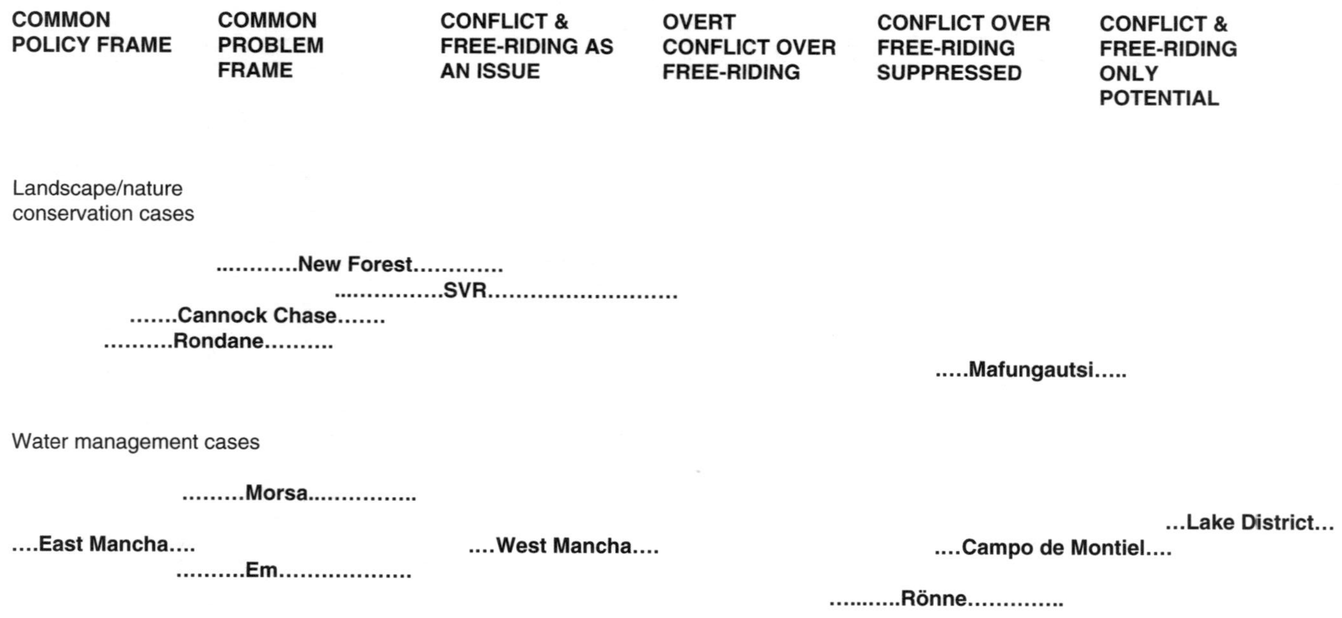

COMMON POLICY FRAME	COMMON PROBLEM FRAME	CONFLICT & FREE-RIDING AS AN ISSUE	OVERT CONFLICT OVER FREE-RIDING	CONFLICT OVER FREE-RIDING SUPPRESSED	CONFLICT & FREE-RIDING ONLY POTENTIAL
Landscape/nature conservation cases					
	..........New Forest..........				
	..........SVR..........				
	......Cannock Chase........				
	..........Rondane..........				
				....Mafungautsi.....	
Water management cases					
	......Morsa..............				
	......West Mancha....				
				....Campo de Montiel.....	
					...Lake District...
...East Mancha....					
	....Em.............				
			..........Rönne..........		

Figure 12.1   The collective action spectrum

collective action. In all other cases bridging capital was in evidence and an active component of the networks. In some cases the bridging capital within the network built on connections that already existed between at least some of the parties. For example in the New Forest there had already been some bridging in an attempt to resolve conflicts over tree-felling before the New Forest Committee came into existence. However the networks went beyond existing contacts, building new bridging capital by bringing together actors who were generally unlike each other and not in frequent contact with each other. Furthermore such bridging activity was not indiscriminate. There was an emphasis on involving relevant stakeholders, including those from outside the locality. For example in the Morsa case there was specific mention of the selective linking of national government and local landowners into the network.

Bridging capital is therefore an essential element within networks, but it seems that while such bridging links can be quite easily created, they can also be rather superficial in character. Making the links is only a first step towards effective collective action. One suggestion might be that networks themselves need to be characterized by bonding not bridging links, that is, strong rather than weak ties. However our cases did not suggest that strong bonding capital within the networks was an important factor. Rather what seemed to be important was selective links from the network to other sites of strong bonding capital. So that in the New Forest, bonding capital was in evidence among the commoners' community and this was an important resource for the New Forest Committee. Again in Rondane, bonding within political parties was harnessed by the network developing the Partial County Plan and, in SVR, the bonding of the mayors' network was drawn upon by the broader and looser networks. One notable weakness of the CAMS processes in the Lake District was the tendency to try and enrol active individuals from various organizations into the bridging networks, rather than build connections to strongly bonded organizations; that is, the individuals already known to the Environment Agency did not necessarily have strong connections to their own organizations.

The cases where there was very direct engagement with local landowners and resources users, notably the Morsa, Mafungautsi and Spanish cases, suggested that care needed to be taken to ensure that the 'dark side' of bonding capital did not influence the collective action. In Morsa efforts were made to build links with local landowners and farmers both directly and through representative organizations. This seemed to be effective. However in the Zimbabwean and Spanish cases strong bonding capital within individual villages was noted alongside a lack of connection between villages. This hindered the building of collective action and allowed a degree of free-riding to continue unchecked.

So it seems as if successful networking requires bridging capital within the network and links out to certain key actors (whether national government or local resource users). But it also relies on strong bonding capital, not within the network itself but in the organizations that are being linked. It would seem that this allows the individual in the network to be fully representative of his or her 'home' organization, since all within that organization are bonded together through strong norms and internal ties of trust and reciprocity. It probably also allows the deliberations and decisions of the network to carry greater weight with the individual organizations, since they are conveyed by an individual already bonded to his or her own organization. This combination of extensive but not indiscriminate bridging capital within the network and bonding capital in selected sites outside the network suggests that the composite bracing capital concept has some explanatory power.

There is however a difficulty in relying just on social capital as an explanation of how networks contribute to collective action. This difficulty lies in the tendency to see social capital (links between actors) as both a causal factor in network building and evidence of the collective action itself. There is often a circularity apparent in social capital analyses. The way out of this is to recognize the dynamics involved in network-building and the subsequent collective actions. It also suggests a need to look beyond the identification and classification of links according to social capital categories to see the importance of different factors in building effective networks.

BUILDING EFFECTIVE NETWORKS

In Figure 12.2 we set out in diagrammatic form our analysis of the factors that link networking to collective action. We understand such collective action in a number of ways. There is simple co-working within a network, the most basic form of collective action. Then there is working together to develop a strategy or plan. This is worthwhile, but clearly any such document needs to be implemented through changed decision-making and action by actors; this is the ultimate collective action that natural resource management aims at. First we discuss the factors that influence patterns of networking and the links with strategy development, before going on to focus on the bottom half of the diagram and the links to implementation.

We see networking as shaped by five key aspects: the importance of strategy development; the role of knowledge resources; the influence of resources including funding and sanctions; the impact of norms; and the role of key individuals. The relationships between these factors and the networking process are not unidirectional. Rather they form a set of virtuous

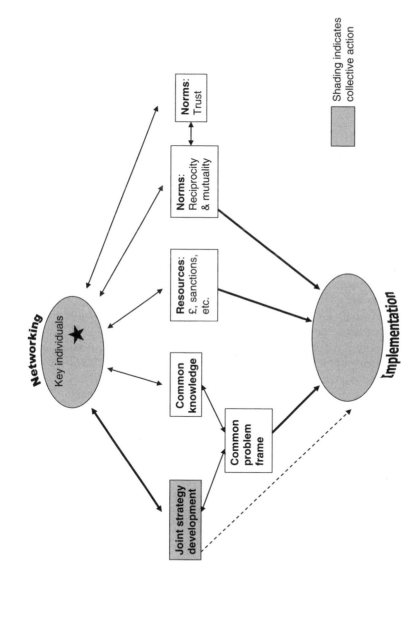

Figure 12.2 The dynamics of network-building

or vicious cycles, with each factor interacting with networking processes to promote or undermine collective action.

We begin with strategy development, which showed up as both a significant impetus to networking and a significant collective output from such networking. Indeed in Figure 12.2 we single out this particular factor as of greater importance than the others we identify. In many of our cases it is notable that the requirement or idea of developing such a strategy lay behind the creation or at least formalization of a network. In Cannock Chase there was the need to devise an AONB plan, in Rondane the Partial County Plan, in SVR the co-management plan at the instigation of the national government and in Morsa the action plan for the project. A focus on a strategy can also act as an impetus for opening up the network, even if the response in some of our cases was more limited. The Lake District CAMS processes are an example here. It seems therefore that under contemporary conditions of governance the requirement or suggestion to prepare a strategy necessarily involves reaching out to stakeholders to some extent. This creates an opportunity for networking towards a fuller and more meaningful form of collective action. The actual production of a document can be taken as evidence of such collective action although, as we emphasize below, this still leaves the need for collective action aimed at implementation.

There is a close relationship between the ability to develop a coherent collective strategy for resource management and the joint framing of the problem requiring such management amongst actors. Our case studies suggest that in many cases the construction of a common knowledge base for networking can be an important factor in creating this common problem frame. Again the process of generating such a common knowledge base is a dialectical one, described by Jasanoff as a process of coproduction of knowledge (1990). The networking activities are influential in both communicating different kinds of knowledge and in filtering and recognizing knowledge claims. In these ways, they actively contribute to the construction of such claims as accepted knowledge. However the knowledge claims themselves can shape the networking activities, with particular actors taking a more central role within networks due to the knowledge resources they hold.

At this point it is important to recognize that knowledge claims regarding natural resource management can take several different forms. One might list scientific, technical, procedural, experiential, local and personal knowledges as different categories of such knowledge. In practice, within our cases the categories collapse into a negotiated relationship between expert and indigenous forms of knowledge in each locality. In some cases, the conflicts between actors at times took the form of conflict between knowledge claims and this inhibited co-working. In SVR actors disagreed over some knowledge claims; in Mafungautsi there was open conflict between the local knowledge of villagers and the dominant scientific knowledge relied on by other actors; and in the Lake District the knowledge held by the Environment Agency while not challenged was not universally accepted. Meanwhile in some of the Spanish cases there was evidence of knowledge claims being used instrumentally to advance certain interests.

However other cases showed the potential for building a common knowledge base and suggested ways of doing this. In both Morsa and Rondane a specific effort was made to produce reports that used a mix of available knowledge resources, including the processing of local knowledge into more generalizable forms. These reports were then used as a base for persuading actors of their mutuality. In the New Forest no such reports were produced but the local expertise of the commoners – as expressed through their everyday land management practices – was recognized as significant by other expert actors. The key to such knowledge mixes supporting networking is therefore its acceptance by network members including a tolerance of any uncertainties inherent in the knowledge claim. On this basis knowledge can play a persuasive role within the network and support collective action. In particular the combination of various personal and processed knowledges (as Bråtå following Friedmann terms it) can be powerful in framing resource management problems. This in turn shapes the development of strategies. Knowledge and strategies are co-produced through the 'lens' of problem framing.

It was notable that a reliance on expert knowledge inputs alone to shape policy development was not successful. By comparison with the impact of climate change predictions (see the Lake District and Morsa cases), local knowledge inputs are much more significant. This might be heralded as a benefit of policy-making through networking, since it seems to offer the space for such local knowledge to have an influence. However it should also be recognized that local networking can be resistant to non-local forms of knowledge and this may adversely affect natural resource management. We return to this at the end of this chapter.

The third factor that we identify is resources, both financial and of other kinds (soft sanctions, regulatory powers and so on). In all our cases we have found these to be significant. There is a tendency in the networks, social capital and institutional capacity literature to sometimes downplay the importance of such resources. Yet they continue to be a primary influence on the incentive structures that actors face and that shape their activities. They also are an indicator of the relative power of different actors within networks, which the Rönne case study reminds us is always important. In

Rönne the distribution of power was significantly unequal, and this was critical for the lack of capacity to act collectively. The hope of networking is that it can overcome the impact of unequal distribution of resources and create new positive-sum outcomes. Thus the flow of resources can act as an impetus to networking, as when a certain grant bid requires evidence of networking to stand any chance of success. In the New Forest a number of collaborative projects were spurred into being by the promise of obtaining funds in this way. The virtuous cycle is then closed if the networking activities result in new sources of funding being identified or resources being released through the bringing together of actors within the network.

It must be recognized that the overall pattern of incentives facing actors can also provide perverse incentives that undermine networking, and there is no guarantee that networking by itself will create resources where there were none before. However our cases suggest that resources, notably financial resources, are particularly important in overcoming the necessary transactions costs involved in linking distant actors (not in regular contact with each other) through networks. Thus bridging networks are highly dependent on the availability of such resources, but the availability of such resources can prompt a potential virtuous cycle of resource availability and networking supporting each other.

The distinctive contribution of the social capital framework to our research was the emphasis it placed on developing common norms and, in particular, norms of reciprocity, mutuality and trust. This goes beyond the discussion of bridging and bonding linkages above. Following the social capital literature, we found that in our cases there was the potential for a virtuous cycle whereby networking generates such common norms and then the norms consolidate the network. Within this process, the norms of trust seem to be particularly important for network consolidation, even if the weaker form of bridging capital is involved.

It is also notable that these different aspects of the common norms – trust, mutuality and reciprocity – reinforce each other. A greater sense of trust between parties to the network strengthens the common norm of reciprocity and mutuality and vice versa. They are however distinct aspects of norms; it is possible to trust another stakeholder without feeling any link of mutual dependence or reciprocity, and the obverse also holds true. In particular a sense of mutuality and the benefits of reciprocity are vital for common problem framing; trust has little direct impact on this. As will be seen, this distinction is also important when we come to consider how jointly developed strategies are implemented. To preview our argument, norms of trust may be most important for building networks but norms of mutuality and reciprocity are more important when it comes to implementation. This is not to suggest that trust is irrelevant when it comes to implementation.

Prevailing norms of trust may set the backdrop for accepting a commonly agreed strategy as the guide for individual actions, as in Rondane. But the internalization of the common frame by individual actors seems to rely on the appreciation of their interdependence.

Finally, in this section, we come to the role of key individuals. Such individuals are variously referred to as policy champions, policy brokers or policy entrepreneurs in the case studies. Where networking has been successful in creating common problem frames and strategies, then such individuals are usually apparent. We found this in Cannock Chase, Rondane, SVR, Eastern Mancha and Morsa in particular. The reasons why such individuals are important lie partly in their individual and personal abilities in forging links and using the language of trust to cement cooperative action (Rydin 2003, Chapter 4). They embody a particular form of political mobilization capacity, to refer to the institutional capacity framework. This can be harnessed to negotiate conflicts between parties (as in SVR for example) or to render latent cooperation more overt (as in Cannock Chase).

Considered more institutionally and less personally, the resources embedded in the post of such individuals become a way of covering the inevitable transaction costs of networking. Such individuals expend considerable effort, time and hence money in bringing network members together and keeping them connected. Fortunately, by acting as a focal point, such individuals also reduce the transactions costs between actors in a network. The various actors can relate to the key individual rather than the range of different possible actors, in the knowledge that the individual will then take the communication further out into the network. In addition to being a focal point for communications, such individuals can become a focal point for the trust generated within the network. Networking also benefits where such individuals remain in their network position for some time. Then they come to embody the collective memory of the network as well as preserving such trust over time.

There seem to be different options open as to whether an outsider or insider fulfils this role of key individual. Where there has been a history of local conflicts, then bringing in someone from outside the local context can be beneficial. Such an individual can be seen as separate from the local history of conflicts and able to mediate, negotiate and operate in a way that is untainted by such conflict. However in some cases the key individual was a local political actor able to use his or her knowledge of local political networks to support the specific collective action effort. In all our Norwegian cases, political actors in the form of an elected mayor played this role.

It seems that local and indeed national context can be important here. Where there is clear separation within the policy process between officers and politicians and where politicians both hold considerable power and command respect, then political parties can be a key resource and political actors can be important. However if the professional activity of resource management is seen as inherently politicized and/or local political actors are not seen as representative of local communities, then party political routes are less important and may even be resisted as inherently containing the potential for corruption and undue influence. While local political actors were not considered in this way in the English cases, elected councillors were not considered as sufficiently powerful or able to command sufficient resources to play this role. Officers instead were the key actors within networks. In Mafungautsi the political leaders were not considered representative and therefore their involvement was not helpful in enabling networks; quite the contrary. Thus the cultural context for networking is an important indicator for identifying where key individuals, important for the success of the networking enterprise, might be found.

We now turn to the links between these different aspects of networking and collective action in terms of implementation, that is, actual changed use of natural resources. While we have emphasized above the links from networking to strategy development – both directly and through developing a common knowledge base and problem frame – when it comes to considering implementation, all our cases suggested a relatively weak link between strategies and action on the ground. The strategies themselves depended on other systems to put them into effect; the networks had then to rely on other organizations, often their constituent organizations, to secure implementation.

In some cases existing resources were relied on for implementation. For example in Rondane the zoning implications of developing a Partial County Plan were the focal point within the network for trusting that the plan would be implemented; however even here the potential for individual local authorities to grant exemptions from zoning could undermine implementation. In Cannock Chase a planning protocol was developed to try and link the AONB Strategy and the planning decision-making of individual local authorities. In several cases external funding sources, usually from central government, were key to achieving implementation. In Morsa and SVR for example, funding was available for implementation.

It is clear from all our cases though that the key factor influencing implementation of collectively agreed strategies is the acceptance of a common framing of the problem and the associated acceptance of mutuality between network members. Where this is absent – as in some of the Spanish cases where illegal wells were not only tolerated but also actively supported – then implementation is hindered. While the common norm of trust was most important in consolidating the networks, it is the common norms of mutuality and reciprocity that spur individual organizations within the network to see the resource problem in different terms and to take action accordingly. The result is effective collective action against free-riding. Thus in the New Forest case, actors emphasized their mutuality and the danger of allowing conflicts to reassert themselves, and used this to justify changes in their own individual strategies and plans.

The reason that this is so effective is that the development of a common problem frame and a common sense of reciprocity and mutuality is likely to alter individual stakeholders' patterns of behaviour in a way that is consonant with the joint strategy. The change occurs back at the site of the individual organizations that make up the network, which is where after all behavioural change is needed. Indeed where networking developed such a common frame and sets of norms, then collective action to overcome free-riding on the resource in question could be expected even if strategy development was not completed. The strategy process acts as a focal point for networking, which then generates and reinforces these more cultural changes within the network of stakeholders with the result that collective action on resource use is fostered.

To summarize, the key to achieving collective action in terms of co-working, joint strategy development and changed resource use is therefore to generate networking activity that releases resources, develops a common knowledge base and problem frame and builds up norms of trust, but also critically of mutuality and reciprocity. Key individuals will be important in generating virtuous cycles within the networking process and there is a need for an appropriate mix of bonding and bridging social capital (also termed bracing capital). The bridging extends across the key stakeholders, particularly involving the local landowners and resource users, while the bonding allows for groups and organizations within the network to be fully represented by individuals within the network and in turn for those groups and organizations to take forward implementation of agreed strategies and approaches. This tension between bonding and bridging networks is crucial for collective action when it comes to the implementation of strategies and decision-making. The actors need to find a balance between their home organizations and the bridging network. The studies indicate that often actors seem to favour their home organizations.

ISSUES OF FRAGMENTATION, INTEGRATION AND DEMOCRACY

By way of conclusion, we wish to reflect on the potential and limits of networking activity. The hope of networking is that it will achieve a degree of policy integration that overcomes the fragmentation bedevilling natural resource management that we outlined in Chapter 1. We have found that such integration is extremely difficult to achieve. This fragmentation appears to be inherent to the natural resource management problematic. It cannot readily be removed by organizational restructuring; each organizational restructuring to resolve one aspect of fragmentation is likely to produce boundaries and barriers elsewhere. Similarly networking, while it can bring together fragmented actors, cannot meld them into one institution. Institutional fragmentation therefore seems to be an intractable aspect of trying to engage with natural resources. Networking can be a helpful if time-consuming response to that fragmentation, but it should not be expected to remove it. The challenge is to ensure that the resources expended on creating and maintaining networks is well spent so that the involvement of actors is meaningful, not token, and that strategies developed represent a common position on how the resources should be managed.

Our cases have highlighted that there are limits to what networking can achieve. Networking involves considerable transactions costs and it can be difficult to maintain virtuous cycles within networks over time. Continuous reinforcement of the positive aspects of networking is required. Each of the links between networking and strategy development, common knowledge base, resources and common norms is a two-way linkage that has to be repeatedly activated. We have emphasized the importance of key individuals in achieving this. Without such constant reinforcement, virtuous cycles can become vicious ones and networking can degenerate into mere consultation or become entirely token.

Furthermore the cooperation built up within networks creates a form of direct co-working, with specific outputs such as plans and strategies and the capacity for further action. However this action is not assured. Another aspect of fragmentation is the dispersed nature of the sites where action is needed to resolve free-riding and promote sustainable resource use. Again networking can bring these different sites of implementation together, but we have emphasized that doing so, even if it results in a common strategy, does not assure joint and several implementation. We have emphasized the need to work on developing a common problem frame and sense of mutuality to enhance the chances of implementation being achieved through action on the ground.

Capacity may also be frustrated by factors internal and external to the network. Our Swedish water management case emphasizes the need to take account of the power of actors within the network and the possibility that they will exercise this power where collective outcomes conflict with their own interests. Several of our cases emphasized the importance of external factors, both broader political and economic dynamics but also the impact of powerful actors external to the networks. Our Morsa case study also highlighted the limitations of focusing on local collective action to improve an aspect of the environment, when that same environment may be threatened by lack of collective action on environmental change at a broader, international scale. Our Lake District case also suggested that it could be difficult to activate local collective action when the impact of such broader environmental change remains predicted rather than immediately apparent to local actors. Visibility of natural resource problems seems to be a necessary prerequisite for local networking to be effective. Even in our more successful cases, such as Rondane and SVR, land fragmentation is still ongoing and threatening the reindeer habitats. All these examples highlight that more than voluntary local collective action may be needed to handle the degradation of natural resources. Some form of national regulatory or fiscal framework or direct public sector action may be necessary. The threat of exercising sanctions arising from these frameworks can be a vital adjunct to the norms holding networks together.

However we would not wish to be too negative about networking; rather we wish to introduce a degree of realism into discussions, so prevalent within governance debates, about the benefits of networks. We believe our case studies show that there are still strong arguments for basing natural resource management on the involvement of key stakeholders and encouraging joint working to build links of trust, mutuality and reciprocity. Such networking remains a necessary supplement to top-down or single agency management, as our Spanish and Lake District cases show. It is the only way to spread the recognition of the need for collective action among the range of actors whose involvement is essential for free-riding to be resisted. It can be a resource-effective way to bring about change particularly if key focal individuals play their part. Networking remains an important way of releasing resources, overcoming conflict and achieving changes in resource management patterns. In order to achieve such behavioural change, we would emphasize the need to build a common problem frame and embed a sense of mutuality so that individual stakeholders change their decision-making processes, and acknowledge the key role of a common knowledge frame in generating this situation in some cases. Networking on its own will not achieve such change, but with careful attention to the dynamics of networking processes then such changes can be achieved.

Furthermore there is a strong democratic imperative to such stakeholder involvement. The legitimacy of the networks depends on open and inclusive forms of networking and actors need to be able to reassure their home organization of the validity of engaging in collective decision-making. We have noted a delicate balance for actors in maintaining legitimacy within the network and within these home organizations also. Inclusiveness and transparency of the network assures the first, while strong bonding capital contributes to the latter. Transparency ensures that political leaders involved in the network are truly representative, and it also contributes to embedding trust within the networks. Thus a commitment to stakeholder involvement is not just a working through of democratic principles, but also an active contribution to effective networking and collective action in all its forms. Should one wish to dismiss networking as just the rhetoric of governance, one should remember these positive contributions that networks, the associated social capital and their internal dialectical dynamics can make to resolving natural resource problems and to embedding a democratic approach to natural resource management.

This means that the literature on social capital and institutional capacity remains an important one. We would however like to suggest that the scope of this literature can be broadened, and indeed we have sought to do this in our case studies. These concepts can be relevant on a larger scale and to a greater range of issues than is often taken to be the case. Our collective action problems have involved large and multi-functional areas rather than the use of a single resource by a local community. This makes collective action much more challenging. It increases the number of actors involved and widens out the perspectives on the collective action problem. With more stakeholders, usually with very different approaches, it can be difficult to find a common policy frame. Extending the collective action problem in terms of size of area or number of topics makes the stakeholders even more heterogeneous. Furthermore the externalities associated with these more complex cases go far beyond the areas that the networks cover. While this reinforces our point that a simple reliance on bridging between actors and some bonding capital within these spatially delimited networks may be insufficient on their own, we would nevertheless urge the greater use of these concepts to analyse and understand the challenges of strategic planning for multi-functional natural resources.

Appendix – Methodology

This book was written in a partnership with NIBR (Norway) and the LSE (UK). Of the nine case studies in the book three are from Norway, three from the UK, one from Sweden, one from Zimbabwe and one from Spain. The three latter case studies mainly form part of the authors' doctoral theses and their research was conducted separately from the partnership between NIBR and LSE, therefore their methodology and theory might differ somewhat from the UK and Norwegian case studies. The starting point for the methodology was to use the same methods as far as possible: semi-structured interviews, observation through participation, surveys (in Norwegian and Swedish case studies) and document analyses.

The book includes four water management cases and five landscape forest management cases; the case study areas were selected for comparative purposes. The Swedish case, Spanish case, Norwegian case of Morsa and the UK case of the Lake District are all case studies with water management issues. They all differ from each other somewhat, but provide for comparison between the practises of water management in the different countries. Landscape management issues exist in Cannock Chase (UK), the New Forest (UK), Rondane (Norway), Setesdal Vesthei-Ryfylkeheiane (Norway) and Mafungautsi (Zimbabwe). In the UK the New Forest with its wild ponies was also furthermore selected to match and provide for a comparative basis with the Norwegian case of Rondane with its wild reindeer. However another Norwegian case, Setesdal Vesthei-Ryfylkeheiane, also has issues concerning wild reindeer. Forestry issues mainly feature in the Zimbabwean case study, but also the New Forest and Cannock Chase have historically been active forestry areas.

The research and interviews for the three UK case studies were carried out throughout 2004. The Norwegian case studies were started a little earlier and were mostly conducted during 2003, except for the case of Rondane where material has been collected since 1995, supplementary documents collected in 1999–2001 and interviews furthermore carried out in 2003–2004. The Swedish case studies were carried out during 2000–2005, the Spanish case studies mainly in 2000 and the Zimbabwean case study in 2000–2002.

As the aim of the research was to look at collective action and social capital in natural resource management in areas showing a high degree of fragmented interests and institutions, and as has been set out in Chapter 1 and 2, the networks in the case study areas were first and foremost identified for the Norwegian and UK cases. From there, key actors within these networks were identified and the snowballing technique used in order to identify interviewees. People from all levels in the local communities were asked for interviews, including local authorities, national agencies, NGOs and other local interest groups. In the Norwegian case studies and the Swedish case, surveys were further used for getting more quantitative data from a wider group of actors.

The Norwegian and UK research team met throughout the research from 2002, when work on this project began, until 2005 when the comparative analysis of all the case studies included in this book was finalized.

Bibliography

Agrawal, A. (2001), 'Common property institutions and sustainable governance of Resources', *World Development*, **29** (10), 1649–72 .

Alcock, F. (2002), 'Bargaining, uncertainty, and property rights in fisheries', *World Politics*, **54**, 437–61.

Amin, A. and N. Thrift (eds) (1994), *Globalisation, Institutions and Regional Development*, Oxford: Oxford University Press.

Amin, A. and N. Thrift (1995), 'Globalisation, "institutional thickness" and the local economy', in P. Healey et al. (eds), *Managing Cities*, London: John Wiley, pp. 91–108.

Andersen, R. and H. Hustad (2005), 'Villrein og samfunn. En veiledning til bevaring og bruk av Europas siste villreinfjell' ['Wild reindeer and society'], *NINA Temahefte*, **27**, Trondheim: NINA.

Baland, J.-M. and J.-P. Platteau (1996), *Halting Degradation of Natural Resources – Is There a Role for Rural Communities?*, New York, Food and Agriculture Organization of the United Nations; Oxford: Clarendon Press.

Bærenholdt, J.O. and N. Aarsæther (2002), 'Coping strategies, social capital and space', *European Urban and Regional Studies*, **9** (2), 151–65.

Bassets, L. (1992), 'El Plan de Recuperacion de Daimiel y Ruidera suscita una buena acogida en la CE', *El Pais*, **21**.

Beall, J. (1997), 'Social capital in waste – a solid investment?', *Journal of International Development*, **9** (7), 951–61.

Beatie, J. (1966), *Other Cultures: Aims, Methods and Achievements in Social Anthropology*, London: Routledge and Kegan Paul.

Berglund, E. (2001), 'Facts, beliefs and biases: perspectives on forest conservation in Finland', *Journal of Environmental Planning and Management*, **44** (6), 833–49.

Berkes, F. (ed.) (1989), *Common Property Resources: An Ecology of Community-based Sustainable Development*, London: Belhaven.

Blackmore, C. with K. Collins, P. Furniss, D. Morris and M. Reynolds (2004), 'The UK policy context for water management: I – The English and Welsh policy context', SLIM Case Study Monograph 12A, Milton Keynes: Open University.

Blomquist, W. (1994), 'Changing rules, changing games: evidence from groundwater systems in Southern California', in E. Ostrom, R. Gardner and J. Walker (eds), *Rules, Games and Common-Pool Resources*, Ann Arbor: University of Michigan Press.

Bogason, P. (2001), *Fragmentert forvaltning. Demokrati og netværkstyring i desentralisert lokalstyre*, Århus: Systime.

Bomberg, E. (1998), *Issue Networks and the Environment: Explaining European Union Policy. Comparing Policy Networks*, Buckingham: Open University Press.

Bourdillon, M.F.C. (1991), *Religion and Society: A Text for Africa*, Gweru: Mambo Press.

Bramwell, A. (1989), *Ecology in the 20th Century: A History*, New Haven, NJ: Yale University Press.

Brandon, K., K.H. Redford and S.E. Sanderson (1998), *Parks in Peril. People, Politics and Protected Areas*, Washington, DC: Island Press.

Bratt, C. (1994), 'Det desentraliserte miljøvern – fortsatt behov for sentral styring', in Naustdalslid, Jon and Sissel Hovik (eds), *Lokalt miljøvern*, Oslo: Tano/NIBR.

Bråtå, H.O. (1985), *Villrein og inngrep i Rondane* [*Wild reindeer and impacts in the Rondane Region*] Lillehammer: Fylkesmannen i Oppland, miljøvernavdelingen.

Bråtå, H.O. (1997), 'Evaluering av fylkesdelplan for Rondane', *NIBR-prosjektrapport*, 1997, **18**, Oslo: Norsk institutt for by- og regionforskning.

Bråtå, H.O. (2001), *Forvaltningen av villreinen og dens ressurssystem i Rondane. Belyst i et arenaperspektiv med makt og kunnskap som teoretiske innfallsvinkler*, PhD thesis, Oslo: University of Oslo.

Bråtå, H.O. (2005), *Kriterier for en bærekraftig villreinforvaltning – et samfunnsvitenskaplig perspektiv på forvaltning av bestander og arealer*, ØF-rapport 2005, **13**, Lillehammer: Østlandsforskning.

Bresser, H., L.J. O'Toole and J. Richardson (1994), 'Networks as models of analysis: water policy in comparative perspective', *Environmental Politics*, **3** (4), 1–23.

Brown, L.D. and D. Ashman. (1996), 'Participation, social capital and intersectoral problem solving: African and Asian cities', *World Development*, **24**, 1467–79.

Bruce, J., L. Fortmann and K. Nhira (1993), 'Tennres in transition, tenures in conflict: examples from the Zimbabwe Social Forest', *Rural Sociology*, **58** (4), 626–42.

Burström, F. (2000), *Environment and Municipalities – Towards a Theory on Municipal Environmental Management*, Stockholm: Royal Institute of Technology (KTH).

Buskerud & Telemark fylkeskommuner (1995), *Fylkesdelplan Hardangervidda Aust*.

Calder, I.R., P.T.W. Rosier, K.T. Prasanna and S. Parameswarappa (1997), 'Eucalyptus water use greater than rainfall input – a possible explanation from southern India', *Hydrology & Earth System Sciences*, **1** (2), 249–59.

Calvert, R.L. (1989), 'Reciprocity among self-interested actors: uncertainty, asymmetry, and distribution', in C. Peter Ordershook (ed.), *Models of Strategic Choice in Politics*, Ann Arbor, MI: University of Michigan Press, pp. 269–93.

Cannock Chase AONB Unit (2003), *Draft Management Plan – A Future Challenge*, Stafford: Cannock Chase AONB Unit.

Cars, Gøran, Patsy Healey, A. Madanipour and C. de Magalhães (2002), *Urban Governance, Institutional Capacity and Social Milieux*, Aldershot: Ashgate.

Castells, Manuel (1996), *The Rise of the Network Society*, Cambridge, MA: Blackwell Publishers.

Cavendish, W.M.P. (1994), 'The economics of natural resource utilisation by communal area farmers of Zimbabwe', University of Oxford, Dphil.

Chitsike, L.T. (2000), 'Decentralization and devolution of campfire in Zimbabwe', CASS, University of Zimbabwe, Harare.

CIDESPA (1988), 'Informe sobre el sistema acuifero 24 del Campo de Montiel', Madrid.

Coleman, J.S. (1990), *Foundations of Social Theory*, Cambridge, MA: Belknap.

Collins, K. (2004), 'The Tweed Forum and the Tweed Catchment Management Plan', SLIM Case Study Monograph 14, Milton Keynes: Open University.

Countryside Agency (2002), 'New Forest National Park – Special arrangements for New Forest National Park Authority', Countryside Agency's Advice to the Secretary of State for Environment Food and Rural Affairs.

Countryside Agency (2005), www.countryside.gov.uk/ WhoWeAreAnd WhatWeDo/changing.asp, 26 April.

Crook, R.C. and J. Manor (1998), *Democracy and Decentralization in South-East Asia and West Africa: Participation, Accountability and Performance*, Cambridge: Cambridge University Press.

Cruces de Abia, J., M. Espino Casado, R. Llamas, A. de la Hera and L. Martinez Cortina (1997), 'El desarrollo sostenible de la cuenca Alta del Guadiana: aspectos hidrologicos', *Revista de Obras Publicas*, **3** (362), 7–18.

Cruces de Abia, J., J.M. Hernandez, G. Lopez-Sanz and J. Rosell (1998), 'De la noria a la bomba: conflictos sociales y ambientales en la Cuenca Alta del Guadiana', Bilbao: Bakpaz.

Dasgupta, P.S. and G.M. Heal (1979), *Economic Theory and Exhaustible Resources*, Cambridge: Cambridge University Press.

Daugstad, K., B.P. Kaltenborg and O.I. Vistad (2000), *'Vern – planer og prosesser. Identifisering av kunnskapsstatus og behov'*, Notat 3/00, Trondheim: NINA-NIKU/Senter for bygdeforskning.

Davoudi, S. and N. Evans (2004), 'The challenge of governance in regional waste planning', paper to AESOP Conference, 1–4 July, University of Grenoble, France.

Dayton-Johnson, J. (2000), 'Choosing rules to govern the commons: a model with evidence from Mexico', *Journal of Economic Behavior and Organization*, 42, 19–41.

Department of Environment, Transport and the Regions (1999), *Taking Water Responsibly*, London: DETR.

DN (2001), 'Områdevern og forvaltning', Directorate for nature management Handbook 17, Norway.

Dobers, P. (1997), 'Styrning eller samarbete? Kommunens förändrade roll vid kontroll av diffusa utsläpp', *Statsvetenskaplig Tidsskrift*, **99** (3), 289–300.

Dolšak, N. and E. Ostrom (2003), 'The adaptation to challenges', in N. Dolšak and E. Ostrom (eds), *The Commons in the New Millennium: Challenges and Adapation*, London: The MIT Press.

Dowding, K. (1995), 'Model or metaphor? A critical review of the policy network approach', *Political Studies*, **43**, 136–58.

Dulsrud, A. (2002), *Tillit og transaksjoner: en kvalitativ analyse av kontraktsrelasjoner i norsk hvitfiskekspor*, PhD thesis, Oslo: University of Oslo.

Dunleavy, P. (1991), *Democracy, Bureaucracy and Public Choice*, London: Harvester-Wheatsheaf.

Eckerberg, K. (1997), 'Comparing the local use of environmental policy instruments in Nordic and Baltic countries – the issue of diffuse water pollution', *Environmental Politics*, **6**, 24–47.

Edney, J. (1979), 'Freeriders en route to disaster', *Psychology Today*, **13** (December), 80–102.

EFEDA (1997), 'EFEDA – an ECHIVAl Field Experiment in desertification-threatened areas', First pilot study conducted in Castille La Mancha.

Elander, I. and M. Blanc (2001), 'Partnerships and democracy: a happy couple in urban governance?', in R. van Kempen and H.T. Andersen (eds), *Governing European Cities Volume III: Social Fragmentation, Social Exclusion and Urban Governance*, Aldershot: Ashgate, pp. 93–124.

Elster, J. (1989), *The Cement of Society. A study of Social Order*, Cambridge: Cambridge University Press.

Environment Agency (2002), *Managing Water Abstraction: The Catchment Abstraction Management Strategy Process*, London: EA.

Environment Agency (2004a), 'Annual Report 2003/04', www.environment-agency.gov.uk/commondata/105385/report_874789.pdf, 15 December.

Environment Agency (2004b), 'Briefing note – General introduction to the Water Framework Directive', www.environment-agency.gov.uk/business, 15 December.

Environment Agency (2004c), 'Leven and Crake CAMS', www.environment-agency.gov.uk/subjects/waterres/564321/309477/309483/314650/?version=1&lang=_e, 9 December.

Etzioni, A. (1988), *The Moral Dimension. Toward a New Economic*, New York: Free Press.

Falk, I. and S. Kilpatrick (2000), 'What is social capital? A study of interaction in a rural community', *Sociologia Ruralis*, **40** (1), 87–110.

Falleth, E.I. (2004), 'Hvordan dannes nettverk: om lokal organisering og kollektiv handling i Setesdal Vesthei-Ryfylkeheiane', *Kart og Plan*, **64** (3), 135–41.

Falleth, E.I., S. Hovik and K.B. Stokke (2003), *Sammenligning av arealplanlegging og landskapsvern som virkemidler i forvaltningen av verneverdige områder*, Utmark 2003:1.

Falleth, E.I. and K.B. Stokke (2000), 'Planlegging i Ringsaker kommune', *NIBR-notat* 2000, 103, Oslo: Norsk institutt for by- og regionforskning.

Fearon, James D. (1998), 'Bargaining, enforcement, and international cooperation', *International Organization*, **52**, 269–305.

Ferguson, J. (1990), *The Anti-Politics Machine: 'Development', Depoliticization, and Bureaucratic Power in Lesotho*, Cambridge: Cambridge University Press.

Fischer, F. (1993), *Policy Discourse and the Politics of Washington Think Tanks. The Argumentative Turn in Policy Analysis and Planning*, London: UCL Press.

Foley, M.W. and B. Edwards (1999), 'Is it time to disinvest in social capital?' *Journal of Public Policy*, **19** (2), 141–73.

Folke, C., J. Colding and F. Berkes (2003), 'Synthesis – Building Resilience and Adaptive Capacity in Social-Ecological Systems', in F. Berkes, J. Colding and C. Folke (eds), *Navigating Social-Ecological Systems – Building Resilience for Complexity and Change*, Cambridge: Cambridge University Press, pp. 352–87.

Forestry Commission (1997), 'Resource Sharing', proceedings report for the seminar held at Kadoma Ranch Motel, Zimbabwe: Forestry Commission, 9–11 April.

Forestry Commission (2004), 'New Forest Fact Files', www.forestry.gov.uk/website/oldsite.nsf/byunique/INFD-62LHYL, 14 September.

Fox, J. and J. Gershman (2000), 'The World Bank and social capital: lessons from ten rural development projects in the Philippines and Mexico', *Policy Sciences*, **33**, 399–419.

Francis, R. (1985), *The Industrial History of Cannock Chase*, Stafford: Association of the Friends of Cannock Chase.

Friedmann, J. (1973), *Retracking America: A Theory of Transactive Planning*, New York: Doubleday.

From, J. and N. Sitter (2002), 'Hva er Governance?' *Plan*, **6**, p. 22.

FM – Fylkesmennene i Rogaland, Vest-Agder og Aust-Agder (1984), 'Setesdal Vesthei – inngrepsoversikt i perioden 1973–1984', Kristiansand: Fylkesmannen i Vest-Agder.

Galaz, V. (2004), 'Stealing from the poor? Game theory and the politics of water markets in Chile', *Environmental Politics*, **13** (2), 414–37.

Galaz, V. (2005), 'Does the EU Water Framework Directive Build Resilience? Harnessing Uncertainty and Complexity in European Water Management', *Policy Report from The Resilience and Freshwater Initiative*, Swedish Water House.

Galaz, V. (forthcoming), *Power in the Commons – The Politics of Water Resources Management in Sweden and Chile*, PhD thesis, Department of Political Science, Göteborg University.

Garcia-Vizcaino, M.J. (2003), 'Legislacion europea, estatel y antonomica de aguas subterraneas', Jornadas sobre las comunidades de Usuarios de Aguas Subterraneas en el marco normatiro actual, Prat de Llobregat.

Gargiulo, M. and M. Benassi (2000), 'Trapped in your own net? Network cohesion, structural holes, and the adaptation of social capital', *Organization Science*, **11** (2), 183–96.

Getches, D.H. (1990), *Water Law in a Nutshell*, Minnesota: West Publishing.

Glosvik, Ø. (1996a), 'Den lokale dimensjonen i norsk nasjonalparkpolitikk', *MILKOM notat*, 6/96, Norges forskningsråd and Norsk institutt for by- og regionforskning.

Glosvik, Ø. (1996b), 'Kommunen og nasjonalparken. Nore Uvdal som dome', *MILKOM – notat*, 2/96, Norges forskningsråd and Norsk institutt for by- og regionforskning.

Gouldson, A. and J. Murphy (1989), *Regulatory Realities*, London: Earthscan.

Granovetter, M. (1973), 'The strength of weak ties', *American Journal of Sociology*, **78**, 1360–80.

Grossman, S. and O. Hart (1980), 'Takeover bids, the free-rider-problem, and the theory of the corporation', *Bell Journal of Economics*, **11** (Spring), 42–64.

Gustafsson, J.-E. (1996), 'Avrinningsområdesbaserade organisationer som aktiva planeringsaktörer', VAV: 64, Solna, Stockholm: Svenska Vatten- och Avloppverksföreningen.

Gwaai Working Group (1997), 'Local-level valuation of village woodlands and state forests: cases from Matabeleland North in Zimbabwe',

Institute of Environmental Studies Working Paper No. 7, Harare: University of Zimbabwe.

Habermas, J. (1984), *The Theory of Communicative Action*, Vol. 1, transl. T. McCarthy, London: Heinemann.

Habermas, J. (1987), *The Theory of Communicative Action*, Vol. 2, transl. T. McCarthy, London: Heinemann.

Hall, P. and R. Taylor (1996), 'Political science and the three new institutionalisms', *Political Studies*, **44**, 936–57.

Hallèn, A. (1994), 'Kommunalt miljøvern frå prosjekt til program', in J. Naustdalslid and S. Hovik (eds), *Lokalt Miljøvern*, Oslo: Tano/NIBR, pp. 205–23.

Hampshire County Council (2004), 'The New Forest', www.hants.gov.uk/newforest/, 24 November.

Hansen, T. and T. Tjerbo (2003), 'Politisk engasjement, borgerroller og social capital', *Makt- og demokratiutredningen*, Report nr 62.

Hardin, G. (1968), 'The Tragedy of the Commons', *Science*, **162**, 1243–7.

Hardin, R. (1982), *Collective Action*, Baltimore, MD: Johns Hopkins University Press.

Healey, P. (1997), *Collaborative Planning: Shaping Places in Fragmented Societies*, London: Macmillan.

Healey, P., D. Magalães and A. Madanipour (1999), 'Institutional capacity-building, urban planning and urban regeneration projects', *Futura*, **18** (3), 117–37.

Healey, P., G. Cars, A. Madanipour and C. de Magalhães (2002), 'Transforming governance, institutional analysis and institutional capacity', in P. Healey, G. Cars, A. Madanipour and C. de Magalhães (eds), *Urban Governance, Institutional Capacity and Social Milieux*, Aldershot: Ashgate.

Healey, P., C. de Magalhães, A. Madanipour and J. Pendlebury (2003), 'Place, identity and local politics: analysing partnership initiatives', in M. Hajer, and H. Wagenaar (eds), *Deliberative Policy Analysis: Understanding Governance in Network Societies*, Cambridge: Cambridge University Press.

Heckathorn, D. and S. Maser (1987), 'Bargaining and constitutional contracts', *American Journal of Political Science*, **31** (1), 142–68.

Helgesen, M. (2002), 'Governance – vil nye former for politisk styring gi større rom for folkelig deltakelse?', i S.I. Vabo, (ed.), *Kommunal governance og bærekraftig utvikling – om governance-begrepet*, NIBR working paper, Oslo, Norway.

Herndl, C. and S. Brown (1996), *Green Culture: Environmental Rhetoric in Contemporary America*, Madison, WN: University of Wisconsin Press.

Hjelseth, A. (1993), 'Rasjonalitet og metodologisk individualisme', *Sosiologisk tidsskrift*, **1** (3), 229–44.

Hobbes, T. (1651/1998), *Leviathan*, Oxford: Oxford University Press.

Holsen, T. (1996), 'Innsigelser som virkemiddel i arealplanlegging', *Rapport*, 1996, 13, Oslo: Norsk institutt for by- og regionforskning.

Hovik, S. (2001), *Statlige målsettinger og lokale interesser i miljøpolitikken. En studie av kommunal iverksetting*, PhD thesis, Oslo: Universitetet i Oslo.

Hovik, S. and E.I. Falleth (2003), 'Vern av Setesdal Vesthei – Ryfylkeheiane landskapsvernområde. Holdninger til vern og forvaltning blant lokalpolitikere og lokale organisasjoner', *Notat* 2003,126, Oslo: Norsk institutt for by- og regionforskning.

Hovik, S. and V. Johnsen (1994), 'Fra forsøk til reform. Evaluering av MIK-programmet', *Rapport*, 1994, 23, Oslo: Norsk institutt for by- og region-forskning.

Hovik, S., J.R. Selvik, N. Vagstad, A.L. Solheim, K.B. Stokke and A. Brabrand (2003), 'Demonstrasjonsprosjekt for implementering av EUs Vanndirektiv i Vansjø-Hobølvassdraget (Morsa)', Phase 1 report, Norwegian Institute for Water Research.

Hovik, S. and S. Vabo (2005), 'Norwegian local councils as democratic meta-governors? A study of networks established to manage cross-border natural resources,' *Scandinavian Political Studies*, **28** (3), 257–75.

Hulgård, L. (2003), 'Weak ties in strong welfare states', paper presented at ACSP-AESOP 3rd Congress, The Network Society – The New Context for Planning. Leuven, 8–12 July.

Hulgård, L. (2004), 'Weak ties in strong welfare states', in K. Nielsen, (ed.), *Social Capital, Trust and Institutions*, Cheltenham, UK and Northampton, MA, USA: Edward Elgar.

Innes, J., J. Gruber, M. Neuman and R. Thompson (1994), 'Co-ordinating growth and environmental management through consensus building', California Policy Seminar Paper, Berkeley, CA: University of California.

Janssen, M.A. (2002), 'Changing the rules of the game: lessons from immunology and linguistics for self-organization of institutions', in M.A. Janssen (ed.), *Complexity and Ecosystem Management – The Theory and Practice of Multi-Agent Systems*, Cheltenham, UK and Northampton, MA, USA: Edward Elgar.

Jasanoff, S. (1990), *The Fifth Branch: Science Advisers as Policymakers*, Cambridge, MA: Harvard University Press.

JCRMO (1999), Dossier 94/99, Albacete, Junta Central de Regantes de la Mancha Oriental.

JCRMO (2001), 'Informe Tecnico para la toma de decisiones en el Plan de Explotacion del acuifero de la Mancha Occidental', *Agua- Boletin*

Informativo de la Junta Centra; de Regantes de la Mancha Oriental, **2** (1), 10–12.

Keohane, R. (2001), 'Governance in a partially globalized world: presidential address', American Political Science Association, 2000, *American Political Science Review*, **95**, 1–13.

Kingdon, J.W. (1984), *Agendas, Alternatives and Public Policies*, Glenvievi Illinois: Harper Collins.

Knight, J. (1992), *Institutions and Social Conflict*, Cambridge: Cambridge University Press.

Koontz, T.M. (2003), 'The farmer, the planner, and the local citizen in the dell: how collaborative groups plan for farmland preservation', *Landscape and Urban Planning*, **66**, 19–34.

Krasner, S. (1991), 'Global communications and national power: life on the pareto frontier', *World Politics*, (43), pp. 336–66.

Krale, S. (1996), *Interviews: An Introduction to Qualitative Research Interviewing*, London: Sage.

Levin, S.A. (1999), *Fragile Dominion: Complexity and the Commons*, Cambridge, MA: Perseus Books.

Li, T.M. (1996), 'Images of community: discourse and strategy in property relations', *Development and Change*, **27**, 501–27.

Liedberg-Jönsson, B. (2004), 'Stakeholder participation as a tool for sustainable development in the Em River Basin', *Water Resources Development*, **20** (3), 345–52.

Llamas, R. (1991), 'Borrador nota preliminar sobre la explotacion del acuifero del Campo de Montiel', Madrid.

Llamas, R., N. Hernandez-Mora and L. Martinez Cortina (2000), 'El uso sostenible de las aguas subterraneas', Fundacion Marcehno Botin Serie A, **1**, 54pp.

Lowndes, V. and D. Wilson (2001), 'Social capital and local governance: exploring the institutional design variable', *Political Studies*, **49**, 629–47.

Lundqvist, L.J. (2001), 'Games real farmers play: knowledge, memory and the fate of collective action to prevent eutrophication of water catchments', *Local Environment*, 6, 407–19.

Lundqvist, L.J. (2004a), 'Integrating Swedish water resource management: a multi-level governance trilemma', *Local Environment*, **9**, 413–24.

Lundqvist, L.J. (2004b), *Sweden and Ecological Governance – Straddling the Fence*, Manchester: Manchester University Press.

MacKenzie, J.M. (1988), *The Empire of Nature*, Manchester: Manchester University Press.

MacNaghten, P. and J. Urry (1998), *Contested Natures*, London: Sage.

Macy, M. and A. Flache (1995), 'Beyond rationality in models of choice', *Annual Review of Sociology*, **21**, 73–91.

Mair, L. (1974), *African Societies*, London: Cambridge University Press.

Mair, L. (1984), *Anthropology and Development*, London: MacMillan.

Majone, G. (1989), *Evidence, Argument and Persuasion in the Policy Process*, New Haven: Yale University Press.

Maloney, W., G. Smith and G. Stoker (2000), 'Social capital and urban governance: adding a more contextualised "top-down" perspective', *Political Studies*, **48**, 802–20.

Mandondo, A. (1997), 'Trees and spaces as emotion and norm laden components of local ecosystems in Nyamaropa communal lands, Nyanga District; Zimbabwe', *Agriculture and Human Values*, **14**, 352–72.

Mandondo, A. (2000), 'Situating Zimbabwe's natural resource governance systems in history', Centre for International Forestry Research Working Paper no. 32, Bogor, Indonesia: Cifor.

March, J. and J. Olsen (1989), *Rediscovering Institutions: The Organizational Basis of Politics*, New York: Free Press.

Mapedza, E. and A. Mandondo (2002), *Co-management in the Mafungautsi Forest Area of Zimbabwe – What Stake for Local Communities?* Washington, DC: World Resources Institute.

Matose, F. (1994), *Local People's uses and Perceptions of Forest Resources: An Analysis of a State Property Regime in Zimbabwe*, MSc thesis, Canada: University of Alberta.

Matowanyika, J.Z.Z. (1991), *Indigenous Resource Management and Sustainability in Rural Zimbabwe: An Exploration of Practices and Concepts in Commonlands*, unpublished PhD thesis, University of Waterloo, Ontario, Canada.

Matzke, G. (1993), 'A study of livestock use of Mafungabusi: Together with a discussion of the planning implications for resource sharing developments', CASS Occasional paper series nr 53/93, Harare: University of Zimbabwe.

Matzke, G. and D. Mazambani (1993), 'Resource sharing schemes for state owned land in Zimbabwe: a discussion of conceptual issues needing consideration in the development and planning of co-management regimes', Occasional Paper Series 54/93, Centre for Applied Social Sciences, Harare: University of Zimbabwe.

Mawhood, P. (ed.) (1983), *Local Government in the Third World*, Chichester: John Wiley.

McNeely, Jeffrey A. (1999), 'The ecosystem approach for sustainable use of biological resources: an IUCN perspective', in Schei, Peter J., Odd T. Sandlund and Rita Strand (eds), *Proceedings*, The Norway/UN Conference on the Ecosystem Approach for Sustainable Use of Biological Diversity, September, Trondheim, Norway: Directorate for

Nature Management and Norwegian Institute for Nature research, pp. 11–18.

Mehta, L. (2001), 'The manufacture of popular perceptions of scarcity: dams and water related narratives in Gujurat, India', *World Development*, **29** (12), 2025–41.

Miljömålsrådet (2004), *Miljömålen – Når ri Dem?*, Stockholm: Naturvårdsverket.

Miller, G.J. (1992), *Managerial Dilemmas – The Political Economy of Hierarchy*, Cambridge: Cambridge University Press.

MIMAM (1998), *El Libro Blanco del Agua Documento de Sintesis*, Madrid: Ministerio de Medio Ambiente.

Mizruchi, M.S. (1994), 'Social network analysis: recent achievements and current controversies', *Acta Sociologica*, **37**, 329–43.

Montgomery, J.D. (2000), 'Social capital as a policy resource', *Policy Sciences*, **33**, 227–43.

Montin, S. (2000), 'A conceptual framework', in E. Amnå, and S. Montin, *Towards a New Concept of Local Self-Government?* Oslo: Fagbokforlaget.

Moore, D.S. (1993), 'Contesting terrain in Zimbabwe's Eastern Highlands: political ecology, ethnography and peasant resource struggles', *Economic Geography*, **69**, 380–401.

Mørk, R. (1990), 'Politiske rammer og faglige rammer for "Miljø-ressurs" – ringens virksomhet', Note presented at meeting for "Miljø-ressurs", Hell, 22–23 August.

Murombedzi, J.C. (1991), 'Decentralizing common property resource management: a case study of the Nyaminyami District Council of Zimbabwe's Wildlife Management Programme', IIED Drylands Network Programme, Issues Paper.

Murphree, M.W. (1990), 'Decentralizing the proprietorship of wildlife resources in Zimbabwe's communal areas', Centre for Applied Social Sciences, Harare: University of Zimbabwe.

Mutizwa-Mangiza, N.D. (1985), 'Community development in pre-independence Zimbabwe: a study of policy with special reference to rural land', *Supplement to Zambezia*.

Naustdalslid, J. (1992), 'Miljøproblema som styringsmessig nivåproblem', *Notat* 1992, **112**, Oslo: NIBR.

Naustdalslid, J. (1994), 'Globale miljøproblem- locale løysingar', in J. Naustdalslid, and S. Hovig, *Lokalt miljøvern*, Oslo: Tano.

Nenseth, V. (1995), Mellom kunnskap og politikk i miljøvernplanleggingen. *MILKOM-notat*, 05/95, Norsk institutt for by- og regionforskning.

NFA – New Forest Association (2004), www.newforestonline.biz/NFA/, 18 October.

NFC – New Forest Committee (2003), *New Forest Strategy*, Lyndhurst: New Forest Committee.

NFC – New Forest Committee (2004), 'New Forest fact file', www. newforestcommittee. org.uk/index.html, 18 October.

NFCDA – New Forest Commoners' Defence Association (2004), www. newforestcommoners.co.uk/index.htm, 18 October.

Newton, K. (1999), *Social Capital and Democracy in Western Europe. Social Capital and European Democracy*, London: Routledge.

NOU (1974:39), *Fjellplan for Setesdal Vesthei*, Oslo: Miljøvern-departementet.

NOU (1986:13), *Ny landsplan for nasjonalparker i Norge*, Oslo: Miljøvern-departementet.

Norges offentlige utredninger (Nov) (2001), 'Bedre kommunal og regional planlegging etter plan- og bygningsloven: planlovutvalgets første delutredning', Oslo: Statens forvaltningstjeneste.

Norges offentlige utredninger (Nov) (2003), '14 Bedre kommunal og regional planlegging etter plan- og bygningsloven II: planlovutvalgets utredning med lovforslag', Oslo: Statens forvaltningstjeneste.

Olson, M. (1965), *The Logic of Collective Action. Public Goods and the Theory of Groups*, Cambridge, MA: Harvard University Press.

Olsson, P., C. Folke and F. Berkes (2004), 'Adaptive comanagement for building resilience in social–ecological systems', *Environmental Management*, **34** (1), 75–90.

Opedal, S. and A.-K. Thoren (1996), 'Fylkesdelplanner for Glomma', *NIBR-notat*, 1996, **119**, Oslo: Norsk institutt for by-og regionforskning.

Ostrom, E. (1998), 'A behavioral approach to the rational choice theory of collective action', *American Political Science Review*, **92** (1), 1–21.

Ostrom, E. (1999), 'Coping with the tragedy of the commons', *Annual Review of Political Science*, **2**, 493–535.

Ostrom, E. (1990), *Governing the Commons: The Evolution of Institutions for Collective Action*, Cambridge: Cambridge University Press.

Ostrom, E. (1992), *Crafting Institutions for Self-Governing Irrigation Systems*, San Francisco, CA: ICS Press.

Ostrom, E., R. Gardner and J. Walker (1994), *Rules, Games and Common-Pool Resources*, Ann Arbor: University of Michigan Press.

Ostrom, E., T. Dietz, N. Dolsak, P.C. Stern, S. Stonich and E.U. Weber (eds) (2002), *The Drama of the Commons*, Washington, DC: National Academy Press.

Peet, R. and M. Watts (1996), *Liberation Ecologies: Environment, Development, Social Movements*, London: Routledge.

Pennington, M. and Y. Rydin (2000), 'Researching social capital in local environmental policy contexts', *Policy and Politics*, **28** (2), 33–49.

Phillips, J., J. Hammond, L.H. Samuels and R.J.M. Swynnerton (1962), 'The Development of the Economic Resources of Southern Rhodesia with particular reference to the Role of African Agriculture: Report of the advisory Committee', *CSAR* 28-1962, Salisbury, Southern Rhodesia: Mardon Rhodesian Printers.

Pierre, J. and B. Guy Peters (2000), *Governance, Politics and the State*, New York: St Martin's Press.

Pitt-Rivers, J. (1971), *The People of the Sierra*, Chicago, IL: University of Chicago Press.

Pretty, J. and H. Ward (2001), 'Social capital and the environment', *World Development*, **29** (2), 209–27.

Purdue, D. (2001), 'Neighbourhood governance: leadership, trust and social capital', *Urban Studies*, **38** (12), 2211–24.

Putnam, R. (1993), *Making Democracy Work: Civic Traditions in Modern Italy*, Princeton, NJ: Princeton University Press.

Putnam, R. (2000), *Bowling Alone: The Collapse and Revival of American Community*, New York: Simon & Schuster.

Raiffa, H. (1982), *The Art and Science of Negotiation*, Cambridge, MA: Belknap Press of Harvard University Press.

Ravenscroft, N., N. Curry and S. Markwell (2002), 'Outdoor recreation and participative democracy in England and Wales', *Journal of Environmental Planning and Management*, **45** (5), 715–34.

Rees, J. (1990), *Natural Resources*, London: Methuen.

Reitan, M. (2004), 'Politicisation and professional expertise in the policy of nature conservation', *Local Environment*, **9** (5), 437–51.

Rhodes, R. (1996), 'The new governance: governing without government', *Political Studies*, **44**, 652–67.

Rhodes, R.A.W. (1997), *Understanding Governance: Policy Networks, Governance, Reflexivity and Accountability*, Buckingham: Open University Press.

Rhodes, R. (1998), 'Governance as theory: five propositions', *International Social Science Journal*, **2**, 17–28.

Rhodes, R. (2000), 'Governance and public administration', in J. Pierre, (ed.), *Debating Governance – Authority. Steering and Democracy*, Oxford: Oxford University Press, pp. 54–90.

Ribot, J.C. (1999), 'Decentralization, participation and accountability in Sahelian forestry: legal instruments of political-administrative control', *Africa*, **69** (1), pp. 23–65.

Ribot, J.C. (2001), *Actors, Powers and Accountability: Implementation and Effects of Decentralized Environmental Management in Africa*, Washington, DC: World Bank.

Richerson, P.J., R. Boyd and B. Paciotti (2002), 'An Evolutionary

Theory of Commons Management', in E. Ostrom, T. Dietz, N. Dolsak, P.C. Stern, S. Stonich and E.U. Webers (eds), *The Drama of the Commons*, Washington, DC: National Academy Press, pp. 403–42.

Rolf, B. (1989), Wittgensteins osägbarhet och Polanyis personliga kunskap, in K. Johannessen, and B. Rolf (red.), *Om tyst kunnskap. Två artiklar*, Uppsala: University of Uppsala, centrum för didaktikk.

Roper, J. and P. Maramba (2000), 'Community based natural resource management. Mid term review', unpublished report, CIDA Project ZW-16883, Harare.

Rothstein, B. (2000), 'Trust, social dilemmas and collective memories', *Journal of Theoretical Politics*, **12** (4), 477–501.

Royal Commission on Environmental Pollution (2002), *Environmental Planning*, 23rd Report, London: RCEP.

Rydin, Y. (2003), *Conflict, Consensus and Rationality in Environmental Planning: An Institutional Discourse Approach*, Oxford: Oxford University Press.

Rydin, Y. and N. Holman (2004), 'Re-evaluating the contribution of social capital in achieving sustainable development', *Local Environment*, **9** (2), 117–34.

Rydin, Y. and N. Holman with V. Hands and F. Sommer (2003), 'Incorporating sustainable development concerns into an urban regeneration project: how politics can defeat procedures', *Journal of Environmental Planning and Management*, **46** (4), 545–62.

Rydin, Y. and M. Pennington (2000), 'Public participation and local environmental planning: the collective action problem and the potential of social capital', *Local Environment*, **5** (2), 153–69.

Sabatier, P.A. (1993), 'Policy change over a decade or more', in P.A. Sabatier and H.C. Jenkins-Smith (eds), *Policy Change and Learning: An Advocacy Coalition Approach*, Boulder: Westview Press, pp. 14–39.

Sabatier, P.A. and H.C. Jenkins-Smith (1988), 'Symposium editor's introduction', *Policy Sciences*, **21**, 123–7.

Sabatier, P.A. and H.C. Jenkins-Smith (1999), 'The advocacy coalition framework', in P.A. Sabatier (ed.), *Theories of the Policy Process*, Boulder: Westview Press.

Samuelson, P.A. and W.D. Nordhaus (1989), *Economics*, Singapore: McGraw-Hill Book Co.

Scharpf, F.W. (1993), *Games in Hierarchies and Networks – Analytical and Empirical Approaches to the Study of Governance Institutions*, Boulder, CO: Westview Press.

Schattschneider, E.E. (1975), *The Semisovereign People. A Realist's View of Democracy in America*, New York: Rinhart & Winston.

Schofelleers, J.M. (1979), *Guardians of the Land*, Gwelo: Mambo Press.

Scott, J.C. (1985), *Weapons of the Weak: Everyday Forms of Peasant Resistance*, New Haven: Yale University Press.

Selman, P. (2001), 'Social capital, sustainability and environmental planning', *Planning Theory and Practice*, **2** (1), 13–30.

Sibanda, B.M.C. (2001), *Wildlife and Communities at the Crossroads: Is Zimbabwe's CAMPFIRE the way forward?* Harare: SAPES Books.

Singleton, S. (2000), 'Co-operation or capture? The paradox of co-management and policy-making', *Environmental Politics*, **9**, 1–21.

Skjeggedal, T., T. Arnesen, G. Markhus, I.-L. Saghe and P.G. Thingstad (2001), *Regimenes slagmark. Om arealutnytting og forvaltningsregimer i LNF-områder*, Steinkjer: Nord-trøndelagsforskning, NTF-rapport 2001:3.

Smith, M. (2005), 'Value judgement', *Guardian*, 23 March.

Solheim, A.L., N. Vagstad, P. Kraft, Ø. Løvstad, S. Skoglund, S. Turtumøygard and J.-R. Selvik (2001), 'Tiltaksanalyse for Vansjø-Hobølvassdraget', *NIVA-rapport* nr. 4377-2001, Norwegian Institute for Water Research.

SOU (1997), *Miljösamverkan i vattenvården*, Stockholm: Swedish Environmental Ministry/Fritzes.

SOU (2002), *Klart som vatten – Betänkande av Utredningen svensk vattenadministration*, Stockholm: Swedish Environmental Ministry/Fritzes.

Stoker, G. (1998), 'Governance as theory: five propositions', *International Social Science Journal*, **2**, 17–28.

Stokke, Knut B. (2004), 'Nettverk og kollektiv handling i Vansjø-Hobølvassdraget', *Kart og Plan*, **64** (3), 142–52.

Stone, C. (1989), *Regime Politics: Governing Atlanta 1946–88*, Lawrence, KS: University of Kansas Press.

Sullivan, H. and C. Skelcher (2002), *Working across Boundaries. Collaboration in Public Services*, London and Basingstoke: Palgrave Macmillan.

Svendsen, L.H. and G.T. Svendsen (2000), 'Measuring social capital: the Danish cooperative movement', *Sociologia Ruralis*, **40** (1), 72–86.

Swyngedouw, E. (1999a), 'Modernity and hybridity: water and modernisation in Spain', paper presented at the SOAS Water Issues Study Group, University of London.

Swyngedouw, E. (1999b), 'Modernity and hybridity: nature, regeneracionismo, and the production of the Spanish waterscape 1890–1930', *Annals of the Association of American Geographers*, **89** (3), 443–65.

Tsing, A. (1999), 'Notes on culture and natural resource management', Berkeley Workshop on Environmental Politics Working Paper 99-4, Institute of International Studies, Berkeley, CA: University of California.

Tennøy, A. (2000), 'Allmennhetens tilgjengelighet i strandsonen', *Notat*, 2000, 131, Oslo: Norsk institutt for by- og regionforskning.

Urban Studies (2001), Special Issue on Social Capital and Urban Regeneration, **38** (12).

Vabo, S.I. (2002), 'Governance og kommunal styring', in S.I. Vabo, (ed.): *Kommunal governance og bærekraftig utvikling – om governance-begrepet*, NIBR-working paper, Oslo, Norway.

Varela-Ortega, C. and J.M. Sumpsi (1998), 'Comparative analysis of CAP agri-environmental programs and water policies in environmentally sensitive areas: the case of La Mancha Wetlands in Spain', Draft Version, Madrid.

Varughese, G. and E. Ostrom (2001), 'The contested role of heterogeneity in collective action: some evidence from community forestry in Nepal', *World Development*, **29** (5), 747–65.

Verderers of the New Forest (1997), *Who Are They? What Do They Do?* Lyndhurst: Verderers.

Vorkinn, M. (2003), 'Ferdsel ut fra hytter i Rondane midt og sør', Lillehammer/Hamar: Oppland fylkeskommune, Hedmark fylkeskommune, Fylkesmannen i Oppland, Fylkesmannen i Hedmark.

Walker, P. (1995), 'Politics of nature: an overview of political ecology', Berkeley, CA: University of California, Department of Geography.

WCED – World Commission on Environment and Development (1987), *Our Common Future*, Oxford: Oxford University Press.

Weale, A. (1992), *The New Politics of Pollution*, Manchester: Manchester University Press.

Wekwete, K.H. and P. de Valk (eds) (1990), *Decentralizing for Participatory Planning?* Aldershot: Gower Publishing Company.

West, K., K. Scanlon, A. Thornley and Y. Rydin (2003), 'The Greater London Authority: problems of strategy integration', *Policy & Politics*, **31** (4), 479–96.

Whitehouse, C.J. and G.P. Whitehouse (1983), *A Town for Four Winters – Great War Camps on Cannock Chase*, Stafford: Staffordshire County Council.

Wilson, K.B. (1986), 'History, ecology and conservation in Southern Zimbabwe', unpublished seminar paper, Department of Sociology, University of Manchester.

Wilson, K.B. (1989), 'Trees in fields in Southern Zimbabwe', *Journal of Southern African Studies*, **15** (2), 369–83.

Wilson, J. (2002), 'Scientific uncertainty, complex systems, and the design of common-pool institutions', in E. Ostrom, T. Dietz, N. Dolsak, P.C. Stern, S. Stonich and E.U. Weber (eds), *The Drama of the Commons*, Washington, USA: National Academy Press, pp. 327–59.

Wilson, P. (1997), 'Building social capital: a learning agenda for the 21st century', *Urban Studies*, **34** (5–6), 745–60.

Wittgren, H.B., S. Westerlund and R. Casterissan (red.) (2000), 'Genevadsåstudien – Ett aktörsspel om genomförande av miljökvalitetsnormer för kväve i ett avrinningsområde', Linköping, Tema Vatten/ Vattenstrategiska forskningsprogrammet (VASTRA).

Wollenberg, E. (1998), 'Methods for assessing the conservation and development of forest products: what we know and what we have yet to learn', in E. Wollenberg and A. Ingles (eds), *Incomes from the Forest: Methods for the Conservation of Forest Products for Local Communities*, Bogor: CIFOR, pp. 1–16.

Woolcock, M. (1998), 'Social capital and economic development: toward a theoretical synthesis and policy framework', *Theory and Society*, **27**, 151–208.

Zachrisson, A. (2004), 'Co-management of natural resources. Paradigm Shifts, Key Concepts and Cases', Report no 1, Umeå: Mountain Mistra Programme Report.

Index